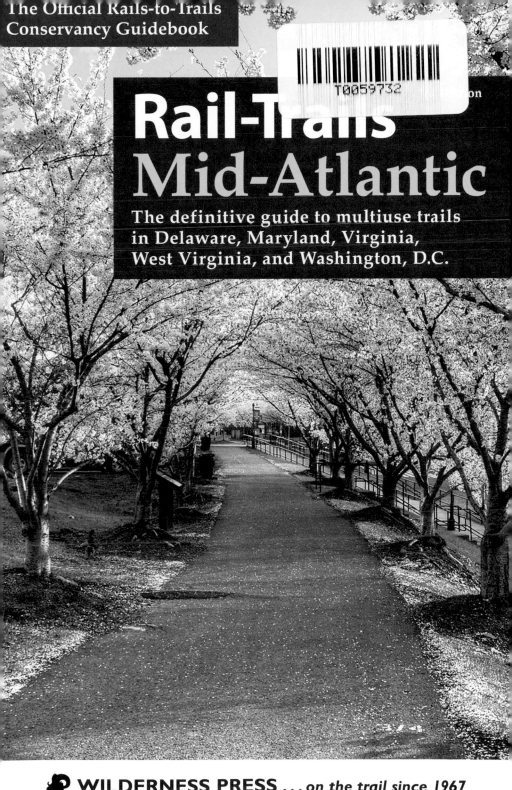

The Official Rails-to-Trails
Conservancy Guidebook

Rail-Trails
Mid-Atlantic

The definitive guide to multiuse trails
in Delaware, Maryland, Virginia,
West Virginia, and Washington, D.C.

WILDERNESS PRESS ... *on the trail since 1967*

Rail-Trails: Mid-Atlantic

3rd Edition
Copyright © 2022 by Rails-to-Trails Conservancy
Cover and interior photographs copyright © 2022 by Rails-to-Trails Conservancy

Maps: Lohnes+Wright; map data © OpenStreetMap contributors
Cover design: Scott McGrew
Book design: Annie Long

Cataloging-in-Publication Data is available from the Library of Congress.
ISBN 978-1-64359-085-1 (pbk.); eISBN 978-1-64359-086-8 (ebook)

Published by: ♟ **WILDERNESS PRESS**
An imprint of AdventureKEEN
2204 First Ave. S, Ste. 102
Birmingham, AL 35233
800-678-7006; fax 877-374-9016

Visit wildernesspress.com for a complete listing of our books and for ordering information. Contact us at our website, at facebook.com/wildernesspress1967, or at twitter.com/wilderness1967 with questions or comments. To find out more about who we are and what we're doing, visit blog.wildernesspress.com.

Manufactured in the United States of America
Distributed by Publishers Group West

Front cover photo: West Virginia's Caperton Trail, part of the Mon River Rail-Trail System (see Hike 54, page 197); photographed by James Riel. *Back cover photo:* One of 47 trestles on the Virginia Creeper National Recreation Trail (see Hike 47, page 169); photographed by Anthony Le.

SAFETY NOTICE: Although Wilderness Press and Rails-to-Trails Conservancy have made every attempt to ensure that the information in this book is accurate at press time, they are not responsible for any loss, damage, injury, or inconvenience that may occur to anyone while using this book. You are responsible for your own safety and health while in the wilderness. The fact that a trail is described in this book does not mean that it will be safe for you. Be aware that trail conditions can change from day to day. Always check local conditions, know your own limitations, and consult a map.

About Rails-to-Trails Conservancy

Headquartered in Washington, D.C., Rails-to-Trails Conservancy (RTC) is a nonprofit organization dedicated to building a nation connected by trails. RTC reimagines public spaces to create safe ways for everyone to walk, bike, and be active outdoors.

Railways helped build America. Spanning from coast to coast, these ribbons of steel linked people, communities, and enterprises, spurring commerce and forging a single nation that bridges a continent. But in recent decades, many of these routes have fallen into disuse, severing communal ties that helped bind Americans together.

When RTC opened its doors in 1986, the rail-trail movement was in its infancy. Most projects, created for recreation and conservation, focused on single, linear routes in rural areas. RTC sought broader protection for the unused corridors, incorporating rural, suburban, and urban routes.

Year after year, RTC's efforts to protect and align public funding with trail building created an environment that allowed trail advocates in communities across the country to initiate trail projects. The ever-growing ranks of these trail professionals, volunteers, and RTC supporters have built momentum for the national rail-trails movement. As the number of supporters has multiplied, so have the rail-trails.

Americans now enjoy nearly 25,000 miles of open rail-trails, and as they flock to the trails to connect with family and friends, enjoy nature, and access places in their local neighborhoods and beyond, their economic prosperity, health, and overall well-being continue to flourish.

A signature endeavor of RTC is **TrailLink.com™**, America's portal to these rail-trails and other multiuse trails. When RTC launched the website in 2000, our organization was one of the first to compile such detailed trail information on a national scale. Today, TrailLink.com continues to play a critical role in both encouraging and satisfying the country's growing need for opportunities to use trails for recreation or transportation. This free trail-finder database—which includes detailed descriptions, interactive maps, photo galleries, and firsthand ratings and reviews—can be used as a companion resource to the trails in this guidebook.

With a grassroots community more than 1 million strong, RTC is committed to ensuring a better future for America made possible by trails and the connections they inspire. Learn more at **railstotrails.org**.

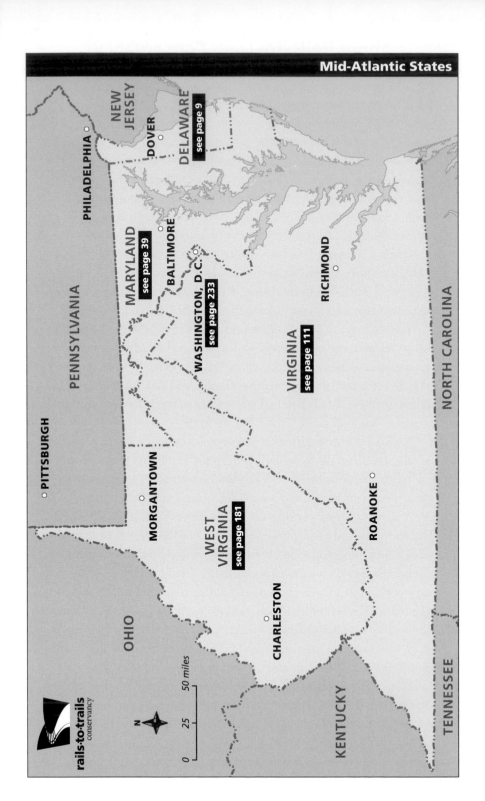

PENNSYLVANIA

NEW JERSEY

DELAWARE
see page 9

DOVER

PHILADELPHIA

MARYLAND
see page 39

BALTIMORE

WASHINGTON, D.C.
see page 233

RICHMOND

VIRGINIA
see page 111

NORTH CAROLINA

PITTSBURGH

MORGANTOWN

WEST VIRGINIA
see page 181

ROANOKE

OHIO

CHARLESTON

KENTUCKY

TENNESSEE

rails-to-trails
conservancy

N

0   25   50 miles

Table of Contents

DELAWARE   9

MARYLAND   39

VIRGINIA   111

WEST VIRGINIA 181

WASHINGTON, D.C. 233

Foreword

Welcome to the *Rail-Trails: Mid-Atlantic* guidebook, a comprehensive companion for discovering the region's top rail-trails and multiuse pathways. This book will help you uncover fantastic opportunities to get outdoors on the region's trails—whether for exercise, transportation, or just pure fun.

Rails-to-Trails Conservancy's (RTC's) mission is to build a nation connected by trails. We reimagine public spaces to create safe ways for everyone to walk, bike and be active outdoors. We hope this book will inspire you to experience firsthand how trails can connect people to one another and to the places they love, while also creating connections to nature, history, and culture.

Since its founding in 1986, RTC has witnessed a massive growth in the rail-trail and active-transportation movement. Today, nearly 25,000 miles of completed rail-trails provide invaluable benefits for people and communities across the country. We hope you find this book to be a delightful and informative resource for discovering the many unique trail destinations throughout Delaware, Maryland, Virginia, West Virginia, and Washington, D.C.

I'll be out on the trails too, experiencing the thrill of the ride right alongside you. Be sure to say hello and share your #TrailMoments with us on social media. You can find us @railstotrails on Facebook, Instagram, and Twitter. Participate in our Trail Moments initiative by sharing your stories of resilience, joy, health, and connection at **trailmoments.org**!

Enjoy the journey,

Ryan Chao, President
Rails-to-Trails Conservancy

Acknowledgments

Special acknowledgment to Amy Kapp and Laura Stark, editors of this guide-book, and to Derek Strout and Bart Wright (with Lohnes+Wright) for their work on the creation of the trail maps included in the book. Rails-to-Trails Conservancy also thanks Gene Bisbee and Amy Ahn for their assistance in writing and editing content.

We also appreciate the following staff and intern contributors, as well as local trail managers, who helped us ensure that the maps, photographs, and trail descriptions are as accurate as possible.

Ethan Abbott	Mary Ellen Koontz
Arielle Bader	Joe LaCroix
Alisa Borland	Anthony Le
Jim Brown	Sophie Mangassarian
Peter Dean	Suzanne Matyas
Cindy Dickerson	Kevin Mills
Khuyen Dinh	Jimmy O'Connor
Andrew Dupuy	Liz Thorstensen
Brandi Horton	Patrick Wojahn
Heather Irish	Tiffany Wu

Summary of Hikes

Trail Number/Name	Page	Mileage	Walking	Cycling	Wheelchair-Accessible	Inline Skating	Mountain Biking	Fishing	Horseback Riding	Cross-Country Skiing
MARYLAND *(continued)*										
25 Sligo Creek Trail	93	10.2	●	●	●	●		●		
26 Torrey C. Brown Rail Trail	97	19.7	●	●	●			●	●	●
27 Trolley Line #9 Trail	101	1.5	●	●	●					
28 Wayne Gilchrest Trail	103	2.1	●	●	●	●				
29 Western Maryland Rail Trail	107	27.5	●	●	●	●		●		●
VIRGINIA										
30 Blue Ridge Tunnel Trail	113	2.3	●				●			
31 Cape Henry Trail	115	7.5	●	●	●		●	●		
32 Devil's Fork Loop Trail	119	7	●				●			
33 Dismal Swamp Canal Trail	123	8.5	●	●	●	●			●	
34 Guest River Gorge Trail	125	5.8	●	●			●	●		●
35 High Bridge Trail State Park	129	31.4	●	●	●			●	●	
36 Huckleberry Trail	133	15.5	●	●	●	●				●
37 Jackson River Scenic Trail	137	14.3	●	●				●	●	●
38 James River Heritage Trail	139	10.1	●	●	●	●		●		
39 Lake Accotink Trail	143	4.5	●	●			●	●		
40 Mount Vernon Trail	145	18	●	●	●	●		●		●
41 New River Trail State Park	149	57.7	●	●	●		●	●	●	●
42 Richmond and Danville Rail-Trail	153	5.5	●	●	●		●		●	●
43 Riverwalk Trail	157	11.9	●	●	●	●		●		
44 Tobacco Heritage Trail	159	22.7	●				●		●	
45 Virginia Blue Ridge Railway Trail	163	6.9	●	●			●	●	●	●
46 Virginia Capital Trail	165	51.7	●	●	●	●				
47 Virginia Creeper National Recreation Trail	169	34	●	●			●	●	●	●
48 Washington & Old Dominion Railroad Regional Park (W&OD)	173	45	●	●	●	●	●		●	●
49 Wilderness Road Trail	177	6.5–8.5	●	●			●	●	●	●

Summary of Hikes

Trail Number/Name	Page	Mileage	Walking	Cycling	Wheelchair-Accessible	Inline Skating	Mountain Biking	Fishing	Horseback Riding	Cross-Country Skiing
WEST VIRGINIA										
50 Blackwater Canyon Trail	183	10.7	●				●	●	●	
51 Brooke Pioneer Trail	185	6.7	●	●	●	●		●		●
52 Glade Creek Trail	189	5.8	●		●		●	●		●
53 Greenbrier River Trail	193	78	●	●			●	●	●	●
54 Mon River Rail-Trail System	197	48.5	●	●	●	●		●		●
55 North Bend Rail Trail	201	72	●	●	●				●	●
56 Otter Creek Trail	205	11.8	●					●		
57 Panhandle Trail	207	29.2	●	●	●		●	●	●	
58 Potts Valley Rail Trail	211	4.5	●			●	●		●	
59 Rend Trail	215	3.2	●			●	●		●	
60 Southside Trail	217	6.9	●			●	●		●	
61 West Fork River/ Ralph S. Larue Trail	221	14	●	●	●	●			●	●
62 West Fork Trail	225	22	●			●		●		●
63 Wheeling Heritage Trails	227	16.5	●	●	●	●		●		●
WASHINGTON, D.C.										
64 Anacostia River Trail	235	12	●	●	●	●				
65 Capital Crescent Trail	239	12.7	●	●	●	●				●
66 Metropolitan Branch Trail	243	4	●	●	●	●				●
67 Rock Creek Park Trails	245	8.5	●	●	●	●			●	●

Introduction

Of the nearly 2,300 rail-trails across the United States, 165 thread through the Mid-Atlantic region of Delaware, Maryland, Virginia, West Virginia, and Washington, D.C. These routes relate a two-part story: The first speaks to the early years of railroading, while the second showcases efforts by Rails-to-Trails Conservancy (RTC), other groups, and their supporters to resurrect these unused railroad corridors as public-use trails. This guidebook highlights 67 of the region's premier trails and routes, including dozens of rail-trails and other multiuse gems.

With the most trails of any state in the region, West Virginia boasts some of the most rural and unique rail-trails. Not always the flat and even pathways you might expect from rail-trails, West Virginia's trails offer a variety of backwoods treks, such as the Glade Creek, Rend, and Southside Trails of the New River Gorge National Park. Complementing these rustic pathways are the well-groomed yet still wild and wonderful Mountain State trails, like the gorgeous and popular 77-mile Greenbrier River Trail and the Morgantown area's Mon River Rail-Trail System, both in the Rail-Trail Hall of Fame.

Next door, Virginia also boasts two Hall of Fame rail-trails: In the southwestern corner of the state, the Virginia Creeper National Recreation Trail offers a premier destination adventure. And in the northern part of the state, right outside the bustle of Washington, D.C., you'll find the Washington and Old Dominion Railroad Regional Park (W&OD), which takes riders out of the city and into rolling farmland and horse country. Northern Virginia's Mount Vernon Trail—full of scenic, cultural, and historical charm—is a great example of a multiuse trail that was not previously a railroad corridor but still has the look and feel of the rail-trails you've come to love. The route is a key segment of the developing 800-mile Capital Trails Coalition network, a TrailNation™ project connecting the greater Washington, D.C., metropolitan region.

Washington, D.C., itself is home to a portion of the Capital Crescent Trail, which begins on its northern endpoint in suburban Maryland before heading to the historical and trendy Georgetown neighborhood. The sprawling C&O Canal Towpath begins in the capital and follows the Potomac River for 184.5 miles to Cumberland, Maryland.

In the state well known for its crabs and waterways, Maryland's Cross Island Trail offers a coastal sojourn. And the largest city in the state is home to the vibrant Baltimore Greenway Trails Network, a 35-mile system of trails that will eventually connect more than 75 neighborhoods.

Last, but certainly not least, Delaware offers Cape Henlopen State Park, a picturesque destination brimming with history and outdoor activities. A trio of stunning pathways run in and around it, including a biking loop, the Junction & Breakwater Trail, and the Georgetown-Lewes Trail.

No matter which route in *Rail-Trails: Mid-Atlantic* you decide to try, you'll be touching on the heart of the community that helped build it and the history that first brought the rails to the region.

What Is a Rail-Trail?

Rail-trails are multiuse public paths built along former railroad corridors. Most often flat or following a gentle grade, they are suited to walking, running, cycling, mountain biking, inline skating, cross-country skiing, horseback riding, and wheelchair use. Since the 1960s, Americans have created nearly 25,000 miles of rail-trails throughout the country.

What Is a Rail-with-Trail?

A rail-with-trail is a public path that parallels a still-active rail line. Some run adjacent to high-speed, scheduled trains, often linking public transportation stations, while others follow tourist routes and slow-moving excursion trains. Many share an easement, separated from the rails by fencing or other barriers. Nearly 400 rails-with-trails exist in 47 states across the country.

What Is the Rail-Trail Hall of Fame?

In 2007, RTC began recognizing exemplary rail-trails around the country through its Rail-Trail Hall of Fame. Inductees are selected based on merits such as scenic value, high use, trail and trailside amenities, historical significance, excellence in management and maintenance of facilities, community connections, and geographic distribution. Hall-of-Fame rail-trails are indicated in this book with a blue icon; for the full list of Hall-of-Fame rail-trails, visit **railstotrails.org/halloffame**.

What Is TrailNation™?

At RTC, we believe communities are healthier and happier when trails are central to their design. Everything we love about trails gets better when we connect them, creating networks that link neighborhoods, towns, cities, and entire regions. That's why we're committed to connecting trails and building comprehensive trail systems that bring people together and get them where they want to go. TrailNation brings to life our vision of trails at the heart of healthy, thriving communities from coast to coast.

We've invested in eight TrailNation projects across the country—in places that are diverse in their geography, culture, size, and scope—to prove what is possible when trail networks are central to our lives. Three of these projects are in the Mid-Atlantic region: the Capital Trails Coalition, connecting the greater Washington, D.C., metropolitan area; the Industrial Heartland Trails Coalition's developing network connecting trails in West Virginia and three surrounding states; and the 35-mile Baltimore Greenway Trails Network. Look for the Trail-Nation logo throughout the book to find trails that are part of these exciting systems. Learn more at **trailnation.org.**

ABOUT THE CAPITAL TRAILS COALITION

 The Capital Trails Coalition seeks to create a world-class network of multiuse trails that are equitably distributed throughout the greater Washington, D.C., metropolitan region. The regional trail network will transform public life by providing healthy, low-stress access to open space and reliable transportation for people of all ages and abilities. The expansive project consists of more than 800 miles of existing and planned trails and connections in Maryland, Virginia, and Washington, D.C. Learn more at **railstotrails.org/ctc.**

ABOUT THE INDUSTRIAL HEARTLAND TRAILS COALITION

 The Industrial Heartland Trails Coalition is working to establish the Industrial Heartland as a premier destination offering a 1,500-miles-plus multiuse trail network. RTC leads the effort to connect the network, which will stretch across 48 counties in four states—Pennsylvania, West Virginia, Ohio, and New York—alongside the Pennsylvania Environmental Council, the National Park Service, and more than 100 partner organizations across the area. Learn more at **ihearttrails.org.**

ABOUT THE BALTIMORE GREENWAY TRAILS NETWORK

 The Baltimore Greenway Trails Network is a developing 35-mile trail system linking together the diverse neighborhoods, cultural amenities, and outdoor resources that make up Baltimore City. The trail network will transform the public realm by providing equitable, healthy, low-stress access to open space and reliable transportation and recreation for people of all ages and abilities. Learn more at **railstotrails.org/baltimore.**

ABOUT THE GREAT AMERICAN RAIL-TRAIL®

 The Great American Rail-Trail is a signature project of RTC and the most ambitious of its TrailNation projects. The developing 3,700-mile route will be the nation's first fully bikeable trail across the country. It traverses 12 states and connects more than 145 host trails between Washington, D.C., and Washington State. Learn more at **great americanrailtrail.org.**

Rail-Trails: Mid-Atlantic provides the information you need to plan a rewarding trek on a rail-trail or other multiuse trail in the region. With words to inspire you and maps to chart your path, it makes choosing the best route a breeze. The key features are described below.

Maps

You'll find three levels of maps in this book: **an overall regional map, state locator maps**, and **a detailed map for each trail.**

Use the state locator maps on the first page of each chapter to find the trails nearest you, or select several neighboring trails and plan a weekend excursion. Once you find a trail on a state locator map, simply flip to the corresponding trail number for a full description. Accompanying trail maps mark each route's access roads, trailheads, parking areas, restrooms, and other defining features.

Key to Map Icons

Parking	Drinking Water	Restrooms	Featured Trail	Connecting Trail	Active Railroad

Trail Descriptions

Trails are listed in alphabetical order within each chapter. Each description begins with a summary of key facts about the trail, including trail endpoints and mileage, a roughness index, the trail surface, and possible uses.

The map and summary information list the trail endpoints (either a city, street, or more specific location), with suggested points from which to start and finish. Additional access points are marked on the maps and mentioned in the trail descriptions. The maps and descriptions also highlight available amenities, including parking; restrooms; and area attractions such as shops, services, museums, parks, and stadiums. Trail length is listed in miles, one way, and includes only completed trail; the mileage for any gaps in the trail will be noted in its description.

Each trail description includes a **roughness index** rating from 1 to 3. A rating of 1 indicates a smooth, level surface that is accessible to users of all ages and abilities. A 2 rating means the surface may be loose and/or uneven and could pose a problem for road bikes and wheelchairs. A 3 rating suggests a rough surface that is recommended only for mountain bikers and hikers. Surfaces can range from asphalt or concrete to ballast, boardwalk, cinder, crushed stone, gravel, grass, dirt, sand, and/or wood chips. Where relevant, trail descriptions address changing surface conditions.

All trails are open to pedestrians. Bicycles are permitted unless otherwise noted in the trail summary or description. The summary also indicates whether the trail is wheelchair-accessible. Other possible uses include inline skating, mountain biking, horseback riding, fishing, and cross-country skiing. While most trails are off-limits to motor vehicles, some local trail organizations do allow ATVs and snowmobiles.

Trail descriptions themselves suggest an ideal itinerary for each route, including the best parking areas and access points, where to begin, direction of travel, and any highlights along the way.

Each trail description also lists a website for further information. Be sure to check these websites in advance for updates and current conditions. **TrailLink.com**™ is another great resource for updated content on the trails in this guidebook.

Key to Trail Use Icons

| walking | cycling | wheelchair access | inline skating |

| fishing | horseback riding | cross-country skiing | mountain biking |

Parking Waypoints

In the Parking section for each trail, we've included GPS coordinates for the main parking waypoints. These latitude and longitude coordinates can be used on a GPS device or in online mapping programs to locate parking areas. If you have a smartphone, you can use this guidebook along with Rails-to-Trails Conservancy's TrailLink app—available from the App Store and Google Play—which provides driving directions at the tap of a waypoint.

Trail Use Guidelines

Rail-trails are popular destinations for a range of users, which makes them busy places to enjoy the outdoors. Following basic trail etiquette and safety guidelines will make your experience more pleasant.

➤ **Keep to the right,** except when passing.

➤ **Pass on the left,** and give a clear, audible warning: "On your left!"

➤ **Be aware of other trail users,** particularly around corners and blind spots, and be especially careful when entering a trail, changing direction, or passing so that you don't collide with traffic.

➤ **Respect wildlife** and public and private property; leave no trace and take out litter.

➤ **Control your speed,** especially near pedestrians, playgrounds, and congested areas.

➤ **Travel single file.** Cyclists and pedestrians should ride or walk single file in congested areas or areas with reduced visibility.

➤ **Cross carefully** at intersections; always look both ways and yield to through traffic. Pedestrians have the right-of-way.

➤ **Keep one ear open and your headphone volume low** to increase your awareness of your surroundings.

➤ **Wear a helmet** and other safety gear if you're cycling or inline skating.

➤ **Consider visibility.** Wear reflective clothing, use bicycle lights, or bring flashlights or helmet-mounted lights for tunnel passages or twilight excursions.

➤ **Keep moving, and don't block the trail.** When taking a rest, pull off the trail to the right. Groups should avoid congregating on or blocking the trails. If you have an accident on the trail, move to the right as soon as possible.

➤ **Bicyclists yield** to all other trail users. Pedestrians yield to horses. If in doubt, yield to all other trail users.

➤ **Dogs are permitted on most trails,** but some trails through parks, wildlife refuges, or other sensitive areas may not allow pets; it's best to check the trail website before your visit. If pets are permitted, keep your dog on a short leash and under your control at all times. Remove dog waste and place in a designated trash receptacle.

➤ **Teach your children** these trail essentials, and be diligent in keeping them out of faster-moving trail traffic.

➤ **Be prepared,** especially on long-distance rural trails. Bring water, snacks, maps, a light source, matches, and other equipment you may need. Because some areas may not have good reception for mobile phones, know where you're going, and tell someone else your plan.

E-Bikes

Electric bicycles, commonly called e-bikes, are similar to standard bikes in appearance and operation but feature a small electric motor to assist the rider by adding power to the wheels. A three-tiered system has been developed to classify e-bikes based on speed capacity and other factors; many states generally allow Class 1 (up to 20 mph; requires pedaling) and Class 2 (uses a throttle) e-bikes to operate on trails, but not Class 3 (up to 28 mph). However, these rules may vary by local jurisdiction, so if you would like to ride an e-bike on one of the trails listed in this book, please visit the website listed for the trail or contact the local trail manager to determine whether the use of e-bikes is permitted.

Learn More

To learn about additional multiuse trails in your area or to plan a trip to an area beyond the scope of this book, visit Rails-to-Trails Conservancy's trailfinder website, **TrailLink.com,** a free resource with more than 40,000 miles of mapped rail-trails and multiuse trails nationwide.

Overlooks on the Junction & Breakwater Trail in Delaware offer views of wetlands (see page 7).
TrailLink.com user hepdj

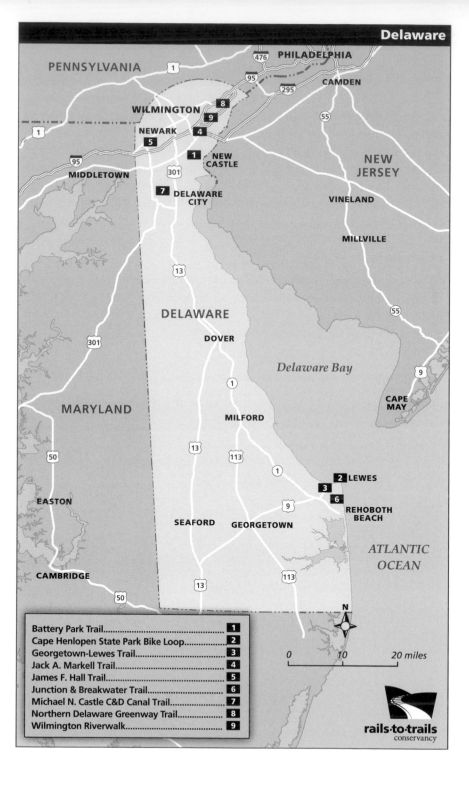

Delaware

PENNSYLVANIA
PHILADELPHIA
CAMDEN
WILMINGTON
NEWARK
NEW CASTLE
MIDDLETOWN
DELAWARE CITY
NEW JERSEY
VINELAND
MILLVILLE
DELAWARE
DOVER
Delaware Bay
MARYLAND
MILFORD
CAPE MAY
EASTON
LEWES
REHOBOTH BEACH
SEAFORD
GEORGETOWN
ATLANTIC OCEAN
CAMBRIDGE

N

0   10   20 miles

Battery Park Trail.. **1**
Cape Henlopen State Park Bike Loop................. **2**
Georgetown-Lewes Trail............................... **3**
Jack A. Markell Trail..................................... **4**
James F. Hall Trail.. **5**
Junction & Breakwater Trail........................... **6**
Michael N. Castle C&D Canal Trail................... **7**
Northern Delaware Greenway Trail.................. **8**
Wilmington Riverwalk.................................. **9**

rails·to·trails
conservancy

Delaware

New Castle's Battery Park Trail traces the Delaware River shoreline (see page 11).
Joe LaCroix

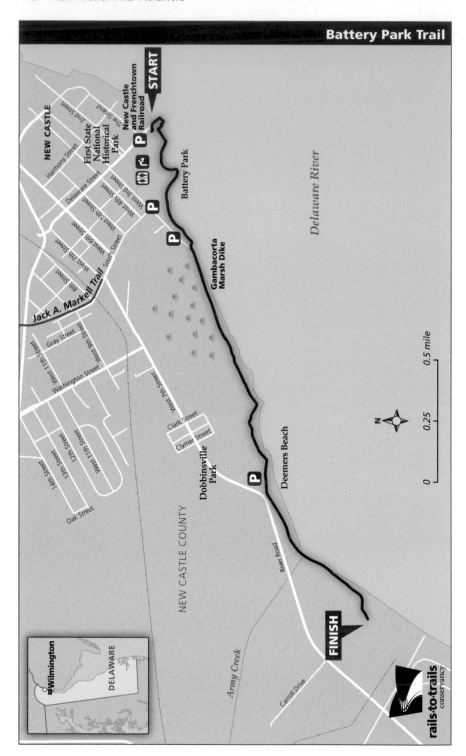

New Castle's Battery Park Trail begins in its eponymous park and extends 1.7 miles along the Delaware River. Battery Park is adjacent to Historic New Castle, a charming downtown area with parks, amenities, shops, and restaurants. The trail is also part of the larger East Coast Greenway, a growing network of multiuse trails connecting 15 states and 450 cities and towns on a 3,000-mile route between Maine and Florida.

The popular park, a draw for residents and visitors alike, gets its name from the cannons once situated there to protect the city from coastal invasion. Another remnant of New Castle's history is the small 19th-century railroad ticket office near the park's entrance. Surrounded by a white picket fence, it was first constructed to serve the short-lived New Castle and Frenchtown Railroad and was restored in the 1950s. You may even catch a glimpse of the

Joe LaCroix

A 19th-century railroad ticket office sits near the entrance to Battery Park.

County
New Castle

Endpoints
Battery Park at Delaware St., 300 feet south of The Strand (New Castle); 0.5 mile southwest of Deemers Beach (New Castle)

Mileage
1.7

Type
Greenway/Non-Rail-Trail

Roughness Index
1

Surface
Asphalt

Kalmar Nyckel, a full-scale replica of a 17th-century Swedish ship (but built by the Dutch) that famously brought Swedish settlers to North America in 1638; it periodically docks at Battery Park as it travels along the Atlantic Seaboard.

On the park's green, you can claim a bench, a picnic table, or a spot on the grass with friends to enjoy the sights and sounds of the river. The paved hike-and-bike path begins on the edge of the green and heads southwest on a levee sandwiched between reedy marsh and the river. At the edge of the park are several short spurs of the trail that connect to a nearby neighborhood, offering immediate trail access to locals.

The Gambacorta Marsh Dike, atop which you'll travel, was constructed to carry a singletrack railroad that led from the park's current location to the Tasker Iron Works plant, which no longer exists. The trail continues past Dobbinsville Park and Deemers Beach, then crosses Army Creek onto another dike before dead-ending. The entire trip is 3.4 miles out-and-back, but if you are interested in extending your run or ride, there is access to the 5.5-mile Jack A. Markell Trail (see page 19) just north of Battery Park; to reach it, take South Street 0.4 mile to Young Street Park.

CONTACT: delawaregreenways.org/trail/battery-park-trail

PARKING

The parking areas below are all within New Castle and are listed from east to west. *Indicates that at least one accessible parking space is available.*

Battery Park*: At the end of Delaware St., 300 feet south of The Strand (39.65801, -75.5620).

Battery Park*: 199 W. Third St. (39.6568, -75.5684).

Deemers Beach River Access: W. Seventh St., 0.2 mile southwest of Clymer St. (39.6533, -75.5825).

Cape Henlopen State Park, on Delaware's Atlantic coast-line, is one of the state's must-see destinations. William Penn (founder of Pennsylvania) once owned much of the land that's now the park, but in 1682, through local resident Edmund Warner, he gave the community free rein to use it for recreation and fishing. After his death, it remained open for public use, officially becoming a state park in 1964.

A trail loop through the state park offers 3.3 miles of paved riding with views of maritime forest, sand dunes, and other picturesque natural settings. In the spring, the Cape is also a stopping point for thousands of migrating birds, and horseshoe crabs lay their eggs on the bayside beaches, providing a food source for the birds. The trail is relatively level, except for two steep sections: one on the

TrailLink user James McGinnis

The paved bike loop offers views of maritime forest and sand dunes.

County
Sussex

Endpoints
Loop trail from Seaside Nature Center on Cape Henlopen Dr. at the Cape Henlopen State Park entrance (Lewes)

Mileage
3.3

Type
Greenway/Non-Rail-Trail

Roughness Index
1

Surface
Asphalt, Concrete

Cape Henlopen State Park Bike Loop

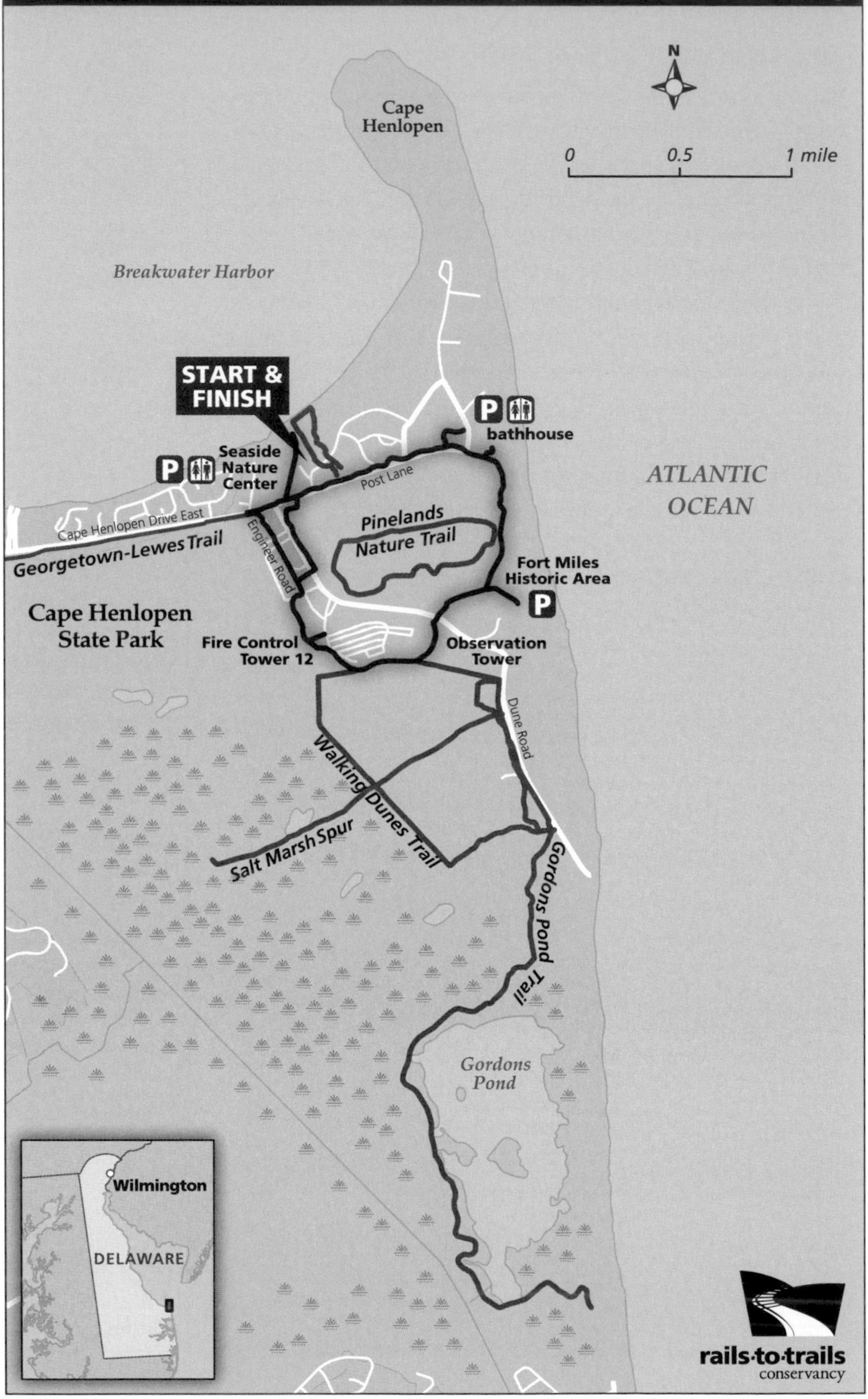

N

Cape
Henlopen

0   0.5   1 mile

Breakwater Harbor

START & FINISH

P 🚻 bathhouse

Seaside
Nature
Center

P 🚻

ATLANTIC OCEAN

Post Lane

Cape Henlopen Drive East

Georgetown-Lewes Trail

Engineer Road

Pinelands
Nature Trail

Fort Miles
Historic Area

P

**Cape Henlopen
State Park**

Fire Control
Tower 12

Observation
Tower

Dune Road

Walking Dunes Trail

Salt Marsh Spur

Gordons Pond Trail

*Gordons
Pond*

Wilmington

DELAWARE

rails·to·trails
conservancy

approach to the Fort Miles Historic Area on the southeast section of the loop, and the other just west of the campground.

Begin your Cape Henlopen State Park Bike Loop adventure at the Seaside Nature Center, where you'll find parking, restrooms, and displays on the area's fascinating wildlife. Heading east from the nature center, you'll cross a park road in 0.5 mile and see a sign for the bathhouse. Here, you'll have access to a coastal swimming beach, a food concession, and restrooms.

In another 0.5 mile, you'll enter the Fort Miles Historic Area and see the remnants of a military base hastily constructed in the early days of World War II to help protect the East Coast from the potential invasion of German forces. The grounds include an orientation building, several barracks, and a fire-control tower that would have located enemy ships and coordinated attacks against them. That history is recounted in a refurbished gun battery that now serves as a museum.

Just west of the Fort Miles parking lot, you'll cross Dune Road and see the observation tower, where visitors can climb a spiral staircase for panoramic views of Delaware's Cape Region. Rounding out the bottom of the loop, you'll travel through a pleasantly wooded section and, in 0.6 mile, reach the historical Fire Control Tower 12. Continuing the route north, you'll largely parallel Engineer Road up to Cape Henlopen Drive, the entrance road to the park, which you can follow east back to the nature center.

If you have more time to explore the park, there are a handful of unpaved nature trails to enjoy, along with two rail-trails: The Junction & Breakwater Trail (see page 25) sits on the western edge of the park, connecting the towns of Lewes and Rehoboth Beach, while the growing Georgetown-Lewes Trail (see page 17) begins in the park along Cape Henlopen Drive and extends nearly 9 miles southwest toward its eventual end in Georgetown.

CONTACT: destateparks.com/beaches/capehenlopen

PARKING

Parking areas are located within Cape Henlopen State Park in Lewes and are listed clockwise from north to south. The parking fee is $5 for in-state vehicles and $10 for out-of-state vehicles. (If you enter the park on foot or bike, there is no fee.) *Indicates that at least one accessible parking space is available.*

Seaside Nature Center: 15099 Cape Henlopen Dr. (38.7840, -75.0979).

McBride Bathhouse*: Cape Henlopen Dr. and Post Road (38.7857, -75.0897).

Fort Miles Historic Area: Dune Road, 0.7 mile south of Cape Henlopen Dr. (38.7771, -75.0919).

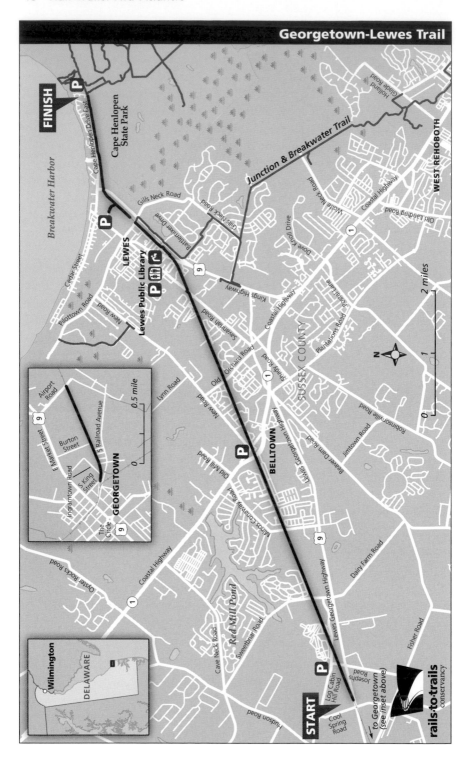

The Georgetown-Lewes Trail is popular for its relatively flat route that runs through tree-lined countryside into the coastal town of Lewes before ending in an oceanside state park. The trail is part of a developing 17-mile trail network that, when completed, will link Georgetown and Lewes to each other and to Cape Henlopen State Park, as well as to Rehoboth Beach by way of a connection to the Junction & Breakwater Trail (see page 25).

Beginning from its western end, a disconnected segment of the trail spanning 0.9 mile runs from Ingramtown Road and South King Street to Airport Road. Opened in late 2021, this section is mere blocks from downtown Georgetown and provides trail access to residents of an adjacent apartment complex and connections to the Georgetown Little League Complex, the Sussex Academy of Arts and Science, and the future Sussex County Park. It's also the first section of rail-with-trail in the corridor as it was built along an active freight line, the Delmarva Central Railroad.

Farther northeast, after a gap of 7 miles, the main segment of the trail begins at Cool Spring Road and the Lewes Georgetown Highway. The route offers plentiful shade and seclusion via a tree tunnel, opening up to meadows and fields as you head east toward Lewes.

The ancestral home of the Indigenous Siconese people, the town of Lewes dates back to 1631 when Dutch colonists

County
Sussex

Endpoints
Ingramtown Road and S. King St. (Georgetown); Airport Road, 0.4 mile southeast of Lewes Georgetown Hwy. (Georgetown); Cool Spring Road and Lewes Georgetown Hwy. (Milton); the Cape Henlopen State Park entrance at Cape Henlopen Dr. and E. Cape Shores Dr. (Lewes)

Mileage
9.6

Type
Rail-Trail/Rail-with-Trail

Roughness Index
1

Surface
Asphalt

Heather Irish

Whimsical art delights visitors along the Lewes end of the trail.

17

settled on this "purchased" tribal land. It became a strategic naval point during the War of 1812, and during World War II, Fort Miles, located in present-day Cape Henlopen State Park, became a vital defense against potential German attacks on Mid-Atlantic port cities. A list of more historical sites is available from the Lewes Chamber of Commerce, located 0.2 mile from the trail near its eastern end.

On the eastern end of the trail's main segment, parking is located at the Lewes Public Library, where the trail runs beside the building. Here you'll find restrooms, benches, a water bottle–filling station, and an information kiosk. A community garden and a set of historical rails are nestled nearby. Flowers and public art dot the stretch of trail between the library and Gills Neck Road.

The easternmost section of the trail leading to Cape Henlopen State Park is separated from the main route by the Lewes-Rehoboth Canal. To reach this disconnected segment, turn left from the eastern terminus of the main segment onto Gills Neck Road. In 0.2 mile, turn right on Savannah Road to cross the canal bridge. Continue 0.3 mile to American Legion Road/Massachusetts Avenue. Take a right and travel 0.2 mile to the trailhead for the Georgetown-Lewes Trail.

After this brief stretch of street traffic, the trail's wide lanes open up to a beautiful mix of sand, sea grass, and pine trees, offering intermittent shade and a fresh scent as you head to Cape Henlopen State Park. The park is home to Delaware's highest sand dune (80 feet tall), where the Henlopen Lighthouse sat until it eroded into the sea in 1926.

Alternatively, just before the canal, you can connect to the Junction & Breakwater Trail by turning right onto the trail at Gills Neck Road. You might even catch a glimpse of a boat or two drifting past you along the canal.

CONTACT: delawaregreenways.org/trail/georgetown-lewes-trail

PARKING

Parking areas are located within Lewes and are listed from west to east. *Indicates that at least one accessible parking space is available.*

Coolspring Presbyterian Church*: 28843 Log Cabin Hill Road (38.7376, -75.2384). Parking for trail users is available behind the church; reach the trail by traveling 0.2 mile east on Log Cabin Hill Road.

Lewes Public Library*: 111 Adams Ave. (38.7674, -75.1407).

American Legion Road Trailhead: Gravel parking area near the eastern terminus of American Legion Road/Massachusetts Ave., 0.1 mile southeast of E. Savannah Road (38.7779, -75.1316). Provides access to the disconnected segment of the Georgetown-Lewes Trail leading to Cape Henlopen State Park.

32191 Nassau Rd.: (38.7525, -75.1874)

Cape Henlopen State Park Seaside Nature Center: 15099 Cape Henlopen Dr., 0.4 mile east of the northern terminus of the Georgetown-Lewes Trail (38.7844, -75.0983).

Spanning 5.5 miles, the Jack A. Markell Trail (JAM Trail)—named after a former Delaware governor—is part of a trail system that connects the Wilmington riverfront with New Castle. The asphalt rail-trail, formerly a freight rail line, was completed in 2018. Connecting to the Wilmington Riverwalk (see page 35) on its northern end and the Battery Park Trail (see page 11) on its southern end, this trail is the center portion of an 8.6-mile trail experience.

The northern end of the JAM Trail begins at the DuPont Environmental Education Center, which offers interactive exhibits and programming about the area's habitats and wildlife. A variety of shopping, restaurants, and a baseball stadium are only about a mile north of the parking lot. A bike repair station is also located at the

Enjoy elevated views of marshland and the Christina River along the trail.

County
New Castle

Endpoints
DuPont Environmental Education Center (Wilmington); Battery Park at South St. and W. Third St. (New Castle)

Mileage
5.5

Type
Rail-Trail

Roughness Index
1

Surface
Asphalt, Boardwalk

Anthony Le

19

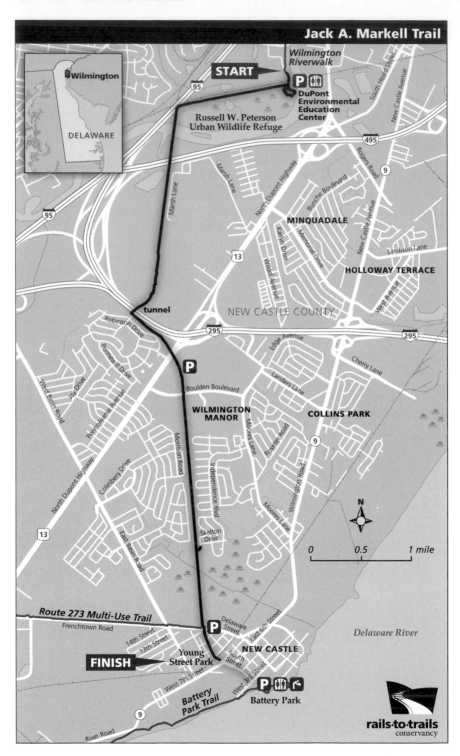

Jack A. Markell Trail

Wilmington

DELAWARE

START

Wilmington Riverwalk

DuPont Environmental Education Center

Russell W. Peterson Urban Wildlife Refuge

South Heald Street

New Castle Avenue

Marsh Lane

Marsh Lane

North Dupont Highway

Rogers Road

MINQUADALE

Burche Boulevard

New Castle Avenue

Lambson Lane

Karlyn Drive

Memorial Drive

HOLLOWAY TERRACE

Wildel Avenue

West Avenue

tunnel

NEW CASTLE COUNTY

Robinson Drive

Pennewill Drive

Edge Avenue

Cherry Lane

West Basin Road

Jay Drive

Boulden Boulevard

Landers Lane

WILMINGTON MANOR

COLLINS PARK

Pennsylvania Avenue

Morrison Road

Moores Lane

Roxeter Road

Colesbery Drive

Independence Blvd

Wilmington Road

North Dupont Highway

East Basin Road

Skelton Drive

Moores Lane

N

0   0.5   1 mile

Route 273 Multi-Use Trail

Frenchtown Road

Delaware Street

East 6th Street

Delaware River

14th Street

13th Street

FINISH

Young Street Park

South Street

NEW CASTLE

West 7th Street

Battery Park Trail

West 3rd Street

Battery Park

River Road

rails·to·trails
conservancy

beginning of the trail. As you continue through the Russell W. Peterson Urban Wildlife Refuge, you will enjoy a beautiful elevated boardwalk over the freshwater tidal marsh with views of the Christina River.

Heading south from the wildlife refuge, you will travel through marshland and wooded areas, over bridges, and through a tunnel under I-295. There are two at-grade road crossings with pedestrian crosswalks to ensure safe crossing.

The trail ends at Young Street Park, where you can visit the New Castle Italian Immigrant Memorial commemorating Italian immigration to the area as early as the 1600s. South of the park, continue the route on-road along South Street for 0.4 mile to Battery Park on the Delaware River. You can pick up the Battery Park Trail in the park along the river and follow the waterway to the southwest. A bike repair station, restaurants, and shopping are also available near the park.

The trail is not only an important local connector but also a part of the larger East Coast Greenway, a growing network of multiuse trails connecting 15 states and 450 cities and towns on a 3,000-mile route between Maine and Florida. Future connections to the JAM Trail include the 2.3-mile Newport River Trail near the marsh and the 2.35-mile Commons Boulevard Pathway near the I-295 tunnel.

CONTACT: delawaregreenways.org/trail/jack-a-markell-trail

PARKING

Parking areas are listed from north to south. *Indicates that at least one accessible parking space is available.*

WILMINGTON*: DuPont Environmental Education Center, 1400 Delmarva Lane (39.7241, -75.5620).

NEW CASTLE: Suburban Little League, Suburba Little League, 0.1 mile north of Boulden Blvd. (39.6922, -75.5769).

NEW CASTLE: Delaware St. and 10th St. (39.6640, -75.5727).

NEW CASTLE*: Battery Park, South St. and W. Third St. (39.6582, -75.5664).

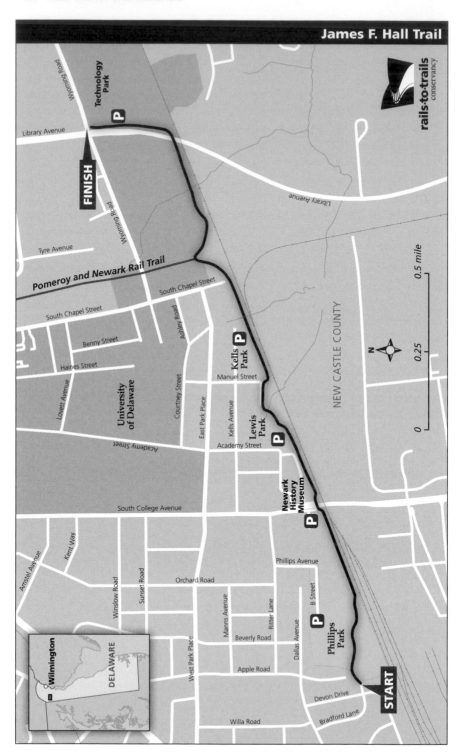

James F. Hall Trail

rails-to-trails
conservancy

Wyoming Road

Technology Park

Library Avenue

FINISH

Wyoming Road

Tyre Avenue

Pomeroy and Newark Rail Trail

South Chapel Street

South Chapel Street

Ashley Road

Benny Street

Haines Street

Lovett Avenue

University of Delaware

Courtney Street

East Park Place

Academy Street

Kells Park

Manuel Street

Kells Avenue

Lewis Park

Academy Street

Newark History Museum

Library Avenue

NEW CASTLE COUNTY

N

0.5 mile

0.25

0

South College Avenue

Kent Way

Amstel Avenue

Winslow Road

Sunset Road

Orchard Road

Manns Avenue

West Park Place

Beverly Road

Ritter Lane

Apple Road

Dallas Avenue

Phillips Avenue

B Street

Phillips Park

Devon Drive

Bradford Lane

Willa Road

START

Wilmington

DELAWARE

The James F. Hall Trail, named for the City of Newark's late parks and recreation director, packs a lot into a short stretch. Its paved surface is great for bicycling, inline skating, and stroller and wheelchair use, and there are multiple access points along the route. The trail runs through a semi-forested area and crosses streams, pristine wetlands, and two tributaries of White Clay Creek Wild & Scenic River—one at Phillips Park and one at Kells Park.

Best of all, this urban trail never crosses a road, so you can ride uninterrupted for its entire length. The trail also functions as a thoroughfare connecting Newark neighborhoods with a regional transit station, the University of Delaware, and shopping centers.

Starting at the southwestern terminus on Bradford Lane, you'll cross wetlands on a boardwalk before heading into Phillips Park—the first of three city parks along the trail. Just 0.3 mile from the park, right after South

The trail runs through a semi-forested area, connecting three Newark parks.

TrailLink user Jamie Herrera

County
New Castle

Endpoints
Phillips Park at Bradford Lane and Devon Dr. (Newark), Delaware Technology Park at Wyoming Road and Library Ave. (Newark)

Mileage
1.8

Type
Rail-with-Trail; Greenway/Non-Rail-Trail

Roughness Index
1

Surface
Asphalt

College Avenue, is the old Newark Train Station, which houses the Newark History Museum. History and rail buffs will also enjoy the various railroad relics, including old switches, that are placed next to the trail.

Train enthusiasts are almost guaranteed a train sighting along the James F. Hall Trail, as the adjacent rail corridor (separated from the path by a large fence) is used by Amtrak, CSX Transportation, and the Southeastern Pennsylvania Transportation Authority (SEPTA). Riders arriving at the Newark Amtrak/SEPTA station off South College Avenue will find themselves only a short walk from the trail.

In another 0.2 mile, you'll hit Lewis Park, and soon thereafter, Kells Park. Families with young children may especially enjoy the multiple playgrounds and picnic areas these parks have to offer. Along the path, trail users will find exercise equipment, baseball diamonds, and soccer fields, as well as basketball, handball, and tennis courts. Police call boxes are placed every 0.1 mile, and the trail is lit for 24-hour use.

Just east of South Chapel Street, 0.2 mile from Kells Park, the trail intersects the 4.4-mile Pomeroy and Newark Rail Trail. This connecting rail-trail leads to White Clay Creek State Park, where it goes on to connect to the 5-mile PennDel Trail for hikers. The James F. Hall Trail ends in 0.6 mile, just east of Library Avenue/DE 72, behind the University of Delaware's Technology Park.

The James F. Hall Trail, a designated National Recreation Trail, is also part of the larger East Coast Greenway, a growing network of multiuse trails connecting 15 states and 450 cities and towns on a 3,000-mile route between Maine and Florida.

CONTACT: newarkde.gov/434/james-f-hall-trail

PARKING

Parking areas are located within Newark and are listed from west to east. *Indicates that at least one accessible parking space is available.*

Phillips Park*: 101 B St. (39.6701, -75.7577).

Lewis Park*: 727 Academy St. (39.6721, -75.7502).

Kells Park*: 201 Kells Ave. (39.6732, -75.7454).

Delaware Technology Park*: 15 Innovation Way (39.6770, -75.7349).

The Junction & Breakwater Trail follows a section of the former Penn Central railroad, connecting the Delaware beach towns of Rehoboth Beach and Lewes. Winding through 4.1 miles of Cape Henlopen State Park, the trail acts as a nature retreat, complete with mature hardwood and conifer forests, open farmland, coastal marshes, and interpretive signs highlighting local flora and fauna. Even though its three endpoints are found in residential and commercial areas, the beautiful, pine-studded rail-trail offers a break from the nearby beaches and shopping centers.

Much of the Junction & Breakwater Trail has been paved in recent years, although the segment within Cape Henlopen State Park has a crushed-stone surface. Be sure to remember your trail etiquette (page 6), as this trail is well traveled by locals and tourists alike. You will be sharing the mostly flat route with bicyclists, walkers, runners, wheelchair users, and families with strollers and dogs.

County
Sussex

Endpoints
Hebron Road, 700 feet northeast of Coastal Hwy./US 1 (Rehoboth Beach); Kings Highway/US 9, between Gills Neck Road/Road 267 and Wells Field Road (Lewes); Gills Neck Road/Road 267, under Theo C. Freeman Memorial Hwy./US 9 (Lewes)

Mileage
8.3

Type
Rail-Trail

Roughness Index
1

Surface
Asphalt, Concrete, Crushed Stone

TrailLink user hepdj

The rail-trail offers a tranquil break from the busy beach towns of Rehoboth Beach and Lewes.

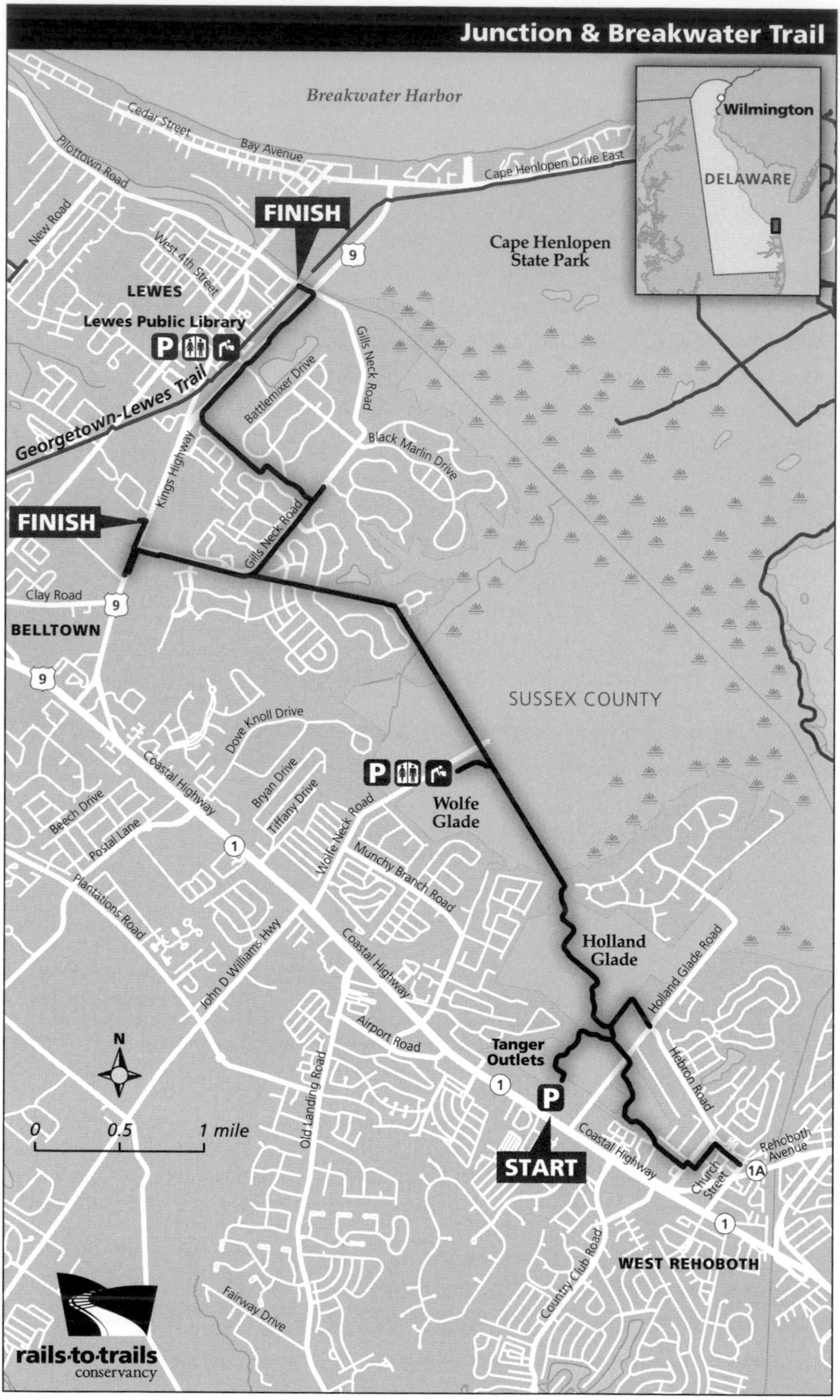

Junction & Breakwater Trail

Breakwater Harbor

Cedar Street

Pilottown Road

Bay Avenue

Cape Henlopen Drive East

Wilmington

DELAWARE

FINISH

9

New Road

West 4th Street

Cape Henlopen
State Park

LEWES

Lewes Public Library

Georgetown-Lewes Trail

Battlemier Drive

Gills Neck Road

Kings Highway

Black Marlin Drive

FINISH

Gills Neck Road

Clay Road   9

BELLTOWN

9

Dove Knoll Drive

SUSSEX COUNTY

Coastal Highway

Bryan Drive

Tiffany Drive

Beech Drive

Postal Lane

Wolfe Neck Road

**Wolfe
Glade**

1

Munchy Branch Road

Plantations Road

Coastal Highway

John D Williams Hwy

**Holland
Glade**

Holland Glade Road

Airport Road

N

Old Landing Road

**Tanger
Outlets**
1

P

Hebron Road

Rehoboth
Avenue

0   0.5   1 mile

Coastal Highway

START

Church Street

1A

1

Country Club Road

WEST REHOBOTH

Fairway Drive

rails·to·trails
conservancy

To begin in West Rehoboth, park at the outlet mall on Seaside Outlet Drive, and follow the bike/pedestrian path leading from the parking lot (between the buildings in the middle) to the trail. The actual southernmost endpoint—from which the trail mile markers originate—is 1.3 miles south, near Hebron Road and Coastal Highway/US 1, but parking is not available at this access point.

Leaving the outlets behind, you'll pass behind some fenced-in condo buildings, visible through the trees. Before long, you'll find yourself flanked by cornfields and forests. Hawks and both snow and Canada geese can be spotted in the air, and deer, squirrels, and other small woodland animals share the trail.

Between mile markers 1.5 and 2.0, you'll hit the Holland Glade Overlook, featuring views of wetlands from a refurbished 80-foot railroad bridge built in 1913. Before mile marker 2.5, you'll see signs for the Wolfe Neck trailhead. For a short side trip, turn left and follow the 0.2-mile spur to access this trailhead. The nearby Wolfe House—a circa 1875 farmhouse—has parking, restrooms, a water fountain, and a bike repair station. Back on the trail, continue north to the Wolfe Glade Overlook at mile marker 3.0, where you can enjoy more scenic views from this forested area of oak, hemlock, and pine.

After the Wolfe Glade Overlook, the trail turns residential as it follows Golden Eagle Boulevard. At the triangular intersection, veer left to access one of the trail's endpoints, opposite Cape Henlopen High School on Kings Highway/US 9 in Lewes (note that parking is not allowed at the high school). Alternatively, turn right to reach the final endpoint in downtown Lewes. This new, northernmost endpoint is located on Gills Neck Road/Road 267 under Theo C. Freeman Memorial Highway/US 9, where the trail connects to the Georgetown-Lewes Trail (see page 17). If you parked at the trail's southern end, retrace your route to the outlet mall, where you can shop and grab a bite to eat at the end of your journey.

CONTACT: delawaregreenways.org/trail/junction-breakwater-trail

PARKING

Parking areas are listed from south to north. *Indicates that at least one accessible parking space is available.*

REHOBOTH BEACH: Tanger Outlet Center, 36470 Seaside Outlet Dr. (outlet mall northwest of Seaside Outlet Dr. and Coastal Hwy./US 1) (38.7199, -75.1113). A bike/pedestrian path leads from the parking lot of the shopping center (between the buildings in the middle) to the actual trail.

REHOBOTH BEACH: 35536 Wolfe Neck Road (38.7409, -75.1207).

LEWES: Monroe Ave. between Theo C. Freeman Memorial Hwy./US 9 and Railroad Ave. (38.7681, -75.1396).

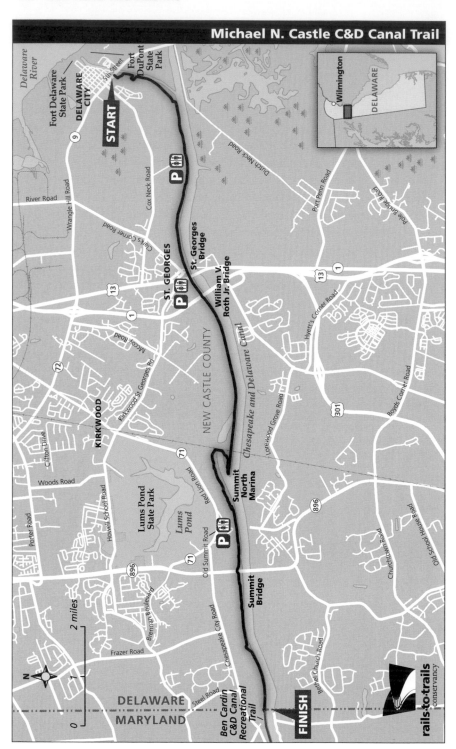

Michael N. Castle C&D Canal Trail

Delaware River

Fort Delaware State Park

DELAWARE CITY

Fort DuPont State Park

5th Street

START

Wilmington

DELAWARE

9

Cox Neck Road

Dutch Neck Road

River Road

Wrangle Hill Road

Clarks Corner Road

ST. GEORGES

St. Georges Bridge

William V. Roth Jr. Bridge

Port Penn Road

Pole Bridge Road

13

13

1

1

McCoy Road

Kirkwood St Georges Rd

Hyett's Corner Road

NEW CASTLE COUNTY

Chesapeake and Delaware Canal

72

KIRKWOOD

Clifton Drive

Woods Road

Lums Pond State Park

Lums Pond

Red Lion Road

71

Summit North Marina

Lorewood Grove Road

Boyds Corner Road

301

Porter Road

Howell School Road

Old Summit Road

896

Churchtown Road

Old School House Road

896

71

Summit Bridge

Brennan Boulevard

2 miles

Frazer Road

N

Chesapeake City Road

Steel Road

Bethel Church Road

DELAWARE

MARYLAND

Ben Cardin C&D Canal Recreational Trail

FINISH

0

rails-to-trails conservancy

The Michael N. Castle C&D Canal Trail offers a scenic 12.4-mile route along the north shore of the Chesapeake and Delaware Canal in northern Delaware. The popular trail is named after the former governor and US representative whose efforts in Congress helped initiate the project on behalf of local trail users.

The C&D Canal opened in 1829, linking the Chesapeake Bay and the Delaware River via a 14-mile route across the Maryland–Delaware peninsula through what was once swampy marshland. Today, the canal continues to be one of the world's busiest, as much of the shipping traffic to and from the Port of Baltimore—one of the largest ports in the United States—makes its way through the channel.

Delaware City is home to two state parks: Fort DuPont State Park (which served as a military base from the Civil War through World War II) and Fort Delaware State Park (popular with birders and accessible via ferry). Along the paved Michael Castle Trail, benches accommodate trail users who wish to watch the ships in the canal. On the edge

In the St. Georges area, the trail offers a view of the Route 1 bridge.

TrailLink user James McGinnis

County
New Castle

Endpoints
Canal St. and Fifth St (Delaware City); Ben Cardin C&D Canal Recreational Trail at the Delaware–Maryland state line (Newark)

Mileage
12.4

Type
Greenway/Non-Rail-Trail

Roughness Index
1

Surface
Asphalt

of Delaware City, the trail also passes the parklike African Union Church Cemetery, which features historical displays.

Heading southwest from Delaware City, the trail passes under three bridges. Nature enthusiasts can be on the lookout for native wildflowers, trees, and wildlife, including deer, turkeys, and raccoons. Birders will enjoy spotting rarer species, such as peregrine falcons, pied-billed grebes, and bald eagles. The only diversion from the canal's edge—and the only exception to the trail's otherwise flat grade—is a brief arc and somewhat steep climb around the Summit North Marina. (*Note:* If riding in the reverse direction, west to east, wayfinding around the marina and up Summit Point can prove challenging.) Horses are not permitted on this short section.

Just west of the boat slips, the trail passes the southern reaches of Lums Pond State Park, which surrounds the largest freshwater pond in the state. Here you can fish and boat but not swim. Several trails inside the park cater to hikers, bikers, horseback riders, and snowmobilers. (Note that the Michael Castle Trail is not open to motorized vehicles.)

From the trailhead south of Lums Pond State Park on Old Summit Road, head 3.4 miles west to reach the terminus of the Michael Castle Trail and the beginning of the Ben Cardin C&D Canal Recreational Trail, at the Delaware–Maryland state line. The Ben Cardin C&D Canal Recreational Trail follows the canal nearly 2 miles to quaint Chesapeake City, Maryland. Note that when going westward past the South Lums Pond parking area, the trail has steep areas that may be difficult for wheelchair users.

CONTACT: delawaregreenways.org/trail/michael-n-castle-c-d-canal-trail

PARKING

Parking areas are listed from east to west. *Indicates that at least one accessible parking space is available.*

NEW CASTLE COUNTY, WEST OF DELAWARE CITY*: Biddle Point (39.5546, -75.6179). Includes horse trailer parking. The 0.6-mile unnamed driveway to the parking lot can be accessed from Cox Neck Road, 0.9 mile east of Clarks Corner Road (look for the brown DELAWARE C&D CANAL WILDLIFE AREA sign at the entrance).

ST. GEORGES*: St. Georges Trailhead (39.5535, -75.6531). The unnamed driveway leading to the parking lot can be accessed from Kirkwood St. Georges Road, 0.2 mile east of Caitlin Way (look for the brown DELAWARE C&D CANAL WILDLIFE AREA sign).

BEAR*: South Lums Pond Trailhead (39.5445, -75.7198). Includes horse trailer parking. The 0.3-mile unnamed driveway leading to the parking lot can be accessed from Old Summit Road, 0.4 mile south of Red Lion Road (look for the brown DELAWARE C&D CANAL WILDLIFE AREA sign at the entrance).

The Northern Delaware Greenway Trail is historically significant as the oldest and longest off-road trail in Delaware. Currently spanning 10.4 miles, the trail was also the impetus for the creation of the Delaware Greenways organization in the 1990s. Designated as a National Recreation Trail, the Northern Delaware Greenway Trail links many of Wilmington's parks and greenways.

Though the mile markers along the trail start from its eastern end in Fox Point State Park, these first 2.7 miles of trail are currently separated from the rest of the path by I-495. A future 9-mile trail connection from Claymont to Fox Point State Park will eventually connect these two segments, but for now trail users will have to make a separate trip to Fox Point if they want to enjoy the picturesque views of the Delaware River that stretch of trail offers.

TrailLink user gogovind

Enjoy vistas of the Delaware River from the segment in Fox Point State Park.

County
New Castle

Endpoints
Cauffiel Pkwy. and
Governor Printz Blvd./
US 13 (Wilmington);
Brandywine Park at
N. Market St. and Glen
Ave. (Wilmington);
Lighthouse Road in Fox
State Park (Wilmington)

Mileage
10.4

Type
Rail-Trail

Roughness Index
1–2

Surface
Asphalt

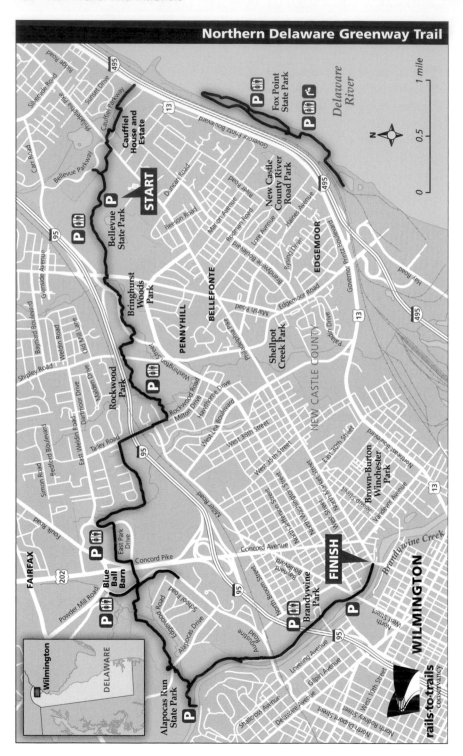

Northern Delaware Greenway Trail

Begin your journey on the 7.7-mile portion of the trail at its eastern terminus in Bellevue State Park. As the trail goes through the park's eastern end, it passes the Cauffiel House and Estate, a Colonial Revival–style home built in the early 1900s. (The trail technically ends at I-495, but the section past the trail sign along Cauffiel Parkway is an overgrown wooded area, so it's recommended for hikers and bikers only.) The park offers amenities for numerous other outdoor activities, including fishing, horseback riding, picnicking, and tennis.

Continuing west, you'll travel through Rockwood Park, home to an 1850s mansion built in the Rural Gothic Revival style and listed on the National Register of Historic Places. From the west side of the park, you'll travel north along Rockwood Road, which becomes Talley Road, and then head west paralleling the residential Weldin Ridge Road.

A particularly scenic, wooded stretch comes next. It runs through Alapocas Run State Park, where visitors can check out the Blue Ball Barn. The converted dairy barn is now home to the Delaware Folk Art Collection, which features works from more than 50 local artists. You can also view historical mills across Brandywine Creek with accompanying historical displays along the trail. Hiking trails provide additional opportunities to explore the wooded park on foot. The state park offers rock climbing as well, though a permit and advance reservations are required.

Much of the trail is filled with rolling curves and short drops, so leave the inline skates at home, and instead enjoy a nice stroll or a fun bike ride with family and friends. (If you do the trail in the reverse direction, note that a very steep uphill section runs from Brandywine Creek to the northeast through Alapocas Run State Park, so plan accordingly.) As the trail heads south from the state park, the segment adjacent to Park Drive, built on a former rail corridor, offers a more level grade.

At its western end, the trail connects with the Brandywine Creek Path at North Market Street and is only 1 mile northeast of the Wilmington Riverwalk (see page 35), offering more access to residential communities, schools, businesses, parks, and cultural sites.

Like many urban trails, the Northern Delaware Greenway Trail is well used by commuters during the workweek. The trail is also part of the larger East Coast Greenway, a growing network of multiuse trails connecting 15 states and 450 cities and towns on a 3,000-mile route between Maine and Florida.

Closure Notice: *The Bancroft Pedestrian Bridge over Brandywine Creek in Alapocas Run State Park is closed indefinitely due to flood damage that occurred in September 2021. Please check the website below for updates.*

CONTACT: delawaregreenways.org/trail/northern-delaware-greenway-trail

Continued on next page

Anthony Le

Much of the greenway traverses wooded parkland.

PARKING

Parking areas are located within Wilmington and are listed from east to west. *Indicates that at least one accessible parking space is available.*

Fox Point State Park*: Lighthouse Road, 0.8 mile northeast of Ellerslie Road (39.7581, -75.4891).

Bellevue State Park*: The park's main parking lot is 0.6 mile south of the park entrance on Carr Road (39.7777, -75.4967). Access the trail from the northern end of the parking lot.

Rockwood Park*: 4671 Washington St. Ext. (39.7738, -75.5208).

Alapocas Run State Park*: Parking lot at the Blue Ball Barn, 1914 W. Park Dr. (39.7768, -75.5457).

Brandywine Park: The parking lot is located under I-95 along N. Park Drive, 0.1 mile north of N. Van Buren St. (39.7572, -75.5526).

A gorgeous addition to the area's trail network, Wilmington Riverwalk (sometimes called the Christina River Walk) allows pedestrians and cyclists to experience Wilmington's renovated urban development along the banks of the Christina River. The trail passes a variety of waterside restaurants and businesses, scenic viewing platforms, and the city's train station just south of downtown.

On the trail's southern end, you'll enjoy a breathtaking boardwalk section leading into the Russell W. Peterson Urban Wildlife Refuge. A statue of the marshy refuge's namesake, a former Delaware governor and prominent environmentalist, greets trail users at the beginning of the boardwalk section. The trail leads to the impressive DuPont Environmental Education Center, where you can check out the visitor center, an essential stop for those interested in learning about the area's ecosystem and biodiversity.

From the education center, the route continues west via the Jack A. Markell Trail (see page 19), starting with another picturesque boardwalk section built to allow trail

The Christina River serves as a picturesque backdrop for the Riverwalk.

Joe LaCroix

County
New Castle

Endpoints
S. Poplar St., 0.1 mile southwest of E. Front St. (Wilmington); the DuPont Environmental Education Center (Wilmington)

Mileage
1.4

Type
Greenway/Non-Rail-Trail

Roughness Index
1

Surface
Boardwalk, Brick, Concrete

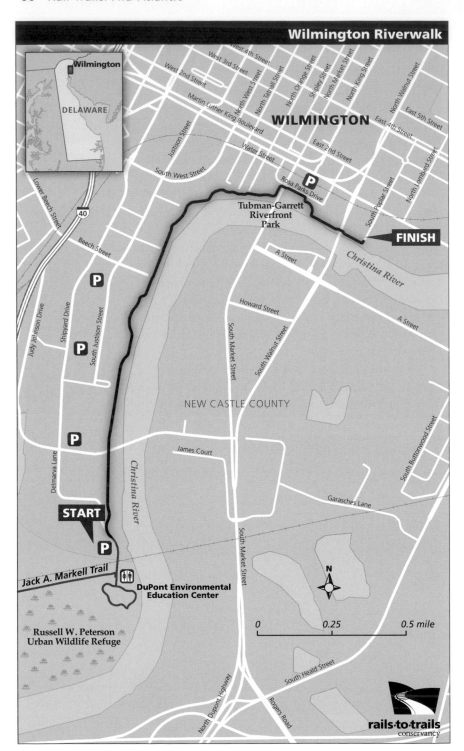

users to explore the preserved wetlands with minimal disruption to the environment. That trail continues all the way into New Castle, allowing for a largely flat, seamless, and scenic journey between the two cities.

With ample benches, numerous trail amenities, beautiful native trees and flowers, and lovely views of the adjacent river, the Wilmington Riverwalk offers great outdoor recreation opportunities for residents and visitors alike.

CONTACT: riverfrontwilm.com

PARKING

Parking areas are located within Wilmington and are listed from north to south. *Indicates that at least one accessible parking space is available.*

Tubman-Garrett Riverfront Park: Parking garage on Rosa Parks Dr. between S. Market St. and S. Walnut St. (39.7370, -75.5524).

Riverfront Wilmington Commuter Lot (Parking Lot K)*: Beech St. between Shipyard Dr. and Justison St. (39.7337, -75.5628). To reach the trail, follow Beech St. 0.1 mile southeast toward the Christina River.

Chase Center on the Riverfront*: 815 Justison St. (39.7309, -75.5640). To reach the trail, travel 0.1 mile east toward the Christina River.

Riverfront Wilmington*: Delmarva Lane and New Sweden St. (39.7278, -75.5635).

DuPont Environmental Education Center: 1400 Delmarva Lane (39.7241, -75.5620).

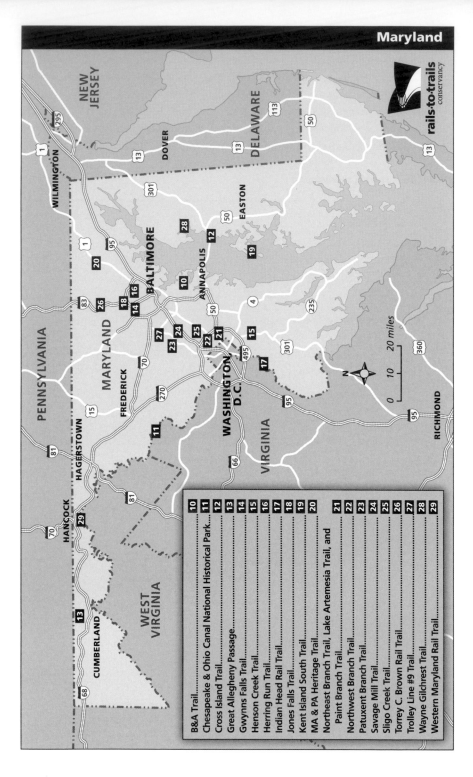

Maryland

rails-to-trails
conservancy

NEW JERSEY

WILMINGTON 295

1

DOVER 13

DELAWARE 13 113

EASTON 50

301

95 1

20

83 26

18 16

14

BALTIMORE

28

12

ANNAPOLIS

19

10

50 4 235

27 24 25

23 22 21 15

495 17 301

70

WASHINGTON D.C.

360

FREDERICK

270

15

95

HANCOCK 70 29

81

HAGERSTOWN

11

VIRGINIA

95 RICHMOND

66

PENNSYLVANIA

MARYLAND

50

N

0   10   20 miles

WEST VIRGINIA

CUMBERLAND 13

68

B&A Trail...	**10**
Chesapeake & Ohio Canal National Historical Park....	**11**
Cross Island Trail...	**12**
Great Allegheny Passage......................................	**13**
Gwynns Falls Trail...	**14**
Henson Creek Trail..	**15**
Herring Run Trail...	**16**
Indian Head Rail Trail..	**17**
Jones Falls Trail..	**18**
Kent Island South Trail..	**19**
MA & PA Heritage Trail..	**20**
Northeast Branch Trail, Lake Artemesia Trail, and	
Paint Branch Trail...	**21**
Northwest Branch Trail..	**22**
Patuxent Branch Trail..	**23**
Savage Mill Trail...	**24**
Sligo Creek Trail...	**25**
Torrey C. Brown Rail Trail.....................................	**26**
Trolley Line #9 Trail...	**27**
Wayne Gilchrest Trail...	**28**
Western Maryland Rail Trail...................................	**29**

Maryland

Chesapeake & Ohio Canal National Historical Park (see page 45)
Khuyen Dinh

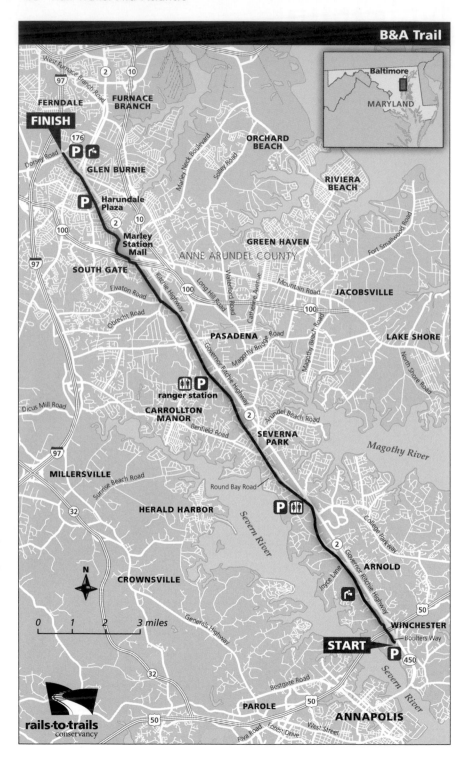

You can augment your physical exercise with a mental workout on the paved B&A Trail, a 13-mile rail-trail that connects the Chesapeake Bay cities of Baltimore and Annapolis. Along with extensive historical markers, this trail features the Planet Walk, a multimile display that might challenge your perception of the solar system.

The B&A Trail follows the former route of the Annapolis and Baltimore Short Line, which began hauling passengers and freight in 1887. Ownership changed over the years, and the trains running to Annapolis—state capital and home to the U.S. Naval Academy—were electrified in 1908. The company was reincorporated as the Baltimore & Annapolis Railroad in 1935, but business dwindled after World War II until service on the remaining segment ended in the 1970s.

In Annapolis, the trail officially begins where Boulters Way intersects Winchester Road, though the nearest parking is available about 0.7 mile south from the trailhead where Boulters Way intersects Governor Ritchie Highway.

Interesting art along the trail provides a good excuse for a short break.

County
Anne Arundel

Endpoints
Boulters Way and Winchester Road (Annapolis); Dorsey Road/MD 170 and Baltimore Annapolis Blvd./MD 648 (Glen Burnie)

Mileage
13.3

Type
Rail-Trail

Roughness Index
1

Surface
Asphalt

TrailLink user dks3405_tl

Heading north, you'll pass a series of historical markers labeled A–Z. The A marker, at 0.1 mile, is the Winchester Station House at Manresa; Z (at 13.3 miles) identifies the Sawmill Branch, a historical source of water and power.

The route rolls through woodsy neighborhoods in Arnold. Be aware that most road crossings are at-grade, and many crosswalks do not have signals. Exceptions are the trestles across Joyce Lane in Arnold and Round Bay Road in Severna Park. Construction work on the Joyce Lane trestle that began in October 2021 was scheduled to be completed in March 2022. Check the county website for updates.

In 3.5 miles, you'll arrive in Severna Park, where you'll find more trail parking and a seasonal farmers market on Saturdays. The trail passes behind pockets of businesses, some that cater to trail users, from here north to Glen Burnie.

At the halfway point, you'll find the circa 1889 general store that now serves as the trail's ranger station and railroad museum. Parking and restrooms are available here, as are pamphlets for the lettered historical markers. This is also the southern terminus of the Planet Walk, a scale model of the solar system that stretches from Pluto, here, to the sun, some 4.6 miles up the trail. It's also as far north as horses are permitted along the trail.

The trail's surroundings become more urban and commercial as you head north past the sprawling Marley Station Mall and Harundale Plaza. The northern terminus is at Dorsey Road, just across from the Cromwell Station on Baltimore's Light RailLink. The John Overstreet Connector heads west for 1.5 miles to the 11-mile BWI Trail, which encircles the Baltimore/Washington International Thurgood Marshall Airport. The closest parking to the endpoint is 0.5 mile south, where Platzner Lane crosses Greenway Street.

The B&A Trail is also included in the East Coast Greenway, a growing network of multiuse trails connecting 15 states and 450 cities and towns on a 3,000-mile route between Maine and Florida. The greenway shadows the length of the B&A Trail, extending across the Severn River and passing through historic Annapolis on its way to Washington, D.C.

CONTACT: aacounty.org/departments/recreation-parks/parks

PARKING

Parking areas are listed from south to north. *Indicates that at least one accessible parking space is available.*

ANNAPOLIS: 1700–1714 Gov. Ritchie Hwy./MD 450 between US 50 and Boulters Way (39.0105, -76.4893).

SEVERNA PARK: Small lot at Jones Station Road and Baltimore Annapolis Blvd./MD 648 (39.05638, -76.5291).

SEVERNA PARK*: Jones Station Road between Baltimore Annapolis Blvd. and Ritchie Hwy./MD 2 (39.05732, -76.5289).

SEVERNA PARK: B&A Trail Station, 50 W. Earleigh Heights Road (39.0974, -76.5699).

SEVERNA PARK*: B&A Trail Station, 51 W. Earleigh Heights Road (39.09689, -76.5698).

GLEN BURNIE: Jumpers Hole Road and Elvaton Road (39.1210, -76.5889).

GLEN BURNIE: Greenway Road SE between Aquahart Road and Pine Terrace (39.15349, -76.6177).

GLEN BURNIE: Greenway St. NW and Platzner Lane near Central Ave. and Crain Hwy./MD 3 (39.1643, -76.6260).

The route rolls through woodsy neighborhoods in a handful of Anne Arundel County communities.
Photo by TrailLink user lapfounts

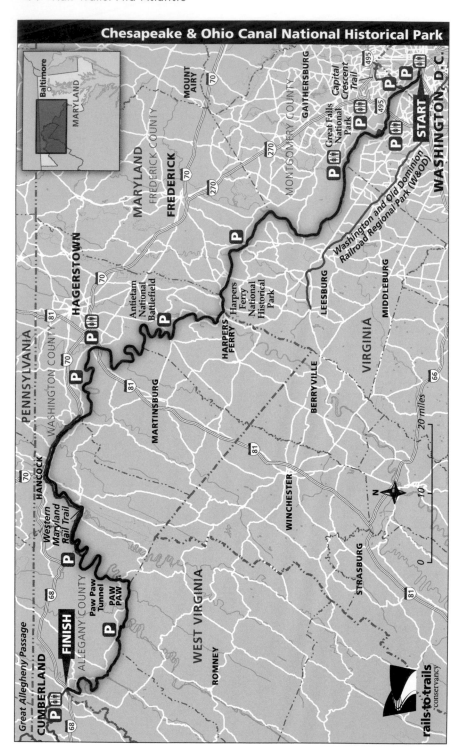

Following the Potomac River, the C&O Canal Towpath traverses the Chesapeake & Ohio Canal National Historical Park for 184.5 miles between Georgetown in Washington, D.C., and Cumberland, Maryland. For its first few miles, the pathway also parallels the paved Capital Crescent Trail (see page 239), which forms an arc around D.C.'s western and northern boundaries. Both trails are part of the Capital Trails Coalition (**railstotrails.org/ctc**)—a Rails-to-Trails Conservancy TrailNation™ project that aims to develop an 800-mile trail network connecting the greater Washington, D.C., metropolitan region.

Hundreds of original features, including locks, lock houses, aqueducts, and other canal structures, are reminders of the canal's role as a transportation system during the Canal Era, which peaked in the mid-19th century. The

Counties
Allegany (MD), Frederick (MD), Montgomery (MD), Washington, D.C.

Endpoints
29th St. and Rock Creek Pkwy. (Washington, D.C.); Canal St., 0.1 mile south of Baltimore St. (Cumberland, MD)

Mileage
184.5

Type
Canal

Roughness Index
2

Surface
Brick, Concrete, Crushed Stone, Dirt

Danielle Taylor

Hundreds of historical features can be seen along the towpath.

45

C&O Canal Towpath was an engineering feat that, unfortunately for investors, was largely outdone by the competing railroad that parallels the towpath in many places.

Today, recreationists of all types can enjoy this mostly level, continuous trail through the spectacular scenery of the Potomac River valley. The towpath is primarily dirt and gravel with about 50 contiguous miles surfaced with crushed stone. (Additional miles are planned to be resurfaced in the coming years.) Every year millions of visitors hike or bike the C&O Canal Towpath. Peak season is May–October. Weekends from spring through fall are busy, especially around Washington, D.C., and Great Falls Park in Potomac, Maryland.

The park provides campgrounds (both private and public), picnic areas, indoor and portable toilets, innumerable historical sites, and lookout points along the way. In adjacent canal towns, you'll also find amenities such as cafés and restaurants, B&Bs and motels, bike shops, museums, and retail shops, as well as additional historical sites. A handful of visitor centers operated by the National Park Service sell guidebooks and provide information about the towpath, its history, and local points of interest. You can even stay the night in one of the restored lock houses (visit **canaltrust.org/programs/canal-quarters** for more information).

Of particular importance is the role the canal played during the American Civil War as a dividing line between North and South. Troops on both sides of the conflict lobbed ammunition across the water and crossed the river and canal numerous times to raid enemy camps, sabotage canal operations, and march to and from battles, including the Gettysburg Campaign. Though many aren't marked, several sites along the canal saw events both tragic and heroic. The guidebooks sold by the National Park Service describe these sites and events.

Most of the trail is heavily wooded, and river views are best during early spring, late fall, and winter, when trees are leafless. Don't miss the Paw Paw Tunnel at milepost 155.2, at the northern end of the trail. Also, because the path requires regular maintenance, some sections may be closed for repairs. Visit the National Park Service website for current information on trail detours.

In Cumberland, the towpath connects to the Great Allegheny Passage (**gaptrail.org**; see page 51), where you can extend your journey all the way to Pittsburgh. Both trails are part of Rails-to-Trails Conservancy's Great American Rail-Trail® (**greatamericanrailtrail.org**), which spans the United States between Washington, D.C., and Washington State. The towpath also has multiple connections to the Western Maryland Rail Trail (see page 107), a paved 27.5-mile route paralleling the Potomac River.

CONTACT: nps.gov/choh

PARKING

Parking areas are listed from southeast to northwest. Select parking areas for the trail are listed below. For a detailed list of parking areas and other waypoints, go to **TrailLink.com™**. *Indicates that at least one accessible parking space is available.*

WASHINGTON, D.C.: Fletcher's Cove, 4940 Canal Road NW (38.9192, -77.1010). Parking is accessible only from northbound Canal Road NW. *Note:* Canal Road NW uses timed, one-way routing. The trail properly begins 3 miles east in the Georgetown neighborhood, but this is the first opportunity for free trailside parking.

BETHESDA*: Lock 6, 6100 Clara Barton Pkwy. (38.9444, -77.1233). Parking lot is accessible only from southbound Clara Barton Pkwy.

POTOMAC*: Carderock Recreation Area, Carderock Road, 0.3 mile south of Clara Barton Pkwy. (38.9726, -77.2000). Four high-capacity parking lots are available.

POTOMAC: Great Falls parking, Macarthur Blvd., 1.1 mile west of Clara Barton Pkwy. (38.9825, -77.2271). Two parking areas are located 150 feet apart and are often filled to capacity.

DARNESTOWN: Riley's Lock (Lock 24), Riley's Lock Road, 0.7 mile south of River Road (39.0691, -77.3408).

POINT OF ROCKS: 3703 Canal Road (39.2731, -77.5401).

SHARPSBURG*: Canal Road, 0.5 mile south of Shepherdstown Pike/MD 34 (39.4339, -77.7955).

WILLIAMSPORT*: Williamsport Visitors Center, 205 W. Potomac St. (39.6005, -77.8260).

CLEAR SPRING: Four Locks, Starliper Road, 300 feet south of Four Locks Road (39.6153, -77.9473).

LITTLE ORLEANS*: Fifteen Mile Creek, High Germany Road, 0.1 mile south of Orleans Road SE (39.6259, -78.3855). Pass through the one-lane tunnel, turn right (south) and cross the one-lane bridge.

OLDTOWN: Lock 70, Green Spring Road SE, 600 feet south of Opessa St. (39.5404, -78.6122).

CUMBERLAND*: Cumberland Visitor Center and Western Maryland Scenic Railroad Station, 13 Canal St. (39.6495, -78.7629).

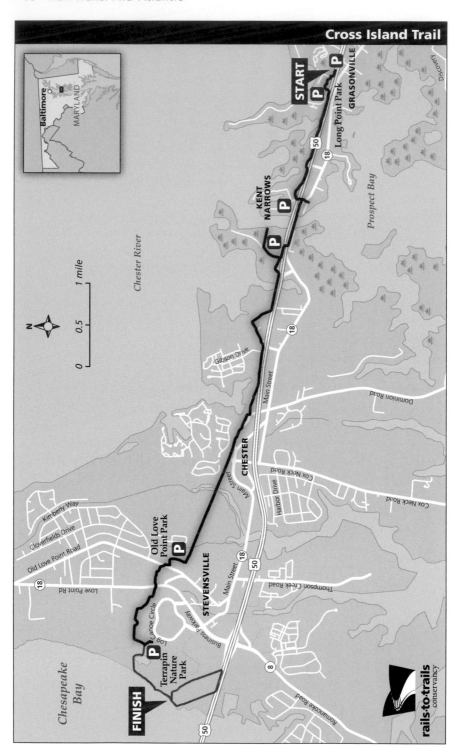

Explore the best of the Eastern Shore on Queen Anne's County's Cross Island Trail, which runs the width of Kent Island from east to west, stretching between two nature parks. With many access points along its route, this tree-lined trail takes you from neighborhood green space to boatyards and wetlands, showing you glimpses of waterfowl and wildlife before depositing you at the Terrapin Nature Center. Over its 6.5-mile course, the trail frequently intersects with water, traversing numerous wetlands and inlets and delivering views of the Chesapeake Bay. Ospreys are frequent visitors along the trail, as they hunt and care for their young in nests built in the wetland areas.

Beginning at Long Point Park in Grasonville, you'll head west along the northern side of the Blue Star Memorial Highway. At Kent Narrows Road, the trail crosses south under US 50/301 and then heads west again, intersecting

The tree-lined trail traverses wetlands and inlets over its 6.5-mile course.

Brandi Horton

County
Queen Anne's

Endpoints
Long Point Park at Long Point Road (Grasonville); Terrapin Nature Park (Stevensville)

Mileage
6.5

Type
Rail-Trail

Roughness Index
1

Surface
Asphalt, Boardwalk

with the causeway across Kent Narrows. There the trail transitions to a protected bicycle and pedestrian lane. Between Old Love Point Park and Kent Island High School, the trail crosses Old Love Point Road, where you'll find clearly marked road crossings. There are several other road crossings over the course of the trail, all of which are well marked and easy to navigate.

Several miles of trail, between Macum Creek in Chester and Old Love Point Park in Stevensville, follow the former Kent Island Railroad. The railroad was operated by Queen Anne's Railroad Company and brought the first passenger rail to the island. Though passenger service was short-lived, the railroad continued to carry freight until the 1950s. At Cox Creek, notice the pilings and lower framing of the bridge, which can be traced to the Baltimore & Eastern Railroad trestle bridge dating back to the 1890s.

Less than 2 miles farther west, the trail reaches Terrapin Nature Park, a 276-acre facility featuring over 3 miles of walking and nature trails. Following signs to beach access will bring you to a sandy shoreline with panoramic views of the Chesapeake Bay Bridge. Nature trails—including a wheelchair-accessible boardwalk—will take you through wildflower meadows, woodlands, wetlands, and tidal ponds.

While the trail provides an escape into nature for locals and visitors alike, it is also an important active-transportation route with access to neighborhoods, community sports fields, schools, and waterfront dining on the Chesapeake Bay. For active tourists, the trail provides pedestrian and bicyclist access to nearby lodging.

The trail is also part of the larger East Coast Greenway, a growing network of multiuse trails connecting 15 states and 450 cities and towns on a 3,000-mile route between Maine and Florida.

CONTACT: rtc.li/cross-island-trail

PARKING

Parking areas are listed from east to west. *Indicates that at least one accessible parking space is available.*

GRASONVILLE*: Long Point Park Trailhead, 113 Jackson Creek Road (38.9664, -76.2236).

GRASONVILLE: Mears Point Marina, Narrows Road, about 360 feet east of Kent Narrow Way N. (38.9705, -76.2446).

CHESTER: Kent Narrows Public Boat Ramp, 100 Piney Narrows Road (38.9717, -76.2497).

STEVENSVILLE*: Old Love Point Park, 300 Old Love Point Road (38.9878, -76.3070).

STEVENSVILLE*: Terrapin Nature Park Trailhead, 191 Log Canoe Cir. (38.9898, -76.3212).

Ever since the Great Allegheny Passage (GAP) was completed in 2013, overnight bicycle riders and backpackers have flocked to the 150-mile rail-trail that travels through Western Pennsylvania and Maryland. The welcoming small towns along the route entice travelers with lodging, camping, markets, and dining. Trail users marvel at the scenery along one of the longest rail-trails in the United States. The biggest allure might be the ability to travel off-road for over 330 miles—all the way from Pittsburgh to Washington, D.C.—when combining the GAP with the Chesapeake & Ohio Canal National Historical Park (see page 45) in Cumberland, Maryland.

The GAP is also a host trail for the 3,700-miles-plus Great American Rail-Trail®—which will one day form a seamless connection between Washington, D.C., and

As one of the longest rail-trails in the country, the GAP offers many dramatic trestles.

Counties
Allegany (MD); Allegheny, Fayette, Somerset, and Westmoreland (PA)

Endpoints
Point State Park near Commonwealth Pl. and Liberty Ave. (Pittsburgh, PA); Chesapeake & Ohio Canal National Historical Park at Canal St. and Harrison St. (Cumberland, MD)

Mileage
150

Type
Rail-Trail; Rail-with-Trail; Greenway/Non-Rail-Trail

Roughness Index
1

Surface
Asphalt, Crushed Stone

51

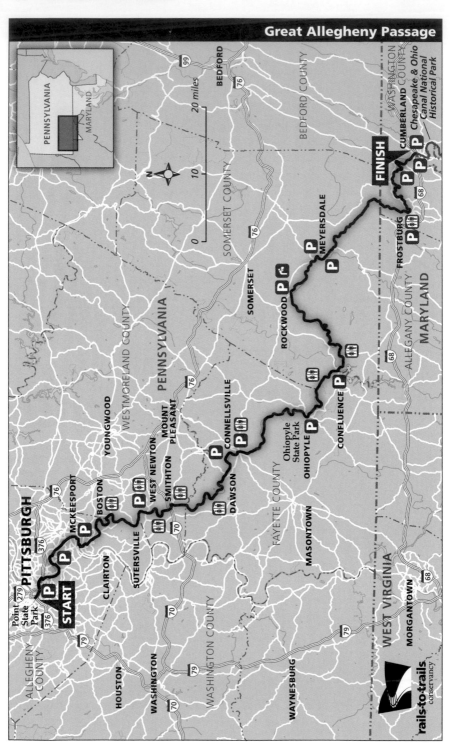

Washington State—and hosts part of the September 11th National Memorial Trail, which connects the World Trade Center, Flight 93, and Pentagon Memorials.

The route mainly follows old railbeds between Pittsburgh and Cumberland, in many cases alongside scenic rivers and streams. Westbound travelers from mile marker 0 in Cumberland will experience a steep grade in the 23.7 miles to the Eastern Continental Divide—the high point of the trail. Eastbound travelers will find a slight but steady grade from Pittsburgh to the Eastern Continental Divide. Abundant historical sites from the French and Indian Wars, as well as from the era of Western exploration, can be found.

While most users are on foot or bike, equestrians are allowed on grassy adjacent paths between Boston and Connellsville; Rockwood and Garrett; and the Pennsylvania–Maryland state line and Frostburg, Maryland. Cross-country skiing and snowshoeing are popular wintertime pursuits. Before setting out, it's a good idea to check the GAP website (**gaptrail.org**) for local trail conditions and for opportunities for dining, lodging, and shuttle services.

The GAP got its start in 1978 when a local nonprofit bought a segment of unused railroad. The first section of trail was completed in 1986. The Allegheny Trail Alliance, formed in 1995, spearheaded the piece-by-piece completion of the route. It was the first pathway in the country to be inducted into Rails-to-Trails Conservancy's Rail-Trail Hall of Fame in 2007.

PENNSYLVANIA

On its western end, the trail begins at historic Point State Park in Pittsburgh. Heading east, it crosses over the Monongahela River on a former railway bridge and travels west along the water until it meets the Youghiogheny River at McKeesport. Along the way, see the remnants of the Steel City's past in the form of a large industrial furnace, a ladle car, and a former steel mill, in addition to an array of interpretive signage.

All along the GAP, you experience a sense of remoteness and tranquility amid the landscape of lush forests, wildflowers meadows, and sparkling rivers, but you're never too far from a town. The former industrial towns along the route that once were vital to the mining, steel, and glass industries now welcome trail users with a variety of amenities and services, the new mainstay of many of their post-industrial economies. Following the meandering Youghiogheny River, you'll pass through several of these towns before reaching Ohiopyle. Here you'll find two dramatic trestles and some of the wildest rapids along the route. Popular with whitewater rafters, the river in this area features rocky outcroppings, boulder-strewn banks, and soothing waterfalls.

Farther east, past the town of Confluence, where the Youghiogheny and Casselman Rivers meet, the GAP makes its way to the Eastern Continental Divide. Highlights of this section include traversing the newly restored 849-foot-long Pinkerton Tunnel; crossing the 101-foot-high Salisbury Viaduct, which spans more than 1,900 feet, and the slightly smaller Keystone Viaduct; and exploring the 3,291-foot-long Big Savage Tunnel, which offers welcome relief on hot summer days. (Note that this tunnel is closed from late November to early April.) Along the way, enjoy spectacular views of the Casselman River Valley, which offers a vivid display of colorful foliage in the fall.

MARYLAND

From the tunnel, it's mostly downhill to Cumberland. Crossing the old Mason–Dixon Line—the traditional border between the North and the South—into Maryland, you'll roll into Frostburg in 5 miles. Home to Frostburg State University, the college town features a vibrant restaurant and art scene. You can visit downtown via a series of uphill switchbacks to a regional museum and a restored 1891 train station that serves as a restaurant. If you're here in mid-September, you can enjoy local music and crafts at the Appalachian Festival (**frostburg.edu /annual-events/afestival**).

On the last 15.5 miles to Cumberland, you'll parallel the Western Maryland Scenic Railroad (**wmsr.com**), which runs steam locomotive excursions on weekends and many weekdays. In fact, 9 miles past Frostburg, the trail shares the 911-foot-long Brush Tunnel with the train. It's recommended to avoid entering the tunnel with the noisy and smoky train; the locomotive emerging from the tunnel makes for a better photo anyway.

Past the tunnel is Cumberland Narrows, where the GAP squeezes through a water gap created by Wills Creek between Wills Mountain and Haystack Mountain. The old National Freeway (US 40), the scenic railroad, and CSX share this historic passage.

The C&O Canal Towpath (see page 45) begins where the GAP ends at the confluence of Wills Creek and the North Branch of the Potomac River in historic downtown Cumberland. Here, in the bike-friendly town, you'll find the Cumberland Visitor Center for the towpath (**nps.gov/choh**) and plenty of places to eat, shop, stay, and grab a beverage. The C&O continues another 184 miles along the Potomac River to Washington, D.C.

CONTACT: gaptrail.org

PARKING

Select parking areas for the trail are listed below. For a detailed list of parking areas and other waypoints, go to **gaptrail.org.** Parking areas are listed from east to west. *Indicates that at least one accessible parking space is available.*

PITTSBURGH, PA*: Second Ave. and 10th St./10th St. Bridge (40.4342, -79.9893).

HOMESTEAD, PA: 191 E. Waterfront Dr. (40.4112, -79.9152).

MCKEESPORT, PA*: Water St. and Fifth Ave. (40.3498, -79.8688). Entrance to parking lot is 200 feet south of intersection.

WEST NEWTON, PA*: W. Main St. and Collinsburg Road (40.2112, -79.7703).

CONNELLSVILLE, PA: Torrance Ave. between N. Sixth St. and N. Seventh St. (40.0203, -79.5993).

CONNELLSVILLE, PA*: Torrance Ave. and N. Third St. (40.0207, -79.5966).

OHIOPYLE, PA*: Sheridan St. and Sherman St. (39.8697, -79.4918).

CONFLUENCE, PA: Ohiopyle State Park, Ramcat Access Point/Ramcat Access Road (at Ramcat Road) (39.8262, -79.3789).

ROCKWOOD, PA: Rockdale Road and Evergreen Dr. (39.9110, -79.1611).

MEYERSDALE, PA: 527 Main St. (39.8163, -79.0206).

MEYERSDALE, PA: 1741 Deal Road (at Old Deal Road), closest to Big Savage Tunnel (39.7613, -78.9309).

FROSTBURG, MD*: New Hope Road NW and Rankin Dr. NW (39.6593, -78.9218).

LA VALE, MD: 11401 Cash Valley Road NW (39.6776, -78.8053). Parking is available alongside trail.

CUMBERLAND, MD: 305 N. Lee St. (39.6549, -78.7686). Parking lot is about 0.1 mile east of entrance to access road.

CUMBERLAND, MD: 119 N. Mechanic St. (39.6503, -78.7628).

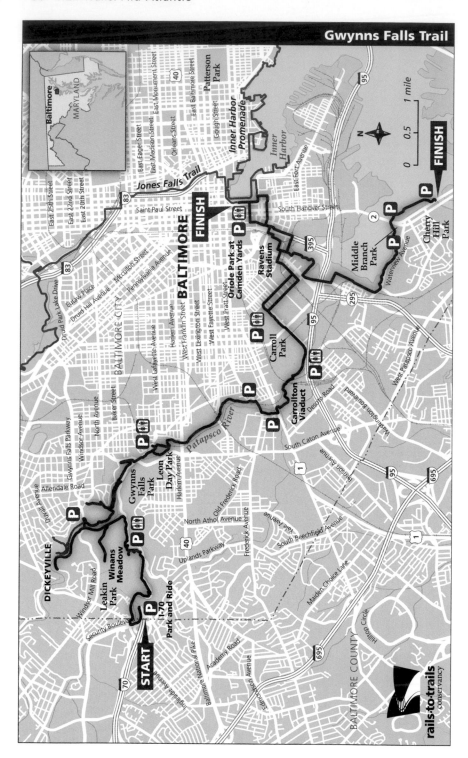

The Gwynns Falls Trail is a nearly 19-mile continuous corridor that winds through dozens of west and southwest Baltimore neighborhoods, parks, and historical and cultural landmarks and the urban business district. It takes a circuitous route through Gwynns Falls/Leakin Park and southeast to downtown and includes side spurs into adjacent parks and a connection to the Jones Falls Trail (see page 69) at Baltimore's famed Inner Harbor. Along the trail are interpretive signs providing opportunities to learn about this impressive valley's historical significance to Baltimore and the nation. Winding through Gwynns Falls/Leakin Park—the largest urban forest east of the Mississippi—to the Middle Branch Patapsco River and the Inner Harbor, the Gwynns Falls Trail serves as a key connector for more than 2,000 acres of publicly owned land and 10 miles of additional hiking trails.

The trail is also a major segment of the developing Baltimore Greenway Trails Network (**railstotrails.org/baltimore**), a Rails-to-Trails Conservancy TrailNation™ project to create a 35-mile network of trails that will connect more than 75 neighborhoods in Baltimore City.

Although the trail can be accessed from dozens of points along the route, its main access points include the

County
Baltimore

Endpoints
Park & Ride, I-70 and Security Blvd. (Baltimore City); Wetheredsville Road, 0.3 mile from Cottondale Lane (Baltimore City); Inner Harbor at Light St. and E. Barre St. (Baltimore City); Middle Branch Park at S. Hanover St. about 400 feet southeast of Redbird Ave. (Baltimore City)

Mileage
18.9

Type
Rail-with-Trail; Greenway/Non-Rail-Trail

Roughness Index
1

Surface
Asphalt, Crushed Stone

The western end of the trail offers views of forests, meadows, and other natural settings.

Arielle Bader

I-70 Park & Ride, Winans Meadow, the Inner Harbor at Light Street, and Middle Branch Park. Starting at the eastern endpoints makes for a moderately uphill trek west.

A good place to start your journey is the I-70 Park & Ride, located adjacent to the northwest section of Gwynns Falls/Leakin Park. From here, the trail heads east alongside Franklin Town Road and through mature forest to Winans Meadow, a popular section of the park with excellent opportunities for bird-watching, turtle-spotting, and historical exploration. This includes remnants of the 19th-century Crimea Estate, which has a preserved waterwheel and root cellar. The Winans Meadow trailhead offers parking, restrooms, a picnic pavilion, and drinking water.

From Winans Meadow, you'll continue eastward on a pleasant, level trail. You'll then turn north through mature forest toward the mill race section of the route, which begins at the Windsor Mill Road trailhead. Just before you reach the trailhead, a short 1-mile detour northeast on the Dickeyville Trail, which travels a former section of Wetheredsville Road, takes you to a historical 18th-century mill village in Dickeyville alongside Gwynns Falls.

Continuing southeast along the Gwynns Falls Trail, you'll follow a former millrace path of crushed stone through forest for 3 miles to Leon Day Park, named for Negro League Hall of Fame baseball player Leon Day. Here, you'll find ball fields, playgrounds, and parking. About 0.5 mile farther southeast, the trail offers views of the fall line between the Piedmont Plateau and the Coastal Plain, marked by a series of waterfalls and rapids.

The trail continues for nearly 3 miles along the wooded stream valley, passing over active railroad tracks, streams, city streets, and smaller parks before passing under the Carrollton Viaduct. Constructed in 1829 to serve the then-growing Baltimore and Ohio Railroad, the viaduct is the oldest railroad bridge in the country. About 0.5 mile beyond the viaduct is Carroll Park—a former plantation and the homestead of Charles Carroll, one of the signers of the Declaration of Independence—where you'll find parking, ball fields, and impressive views of downtown Baltimore from the historic mansion.

The final 2 miles are decidedly urban compared to the stream-valley setting of the rest of the trail. Leaving Carroll Park, the trail becomes an on-road cycle track along Bush Street. Be sure to look for trail signs indicating you are on the official route.

After Bush Street, the trail hits the Middle Branch of the Inner Harbor near Ravens Stadium. Here, you can head south to Middle Branch Park on the Middle Branch Spur of the Gwynns Falls Trail for expansive water views, fishing, and boating. Alternatively, heading north will take you through the historic neighborhoods of South Baltimore until you reach the many attractions of the city's Inner Harbor.

At the Inner Harbor, extend your route by connecting to the Jones Falls Trail (see page 69), which heads north for 11 miles through parks and other popular destinations.

CONTACT: bcrp.baltimorecity.gov/trails or gwynnsfallstrail.org

PARKING

Parking areas are located within Baltimore City and are listed from west to east. *Indicates that at least one accessible parking space is available.*

Park & Ride: I-70 and Security Blvd. (39.3015, -76.7104).

Gwynns Falls Park/Leakin Park*: Winans Meadow, 4500 Franklintown Road (39.3046, -76.6936).

4300 Windsor Mill Road*: (39.3122, -76.6877).

Leon Day Park*: 1200 block of N. Franklintown Road (39.2997, -76.6706 and 39.3000, -76.6715).

2700 Frederick Ave.*: (39.2816, -76.6592).

Carroll Park Golf Course: 2100 Washington Blvd. (39.2718, -76.6475).

Carroll Park: Bayard St. and Herkimer St. (39.2812, -76.6390).

Carroll Park*: Park access road at 1600 block of Washington Blvd. (39.2803, -76.6424).

Light St. and E. Barre St.*: (39.2835, -76.6126); parking only at limited times.

Middle Branch Park: 3301 Waterview Ave. (39.2546, -76.6227).

Middle Branch Park: 2825 S. Hanover St. (39.2546, -76.6158).

Middle Branch Park: 3131 S. Hanover St. (39.2495, -76.6124).

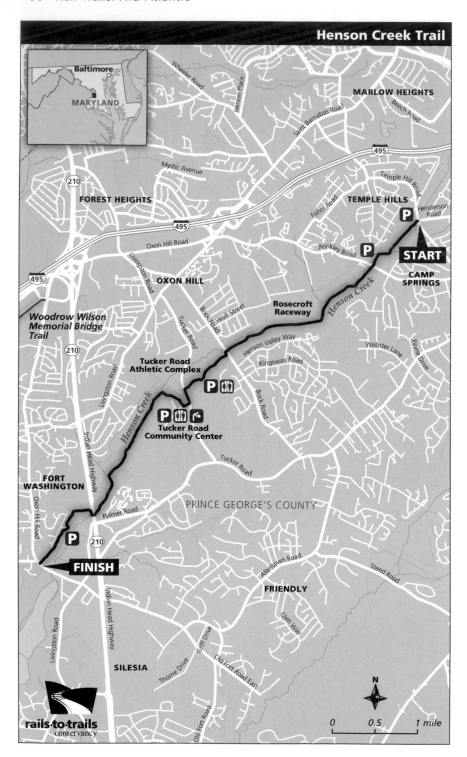

Visitors to the Henson Creek Trail in the sprawling suburbs of southwestern Prince George's County may be surprised by the extent of woodlands and open space along this corridor that lies just outside the Capital Beltway.

The 5.7-mile paved greenway trail runs the length of Oxon Hill, linking Fort Washington on the Potomac River to Camp Springs. A favorite of cyclists, joggers, and inline skaters, the paved path also has a grassy shoulder for equestrians. The trail is open from dawn to dusk, except for bicyclists with lights, who are permitted to use the trail from 5 a.m. to midnight.

The Prince George's County Department of Parks and Recreation manages the trail as part of its 85-mile network of multiuse trails. Be aware that because the trail runs alongside Henson Creek, erosion and washouts can occur after heavy storms, and trail users may be directed

Many recreational amenities dot this community connector in Prince George's County.

TrailLink user edee.ocampo

County
Prince George's

Endpoints
Temple Hill Road and Henderson Road (Camp Springs); Oxon Hill Road and Fort Foote Road (Fort Washington)

Mileage
5.7

Type
Greenway/Non-Rail-Trail

Roughness Index
1

Surface
Asphalt

onto temporary crushed-stone paths around the trouble areas. For questions, please contact the parks department.

A visit to the trail can start at the Henson Creek Park trailhead off Temple Hill Road, about a mile south of the Capital Beltway. You can park there or take the Route 32 bus on the Prince George's County Transit System to the stop at Temple Hill Road at Henderson Road.

The trail crosses under Brinkley Road in less than a mile and passes the 125-acre Rosecroft Raceway, a destination for harness racing that opened in 1949 and drew some 7,000 spectators daily during its heyday. Crossing under Bock Road, you'll arrive at the Tucker Road Athletic Complex, which features picnic shelters, tennis courts, ball fields, ice-skating, an archery range, and a kid-friendly fishing pond and pier.

Pass through the parking lot or adjacent pedestrian paths, and turn left onto a wide paved shoulder along Tucker Road for 0.2 mile to pick up the trail again at Ferguson Lane. The Tucker Road Community Center here has a playground, more tennis courts, picnic tables, and a gym.

The trail goes beneath MD 210/Indian Head Highway in 1.5 miles and then passes the Tor Bryan Estates Neighborhood Playground before ending at Oxon Hill Road, about a mile south of the 300-acre National Harbor Waterfront development on the Potomac River. Commuters can reach that area and Virginia via bike lanes along Oxon Hill Road that connect to a bike trail across the Woodrow Wilson Memorial Bridge.

CONTACT: pgparks.com/4604/henson-creek-trail

PARKING

Parking areas are listed from east to west. *Indicates that at least one accessible parking space is available.*

CAMP SPRINGS*: Henson Creek Neighborhood Park, Temple Hill Road between Henderson Road and Weldon Dr. (38.8075, -76.9366).

OXON HILL*: 7401 Bock Road between Haverhill St. and Henson Valley Way (38.7899, -76.9715).

FORT WASHINGTON*: Tucker Road Athletic Complex, 1862 Tucker Road, between Ferguson Lane and St. Barnabas Road (38.7852, -76.9780).

OXON HILL*: Tucker Road Community Center, 1771 Tucker Road at Ferguson Lane (38.7829, -76.9795).

FORT WASHINGTON*: Tor Bryan Estates Neighborhood Playground, Harg Lane at Branchview Dr. (38.7657, -76.9993).

The 2.5-mile Herring Run Trail is a neighborhood gem that runs through Herring Run Park, a scenic 375-acre stream-valley oasis in Northeast Baltimore. This loop trail, bordered by Harford Road to the west and Sinclair Lane to the east, gives residents ample opportunities to walk, run, bike, or enjoy nature right in their backyard. The trail runs parallel to Herring Run, which meanders through the park. Multiple side hiking trails are also available in the park between Harford Road and Belair Road.

One of the city's three major trails, the Herring Run Trail is a cornerstone of the developing Baltimore Greenway Trails Network (**railstotrails.org/baltimore**), a Rails-to-Trails Conservancy TrailNation™ project to create a 35-mile network of trails that will connect more than 75 neighborhoods in Baltimore City.

This neighborhood gem runs through scenic Herring Run Park in northeast Baltimore.

Location
Baltimore City

Endpoints
Harford Road/MD 147 and Chesterfield Ave. (Baltimore City); 0.5 mile south of Sinclair Lane (Baltimore City)

Mileage
2.5

Type
Greenway/Non-Rail-Trail

Roughness Index
1

Surface
Asphalt, Dirt

TrailLink user yugo69

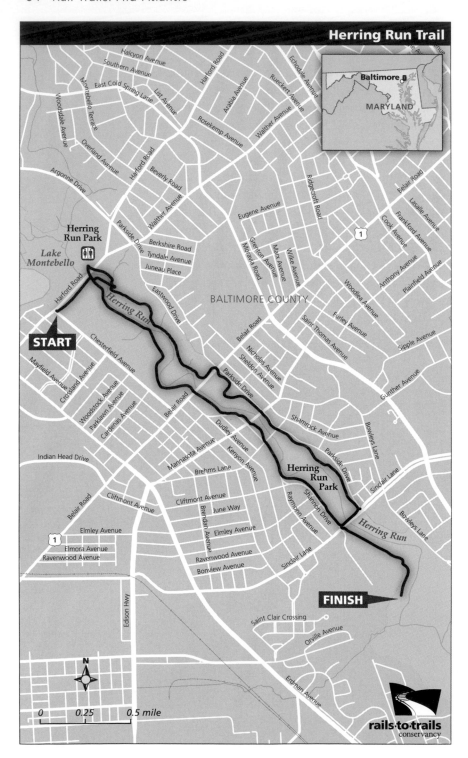

A good place to access the trail is on the western side of the park at Harford Road and Chesterfield Avenue, where street parking is available. This busy section of the park provides areas for recreation and relaxation, with picnic tables, ball fields, playgrounds, basketball courts, and multiple views of the stream from pedestrian bridges that cross over Herring Run.

The northwestern endpoint sits just south of the northeast end of Lake Montebello, another popular recreation attraction for students and families. Located adjacent to Herring Run Park to the southeast and Morgan State University to the north, the scenic reservoir is encircled by a 2.5-mile shared-use path and roadway that is a haven for walkers, runners, and bikers. Users can access the Herring Run Trail from Lake Montebello via a trail crossing over Harford Road at Chesterfield Avenue.

Just past Harford Road, the Herring Run Trail splits into two sections—flanked by trees and neighborhoods—that travel southeast on either side of the stream and then reconnect at Sinclair Lane between Shannon Drive and Parkside Drive. Trail users can access the eastern side of the park here, where street parking is available.

Recreational amenities are available along the western sections of trail, including playgrounds at Brehms Lane and Chesterfield Avenue on the southwest leg, and at the intersection of Parkside Drive and Roberton Avenue on the northeast side. Football fields are dispersed throughout and are often the site of local Little League games. A lesser-known section of the park, referred to as Lower Herring Run Park, extends for 0.5 mile past Sinclair Lane into the Armistead Gardens neighborhood. This portion of the park—whose undulating landscape reflects its former life as a city landfill—is largely unmanaged and consists mostly of unpaved dirt trails. Please note that while the rest of Herring Run Trail and the park are ADA-accessible, this lower portion is not.

A forested treasure in the middle of an urban setting, the Herring Run Trail presents a unique opportunity for residents and visitors to experience the natural world and spot local wildlife, including the many foxes, deer, beavers, great blue herons, hawks, and other fowl that call the park home.

CONTACT: friendsofherringrun.org/trail-maps.html

PARKING

Although there are no designated parking lots for the trail, street parking around Herring Run Park can be found along Chesterfield Ave., Shannon Dr., and Parkside Dr.. Limited street parking can also be found along Easterwood Dr.

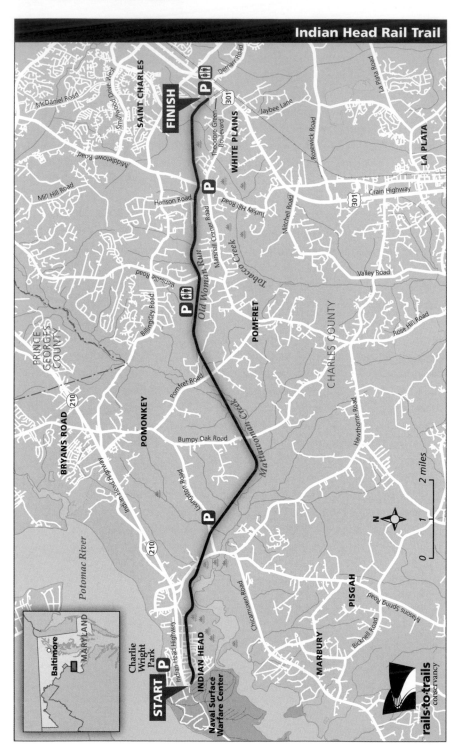

Indian Head Rail Trail

Although located within easy reach of the Washington, D.C., metro area, the Indian Head Rail Trail in southern Maryland seems far removed from the hectic pace of urban life. The 13-mile paved rail-trail travels alongside creeks and through woods halfway across Charles County from the town of Indian Head on the Potomac River to the inland community of White Plains.

The trail follows a former railroad line built in 1918 to transport supplies to the U.S. Navy's weapons facility built on the Indian Head peninsula overlooking the Potomac River. The facility, whose name and mission has changed over the years, still exists, but the railroad corridor is no longer needed and was transferred to Charles County under the Department of the Interior's Federal Lands to Parks Program. The eastern end of the trail opened in 2009.

The trail starts on Mattingly Avenue near the gates of the Naval Surface Warfare Center, a facility that got its start in 1890 as a weapons base. The town of Indian Head grew up around the base and was incorporated in 1920. Local leaders say the town's name is most likely derived from the peninsula where the town sits (known as the

Spanning half of Charles County, this rail-trail offers a panoply of beautiful backdrops.

County
Charles

Endpoints
Mattingly Ave. near Naval Station (Indian Head); Theodore Green Blvd. west of US 301 (White Plains)

Mileage
13.4

Type
Rail-Trail

Roughness Index
1

Surface
Asphalt

Indian Headlands) and the Algonquian peoples who once lived here. The area's Indigenous community has petitioned for the name to be changed, however, asserting that it alludes to violence inflicted on them in years past.

There's no parking at the trailhead on Mattingly Way. Trail users can park at Charlie Wright Park or Village Green Park, about 0.3 mile north of the trailhead, and follow signs across Indian Head Highway/MD 210 to the trailhead.

Heading eastward, the trail leaves the town and passes a wide-open view of the wetlands surrounding Mattawoman Creek, a tributary of the Potomac River and a productive breeding estuary for migratory fish. The trail also passes two other tributaries, Old Woman Run and Tobacco Creek, as well as three wildlife management and environmental areas. Sharp-eyed visitors may spot wild turkeys, deer, herons, bald eagles, egrets, and a variety of waterfowl from the trail. Bird-watchers have identified nearly 150 different species of birds along the corridor.

The trail makes a flat and often straight run to White Plains on a 10-foot-wide paved path with grassy shoulders regularly maintained by the county. You'll pass a lily pond at Bumpy Oak Road about 5.5 miles out from Indian Head, but most of the route is bordered by forests and farmland. Except for parking at crossroads and occasional portable toilets, there are no services (such as food) until you reach White Plains, where there is parking at the trailhead.

County officials are currently planning an extension east to Hughesville that could double the trail's length and connect it to the Three Notch Trail, a 13-mile trail that heads into St. Mary's County.

CONTACT: rtc.li/indian-head-rail-trail

PARKING

Parking areas are listed from west to east. *Indicates that at least one accessible parking space is available.*

INDIAN HEAD*: Charlie Wright Park, 101 Dr. Mitchell Ln., between Pye St. and Dr. Andrews Way (38.6012, -77.1676). Lot is about 0.3 mile north of the trailhead.

INDIAN HEAD*: Village Green Park, Lackey Dr. and Walter Thomas Road (38.6004, -77.1674).

INDIAN HEAD*: Livingston Road/MD 224, 0.4 mile east of Hawthorne Road/MD 225 (38.5916, -77.1125).

WHITE PLAINS*: Bensville Park, 6980 Bensville Road (at Robie Manor Dr.) (38.5998, -77.0199). The park is 0.5 mile north of the trail along Bensville Road.

WHITE PLAINS*: Middletown Road, 0.2 mile north of Marshall Corner Road/MD 227 (38.5950, -76.9795).

WHITE PLAINS*: Indian Head Trailhead, 10410 Theodore Green Blvd., between Austin Lane and Charles Crossing Dr. (38.5913, -76.9468).

Running north to south for 11 miles along the Jones Falls Stream Valley, the Jones Falls Trail is one of the Baltimore region's premier urban trails. Combining pristine forested stream valleys and busy parks, plazas, and streets, it's a perfect blend of the city's built and natural environments. The multiuse trail connects the Mount Washington Light Rail Station with the Inner Harbor and features some of the city's most popular attractions, parks, green spaces, and cultural landmarks.

One of the city's three major trails, the Jones Falls Trail is a cornerstone of the Baltimore Greenway Trails Network (**railstotrails.org/baltimore**), a Rails-to-Trails Conservancy TrailNation™ project to create a 35-mile network of trails that will connect more than 75 neighborhoods in Baltimore City. The trail is also part of the larger East Coast

Druid Hill Park, with a lake, zoo, and botanic garden, is a highlight of the route.

Milo Bateman

Location
Baltimore City

Endpoints
Greenspring Ave./Pimlico Road and Cross Country Blvd. (Baltimore City); Gwynns Falls Trail/Light St. and E. Barre St. (Baltimore City)

Mileage
11.1

Type
Rail-Trail; Greenway/Non-Rail-Trail

Roughness Index
1

Surface
Asphalt

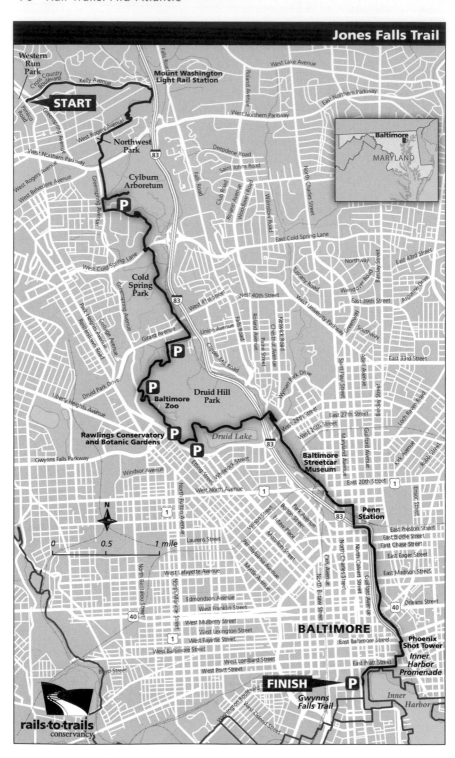

Greenway, a growing network of multiuse trails connecting 15 states and 450 cities and towns on a 3,000-mile route between Maine and Florida.

Beginning at the northern endpoint at Greenspring Avenue, you'll head east on the trail along Cross Country Boulevard/Kelly Avenue for about 1.5 miles, and then south to Rogers Avenue via an elevated boardwalk that whisks you through a peaceful wooded area. From here, the route winds through Northwest Park and along a 400-foot bike/pedestrian bridge that crosses over Northern Parkway and connects to Cylburn Arboretum. This is the newest segment of the Jones Falls Trail, completed in 2020.

After about 4.5 miles, the trail meets Druid Hill Park, which offers a natural escape from city life with many historical and cultural amenities, including the Baltimore Zoo and the Rawlings Conservatory and Botanic Gardens.

Upon exiting the southeastern side of the park, you'll head south along Falls Road, where the trail's surroundings become more urban. Along the way, the Baltimore Streetcar Museum is a worthwhile stop.

An on-road portion of the trail begins just past Penn Station, taking you south via a separated shared-use path to the Inner Harbor, a major tourist destination with restaurants, shops, museums, and other attractions. While navigating this section of the trail, look for painted green trail markings along the ground to help guide you. Hop on the Gwynns Falls Trail (see page 57) at the Inner Harbor at Light Street and East Barre Street to extend your trek another 3.5 miles through southwest Baltimore to Middle Branch Park and Cherry Hill Park.

Just before the Inner Harbor, you'll pass the Phoenix Shot Tower, a redbrick pillar built in 1828 that stands more than 200 feet above downtown. Molten lead was once dropped from its top into a vat of cold water at the bottom to produce shot for pistols, rifles, and other weapons. Today, it is one of only a handful of similar structures around the country.

CONTACT: bcrp.baltimorecity.gov/parks/trails/jones-falls

PARKING

While there are no official parking lots for the trail in Druid Hill Park, abundant on-street parking is available at the park's entrances: Parkdale Ave., 0.2 mile south of Clipper Park Road (39.3296, -76.6478); Gwynns Falls Pkwy. and Beechwood Dr. (39.3187, -76.6470); Swann Dr. and East Dr. (39.3198, -76.6421); and 3300 Crow's Nest Road (39.3261, -76.6515).

Cylburn Arboretum: 4915 Greenspring Ave. (39.3525, -76.6557).

Light St. and E. Barre St.*: (39.2835, -76.6126). Parking only at limited times.

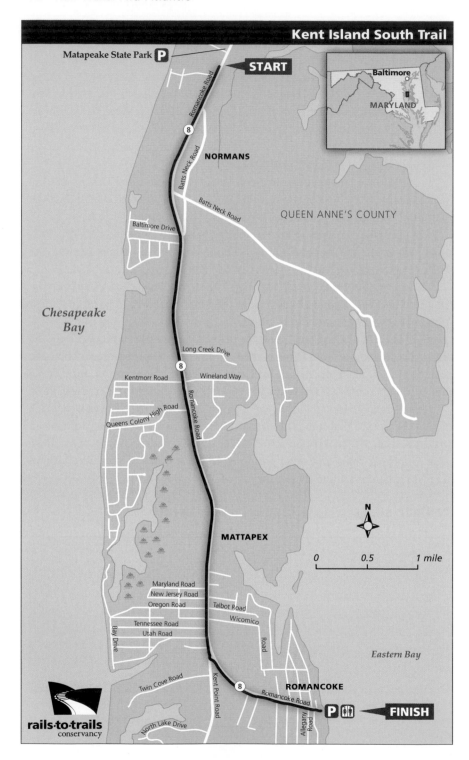

The Kent Island South Trail is one of two popular recreational trails on Maryland's Kent Island, the largest island in the Chesapeake Bay (the other is the Cross Island Trail; see page 49). The trail runs parallel to Romancoke Road/MD 8 in Stevensville for its entire length. It begins at Matapeake State Park and ends at Romancoke Pier, offering an off-road route for bicyclists, walkers, runners, and rollers from the Chesapeake Bay to the Eastern Bay. Along the way, it passes several residential neighborhoods and the Blue Heron Golf Course. Nearly half of the route runs through woods, while the other half passes through open fields. The trail is paved and mostly flat, with small hills throughout.

The trail can make for a wonderful day trip that includes Matapeake State Park at the northern terminus. The park is located on the Chesapeake Bay and includes a

County
Queen Anne's

Endpoints
Matapeake State Park at Marine Academy Dr., 0.1 mile west of Romancoke Road/MD 8 (Stevensville); Allegany Road and Romancoke Road/MD 8 (Stevensville)

Mileage
5.8

Type
Greenway/Non-Rail-Trail

Roughness Index
1

Surface
Asphalt

Nearly half the route of this Kent Island trail runs through woodlands.

Brandi Horton

73

public swimming beach, an outdoor amphitheater, a family picnic area, and a 1-mile trail through the surrounding woods, with views of the Bay Bridge. The beach is open daily, from sunrise to sunset.

At the southern terminus of the trail is the Romancoke Pier, a 600-foot fishing pier located at the southern end of Romancoke Road/MD 8. Fishing and crabbing are the highlights at the pier, which is open daily, from sunrise to sunset. There is a small picnic area for you to enjoy as well.

CONTACT: qac.org/facilities/facility/details/southislandtrail-136

PARKING

Kent Island is located directly across the Bay Bridge from Annapolis. Parking areas are located in Stevensville and are listed from north to south.

Matapeake State Park: 1112 Romancoke Road, Marine Academy Drive, 0.1 mile west of Romancoke Road/MD 8 (38.9533, -76.3518).

Romancoke Pier: 9700 Romancoke Road, where Romancoke Road/MD 8 meets the Eastern Bay (38.8808, -76.3339). Parking at the pier is $2.50/hour.

The MA & PA Heritage Trail is not your typical rail-trail. Named for the Maryland and Pennsylvania Railroad, which chugged through the Harford County countryside for the first half of the 20th century, the trail has some tight turns and short, steep climbs that are uncharacteristic of a railroad grade.

The trail is currently in two sections separated by a 2-mile gap, but efforts by county and city officials, as well as trail foundation members are expected to close the gap between Bel Air and Forest Hill by late 2023 or early 2024. You'll be able to take a 7-mile trail from Annie's Playground in Bel Air's Edgeley Grove Park to Friends Community Park in Forest Hill. Along the way, you can read about historical and environmental features on trailside signs or speak with volunteer trail monitors who clear trash and debris.

County
Harford

Endpoints
Edgeley Grove at Smith Lane, 0.6 mile north of Connolly Road (near US 1) (Bel Air); N. Main St. near W. Ellendale St. (Bel Air); Melrose Lane about 300 feet north of Bynum Road (Forest Hill); Friends Community Park at Friends Park Road, 0.1 mile south of E. Jarrettsville Road (Forest Hill)

Mileage
5.1

Type
Rail-Trail

Roughness Index
1–2

Surface
Boardwalk, Crushed Stone, Dirt

The southern section of the trail connects many recreational amenities in the suburb of Bel Air.

TrailLink user James McGinnis

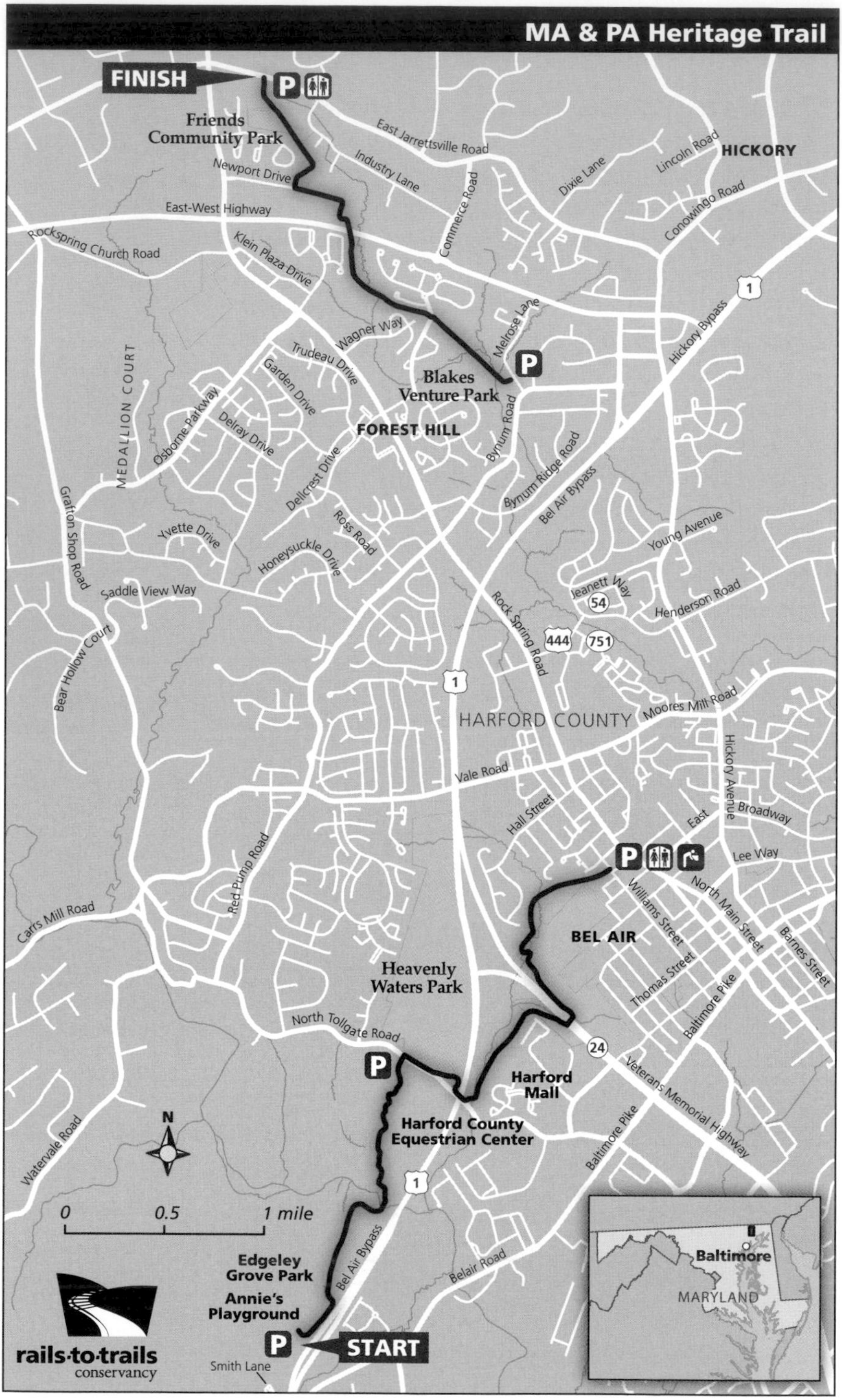

MA & PA Heritage Trail

FINISH

P

Friends
Community Park

East Jarrettsville Road

Industry Lane

Newport Drive

Commerce Road

Dixie Lane

Lincoln Road

HICKORY

Conowingo Road

East-West Highway

Rockspring Church Road

Klein Plaza Drive

Melrose Lane

Hickory Bypass

1

Wagner Way

Trudeau Drive

MEDALLION COURT

Garden Drive

Blakes
Venture Park

P

Osborne Parkway

Delfay Drive

FOREST HILL

Bynum Road

Grafton Shop Road

Dellcrest Drive

Bel Air Bypass

Bynum Ridge Road

Yvette Drive

Ross Road

Young Avenue

Saddle View Way

Honeysuckle Drive

Jeanett Way

54

Henderson Road

Bear Hollow Court

Rock Spring Road

444 751

1

HARFORD COUNTY

Moores Mill Road

Vale Road

Red Pump Road

Hall Street

East

Hickory Avenue

Broadway

P 🚻 🧍 🚻

Lee Way

North Main Street

Barnes Street

Carts Mill Road

Williams Street

BEL AIR

Thomas Street

Baltimore Pike

Heavenly
Waters Park

North Tollgate Road

P

24

Veterans Memorial Highway

Harford
Mall

Harford County
Equestrian Center

Baltimore Pike

N

Watervale Road

0   0.5   1 mile

1

rails·to·trails
conservancy

Edgeley
Grove Park

Annie's
Playground

P

Smith Lane

Bel Air Bypass

START

Belair Road

Baltimore

MARYLAND

The railroad originated in the late 1800s, and in the early 1900s a merger created the Maryland and Pennsylvania Railroad, which ran between Baltimore and York, Pennsylvania. Passenger service ended in the 1950s, and freight service through Bel Air and Forest Hill ended soon thereafter. A community effort to create a trail started 40 years later.

While the trail generally follows the corridor of the MA & PA, long sections don't use the old railbed because of the development that took place in the intervening years. These sections rely instead on available rights-of-way through parks and easements, leading to sharp turns and rougher terrain.

Bel Air's 3.4 miles of trail rise and fall with the landscape as the route passes through Annie's Playground, Edgeley Grove Park, and Heavenly Waters Park west of US 1. You'll find bridges, overlooks, an old stand of trees, and a boardwalk in this area. Horseback riding is allowed on the trail in the vicinity of the Harford County Equestrian Center.

To explore off-trail, take the spur leading to Harford Mall just before the lighted tunnel under Veterans Memorial Highway. Another spur leads to the restored Liriodendron Mansion and art gallery (see **liriodendron.com** for free-admission schedule). If you're looking for refreshment, you can choose from many eateries or a brewery in the vicinity of North Main Street.

When the new segments open, the trail will follow the old railroad grade next to Bel Air Memorial Gardens before arriving at a woodsy area alongside Bynum Creek. North of the Bel Air Bypass/US 1, the trail will connect to an established 1.7-mile segment at Blakes Venture Park in Forest Hill that follows the railbed to the pond at Friends Community Park, located just off East Jarrettsville Road on Friends Park Road.

CONTACT: mapatrail.org

PARKING

Parking areas are listed from south to north. *Indicates that at least one accessible parking space is available. The trail manager does not generally recommend the trail for wheelchair use due to hills and the gravel surface.*

BEL AIR*: Edgeley Grove Park, Smith Lane, 0.6 mile north of Connolly Road (39.51328, -76.3808).

BEL AIR*: County Home Road and N. Tollgate Road (39.5289, -76.3727).

BEL AIR*: Williams St. and W. Ellendale St. (39.5390, -76.3576).

FOREST HILL*: Blakes Venture Trailhead, Melrose Lane, 300 feet north of Bynum Road (39.5671, -76.3651).

FOREST HILL*: Friends Community Park, 37 E. Jarrettsville Road, between Rocks Road/ MD 24 and Maxa Meadows Lane (39.5836, -76.3834).

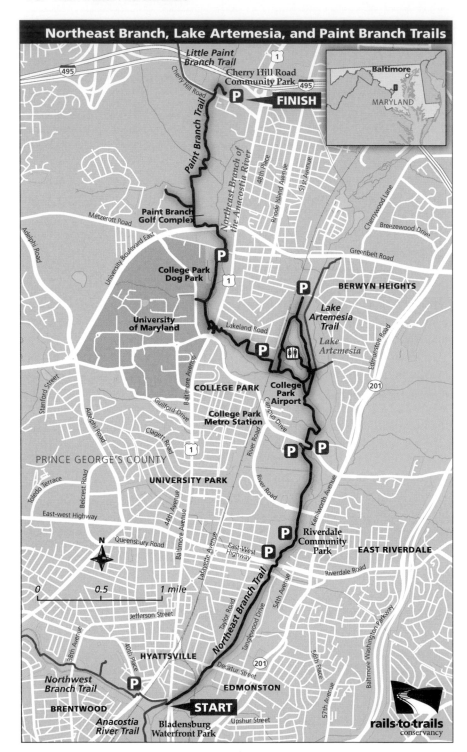

Northeast Branch, Lake Artemesia, and Paint Branch Trails

The Northeast Branch Trail, Lake Artemesia Trail, and Paint Branch Trail combine to form an 8.3-mile segment of the Anacostia Tributary Trail System in Prince George's County. Connecting in the south with both the Anacostia River Trail (see page 235) into Washington, D.C., and the Northwest Branch Trail (see page 83) into Silver Spring, Maryland, and in the north with the Little Paint Branch Trail into Laurel, Maryland, the trails represent a well-traveled section of off-road routes around College Park. They are also part of the Capital Trails Coalition (**railstotrails.org/ctc**), a Rails-to-Trails Conservancy TrailNation™ project that aims to develop an 800-mile trail network connecting the greater Washington, D.C., metropolitan region.

The 3.5-mile Northeast Branch Trail follows the levee along—you guessed it—the Northeast Branch of the Anacostia River. Starting in the south from Bladensburg

County
Prince George's

Endpoints
Anacostia River Trail/
Northwest Branch Trail/
Bladensburg Waterfront
Park at Charles Armentrout Dr. and 42nd Pl.
(Hyattsville); Little Paint
Branch Trail/Cherry Hill
Road Community Park at
Cherry Hill Road between
Park Dr. and 47th Ave.
(College Park)

Mileage
8.3

Type
Greenway/Non-Rail-Trail

Roughness Index
1

Surface
Asphalt

Kevin Belanger

This trail system provides access to greenspace, parks, and waterways.

79

Waterfront Park in Hyattsville, head northeast following the Northeast Branch about 2 miles to the popular Riverdale Community Park, which has playgrounds, ball fields, restrooms, and a water fountain. One mile north, a short spur to the left connects to a trail parking lot and access to Campus Drive, which leads to the College Park–U of MD Metro Station on Metro's Green Line; access the station by heading west on Campus Drive for 0.3 mile and turning right onto River Road.

Back on the trail, you'll travel north under Campus Drive and skirt the edge of the College Park Airport—the oldest continuously operating airport in the world—which features an aviation museum. About 0.5 mile farther north lies scenic Lake Artemesia, which has taken on a de facto role in the area as a trail hub and a community meeting spot. It is named after local resident Artemesia Drefs, who donated the land in the 1970s to allow for the lake to be expanded and a nearby natural area to be preserved. The lake is popular with birders and fishers and boasts a renovated ADA-accessible fishing pier. An approximately 1.3-mile paved trail circumnavigates the lake and is a favorite spot for daily walkers and bicyclists. The trail has many benches for sitting and relaxing, as well as a bathroom facility.

The 3.5-mile Paint Branch Trail originates at the southwestern end of Lake Artemesia, traveling underneath Metro's Green Line tracks and through a forested area toward the University of Maryland. At the crossing of Baltimore Avenue/US 1, you can either cross at grade or take a tunnel underneath the busy road. The next 0.5 mile of trail travels through the eastern end of the University of Maryland campus, passing by the Clark School of Engineering and the Xfinity Center, where the storied men's and women's Big Ten basketball teams play. The trail also connects to commercial areas and high-rise student housing along Baltimore Avenue, and students can be seen rushing to and from class along the trail.

Traveling north along the Paint Branch Trail from the university, you'll pass the College Park Dog Park and the Paint Branch Golf Complex before intersecting with the newly finished College Park Woods Connector, complete with a boardwalk highlighting species native to Maryland that can be seen from the trail with a keen eye. The Paint Branch Trail ends 1.5 miles farther north at the Cherry Hill Road Community Park on the north side of Cherry Hill Road. From there, you could continue northeast toward Laurel, Maryland, for about 1 mile on the Little Paint Branch Trail, which currently exists in two non-contiguous sections.

CONTACT: pgparks.com/3168/trails

PARKING

Parking areas are listed from south to north. *Indicates that at least one accessible parking space is available.*

HYATTSVILLE*: Melrose Park, 4700 Rhode Island Ave. (38.9463, -76.9462).

RIVERDALE*: Two lots at Riverdale Recreation Center, 5400 Haig Dr. (38.9637, -76.9235).

COLLEGE PARK*: Herbert W. Wells Ice Skating Center, 5211 Campus Dr. (38.9756, -76.9215).

BERWYN HEIGHTS*: Lake Artemesia, 55th Ave. and Berwyn Road (38.9931, -76.9205).

COLLEGE PARK*: College Park Community Center, 5051 Pierce Ave. (38.9868, -76.9274).

COLLEGE PARK*: Acredale Community Park, 4200 Metzerott Road (38.9985, -76.9335).

COLLEGE PARK*: Cherry Hill Road Community Park, 4620 Cherry Hill Road (39.0170, -76.9326).

The trail circumnavigating Lake Artemesia is a favorite spot for daily walkers and bicyclists.
Kevin Belanger

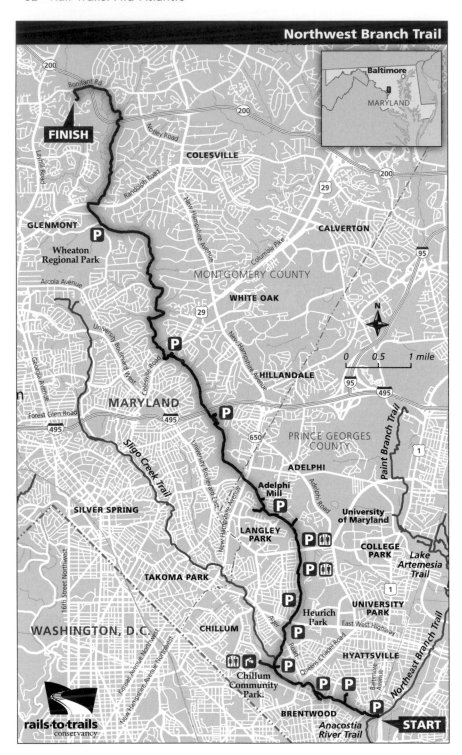

Northwest Branch Trail

The Northwest Branch Trail travels a sylvan setting through a string of parks in the Maryland suburbs northeast of Washington, D.C. The 15.8-mile greenway connects the commercial-residential centers of Hyattsville and Wheaton on a trail that's paved for 7 miles through Prince George's County and then mostly soft-surfaced in Montgomery County.

It's part of the 40-mile Anacostia Tributary Trail System, which begins in Hyattsville where the tidal main stem of the Anacostia River splits into the Northwest and Northeast Branches. The trail system is bordered by stream-valley parkland acquired by the Maryland–National Capital Park and Planning Commission beginning in the 1930s.

The Northwest Branch Trail begins in Hyattsville, where it joins the Northeast Branch Trail (see page 79) and the Anacostia River Trail (see page 235). It also hosts the

TrailLink user dtread

Counties
Montgomery,
Prince George's

Endpoints
Anacostia River Trail/
Northeast Branch Trail/
Bladensburg Waterfront
Park at Charles Armen-
trout Dr. and 42nd Pl.
(Hyattsville); Alderton
Road near Alderton Lane
(Wheaton-Glenmont)

Mileage
15.8

Type
Greenway/Non-Rail-Trail

Roughness Index
1–2

Surface
Asphalt, Dirt

The leafy trail connects a string of parks in the Maryland suburbs northeast of D.C.

cross-country American Discovery Trail and is part of the 3,000-mile East Coast Greenway—a growing network of multiuse trails connecting 15 states and 450 cities and towns between Maine and Florida—for its first 2 miles through Prince George's County, until the greenway network splits off toward the District of Columbia at Chillum Community Park. That's just after the Northwest Branch Trail passes a junction to the West Hyattsville Metro Station at 1.8 miles, and before the fork to Sligo Creek Trail (see page 93) at 2.2 miles.

Although the trail follows parkland for its entire distance, there's scarce tree cover at the beginning. A thicker tree canopy emerges around Heurich Park at mile 3, and the trail becomes very woodsy after a power line corridor at about 4.5 miles.

A notable historical site is the Adelphi Mill at mile 5, just past Riggs Road. Built in 1796, the gristmill was served by boats using the tributary in the early 19th century. It was restored in the 1950s and is now a meeting place, open by reservation only.

The trail's character changes about a mile after crossing into Montgomery County at New Hampshire Avenue/MD 650. The pavement ends just shy of the Capital Beltway (a utility access road connects to Oakview Drive) and the path continues as a dirt trail northward along the Northwest Branch for 8.5 miles to Alderton Road in Wheaton.

Mountain bikes are recommended on the narrow dirt trail. At Burnt Mills East Special Park on Columbia Pike, a junction puts mountain bikers on the Copperhead Run Trail, which follows a snaky, singletrack course along the hillside overlooking the creek.

Across Columbia Pike, at Burnt Mills West Special Park, the Northwest Branch Trail passes a dam used by an 18th-century gristmill. The Rachel Carson Greenway Trail—named for the noted conservationist who lived nearby as she wrote Silent Spring—runs through the woods across the creek and is reserved for hikers and equestrians only.

In 3.8 miles, the Northwest Branch Trail comes to an access trail for Wheaton Regional Park at Kemp Mill Road. The trail takes a right turn, following an on-road route for 0.4 mile. The off-road trail resumes on the north side of Randolph Road and winds through the woods for another 3 miles to its endpoint on Alderton Road.

Be aware that cross-country skiing is allowed on Prince George's County trails but is prohibited on trails in Montgomery County. The trails are open from dawn to dusk, although Prince George's County allows commuting cyclists to use the trails from 5 a.m. to midnight.

CONTACT: pgparks.com/4602/anacostia-stream-valley-trail, rtc.li/montgomery
-northwest-branch, or rtc.li/montgomery-northwest-branch-map

PARKING

Parking areas are listed from south to north. Select parking areas for the trail listed below. For a detailed list of parking areas and other waypoints, go to **TrailLink.com™**. *Indicates that at least one accessible parking space is available.*

HYATTSVILLE*: Melrose Skatepark, 4666 Rhode Island Ave. (38.9464, -76.9461).

HYATTSVILLE*: Driskell Park, 0.1 mile south of Hamilton St. and 40th Ave. (38.9510, -76.9514).

HYATTSVILLE: Kirkwood Neighborhood Park (street parking), Nicholson St., 0.4 mile west of the intersection with Ager Road (38.9581, -76.9725).

ADELPHI*: Adelphi Manor Recreation Center, 8000 W. Park Dr. (at Lyndon St.) (38.9878, -76.9660).

ADELPHI*: Adelphi Mill Recreation Center, 8402 Riggs Road/MD 212, 450 feet south of Cool Spring Road (38.9932, -76.9726).

SILVER SPRING*: Roscoe Nix Elementary School, 1100 Corliss St., at Hedin Dr. (39.0170, -76.9891).

WHITE OAK: Burnt Mills East Special Park, 10701 Columbia Pike/US 29, between Crestmoor Dr. and Hillwood Dr. (39.0304, -77.0047).

WHITE OAK: Burnt Mills West Special Park, 10700 Columbia Pike/US 29, between Crestmoor Dr. and Hillwood Dr. (39.0307, -77.0059).

WHEATON: Glenallan Ave. and Kemp Mill Road (39.0621, -77.0269).

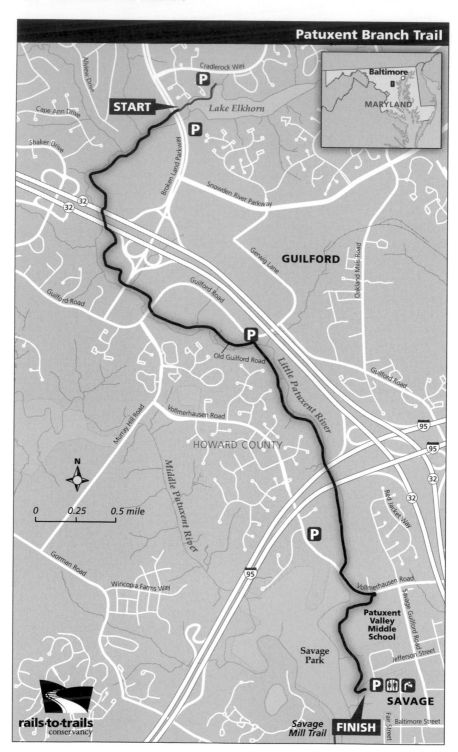

Patuxent Branch Trail

Whether by wheel or foot, many off-road trips in southern Howard County involve the Patuxent Branch Trail. Opened in 1997, the 4.5-mile regional trail connects to an extensive network of local trails that serve neighborhoods, parks, and commercial areas, making it ideal for recreation or commuting.

The trail takes a generally flat route, following the Little Patuxent River from Lake Elkhorn reservoir south of Columbia to the athletic fields at Savage Park near Laurel. It is currently surfaced with crushed stone for 1.3 miles—from Old Guilford Road to Vollmerhausen Road—and asphalt for the remainder, but Howard County plans to completely pave the trail in 2023. The trail passes under several major highways. Horseback riding is prohibited.

A 2-mile segment follows the Baltimore and Ohio Railroad's (B&O's) Patuxent Branch, which at one time served a major granite quarry in Guilford and a cotton

County
Howard

Endpoints
Lake Elkhorn Loop at Broken Land Pkwy., 0.7 mile south of Cradlerock Way (Columbia), Savage Park, 0.2 mile north of Fair St. and Baltimore St. (Savage)

Mileage
4.5

Type
Rail-Trail

Roughness Index
1

Surface
Asphalt

TrailLink user dks3405_tl

The north end of the trail begins at a paved loop around Lake Elkhorn.

87

mill complex in Savage. Built in the 1880s from the main B&O line passing through nearby Savage Station, the Guilford section was closed in 1928, leaving Savage Mill as the end of the line.

Park at either lot near the reservoir, and take the Lake Elkhorn Loop trail to an intersection with the Patuxent Branch Trail just west of the dam. As the trail enters the wooded valley alongside the Little Patuxent River, remember to consult trail markings at frequent junctions to stay on the correct path.

After 2 miles, the trail comes to the Guilford Road parking lot at the beginning of the former B&O branch line. Signs along the trail explain the historical significance of the B&O and the quarry that operated here until 1928. Leaving the trailhead, you'll cross the picturesque 83-foot Pratt Truss Bridge, installed in 1902.

The trail follows a wooded area alongside the Little Patuxent River for 1.3 miles until it emerges at Vollmerhausen Road. Cross the road and take the sidewalk or bike lane for 0.2 mile, and then make a sharp right back onto the trail at Patuxent Valley Middle School. (To visit 4 miles of mountain biking trails, turn right at Vollmerhausen Road, go 0.1 mile, and turn left into the Wincopin Loop trailhead parking lot.) The Patuxent Branch Trail ends in 0.7 mile at the sports complex at Savage Park, which has restrooms, drinking water, and parking, as well as 3 miles of hiking or mountain biking trails.

About 0.5 mile south, the historic Savage textile mill complex, which dates to the early 1800s, is now a tourist spot housing restaurants and shops. Follow the signs from Savage Park for street access. The mile-long Savage Mill Trail (see next page) starts there and offers scenic views of the Little Patuxent rapids.

CONTACT: howardcountymd.gov/recreation-parks/location/patuxent-branch-trail

PARKING

Parking areas are listed from north to south. *Indicates that at least one accessible parking space is available.*

COLUMBIA*: Lake Elkhorn Park, Dockside Lane and Cradlerock Way (39.1849, -76.8450).

COLUMBIA*: Lake Elkhorn parking lot, Broken Land Pkwy. between Snowden River Pkwy. and Cradlerock Way (39.1804, -76.8471).

COLUMBIA*: Old Guilford Road and Guilford Road (39.1660, -76.8410).

JESSUP: Wincopin Trailhead, 9299 Vollmerhausen Road between Spring Water Path and Savage Guilford Road, 0.1 mile north of the Patuxent Branch Trail (39.1500, -76.8345).

SAVAGE*: 8400 Fair St., 0.1 mile north of Baltimore St. (39.1396, -76.8285).

O nly a mile long, the Savage Mill Trail rolls through a significant piece of Howard County's industrial heritage as it crosses the grounds of an old textile mill complex on the Little Patuxent River. The mill has been renovated into a restaurant and shopping destination and, together with the former company town located just north, is listed on the National Register of Historic Places.

Start alongside a four-story brick-and-stone building at the edge of the complex, parts of which date to 1822. The compound harnessed the power of the Little Patuxent River to run the textile looms, as well as a gristmill and sawmill. Upwards of 300 people were employed at the mill during peak production.

The trail crosses the river on the unique Bollman Truss Bridge, an iron structure used to carry a spur from the Baltimore and Ohio Railroad's (B&O's) Patuxent Branch into

The Bollman Truss Bridge once carried a spur of the B&O Railroad's Patuxent Branch.

County
Howard

Endpoints
0.1 mile north of Foundry St. at Gorman Road (Savage); Savage Park near the Little Patuxent River, about 0.3 mile north of Gorman Road and Horsham Dr. (Savage)

Mileage
1.2

Type
Rail-Trail

Roughness Index
1

Surface
Asphalt, Dirt, Gravel

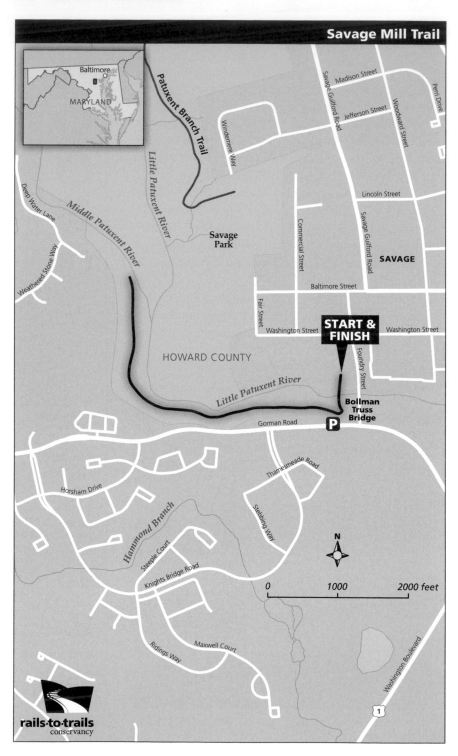

the plant. Built for another location in 1852, the twin-span bridge was installed here in 1887 to replace a stone arch bridge. As the lone surviving example of a style of iron bridge widely used in the 1800s, it has earned a National Historic Landmark plaque.

Crossing the 160-foot span, you'll notice the train tracks have been left in place on one side so you can imagine the train rolling past. Across the river, the trail follows the old corridor of the B&O branch that heads upstream. The B&O built the connection from the main line a few miles south in the 1880s but closed it beyond Savage Mill in 1928.

The trail on the south bank runs on compacted ground-up asphalt and then becomes dirt before ending abruptly in the woods. Stairways lead down to the river's edge, where you can get views of the mill complex and fishermen.

Although you are near a major highway and a bustling shopping center, the white oaks surrounding the trail and the music of the river spilling over large boulders create the impression that you're in the wilderness. It's easy to stop and savor the natural oasis at one of the trail's many picnic tables.

About 0.5 mile north of the mill complex, in Savage Park, you can find the trailhead for the 4.5-mile Patuxent Branch Trail (see page 87) that roughly follows the B&O railroad corridor and the river valley to Lake Elkhorn near Columbia and connects to many trails in the southern part of the county.

CONTACT: howardcountymd.gov/recreation-parks/parks

PARKING

LAUREL: Savage Mill Trailhead, Gorman Road and Foundry St. (39.1340, -76.8250).

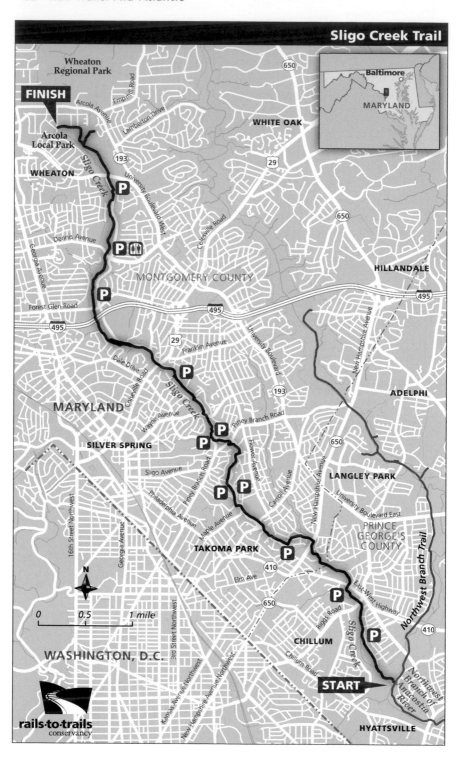

Sligo Creek Trail

The bustling D.C. metro area seems light-years away from the parklands bordering the Sligo Creek Trail in the Maryland suburbs northeast of the city. The paved stream-valley trail follows the meandering creek for about 10 miles from its junction with the Northwest Branch Trail (see page 83) in Hyattsville in Prince George's County to the town of Wheaton in Montgomery County.

Named for the creek it follows, the Sligo Creek Trail is just one arm of the 40-mile Anacostia Tributary Trail System. That trail network starts in Hyattsville where the tidal Anacostia River splits into the Northwest and Northeast Branches, each with its corresponding creekside trail. The trail corridors run through parkland that the Maryland–National Capital Park and Planning Commission started acquiring in the 1930s.

Counties
Montgomery,
Prince George's

Endpoints
Northwest Branch Trail at Nicholson St. (Hyattsville); Arcola Local Park at Channing Dr. and Ventura Ave. (Wheaton)

Mileage
10.2

Type
Greenway/Non-Rail-Trail

Roughness Index
1

Surface
Asphalt

The trail courses through lush parklands along meandering Sligo Creek.

TrailLink user jpreeg51

The Sligo Creek Trail begins where it splits off from the Northwest Branch Trail at the confluence of Sligo Creek and Northwest Branch of Anacostia River in Hyattsville. The playing fields at Green Meadows Park are the first of many you'll pass as you head northwest.

Throughout the trail, be aware of side trails that can carry you off the main trail and into nearby neighborhoods. Also, activate the flashing lights for pedestrian crosswalks at the Riggs Road and East–West Highway crossings.

The trail enters Montgomery County just before New Hampshire Avenue and begins long passages through woodland, where occasional small bridges cross the creek. Heading north, you may notice low dams crossing the creek. Some mark the locations of old gristmills, and one was part of Takoma Park's public drinking-water system until the 1930s.

Commuters can use the winding 8-foot-wide trail from 5 a.m. to midnight, although general hours are sunrise to sunset. Dozens of picnic tables and benches allow recreational users to relax and watch deer browsing in the woodsy sections or herons stealthily fishing in the creek.

The two-lane Sligo Creek Parkway runs alongside the trail most of the way through Montgomery County until the trail crosses University Boulevard/MD 193. The narrow trail gets crowded on the weekends with walkers, joggers, and bicyclists, so two sections of the parkway are closed to motor vehicles from 9 a.m. Friday to 6 p.m. Sunday. One stretches from Old Carroll Avenue to Piney Branch Road in Takoma Park; the other is from Forest Glen Road in Forest Glen to University Boulevard West in Wheaton.

The trail ends in a residential area about 0.4 mile from a pedestrian entrance to the 530-acre Wheaton Regional Park, a popular family destination featuring a large playground, an ice rink, a fishing lake, picnic shelters, and even a merry-go-round and miniature train for the kids.

CONTACT: pgparks.com/4602/anacostia-stream-valley-trail and montgomeryparks.org/parks-and-trails/sligo-creek-stream-valley-park

PARKING

Parking areas are listed from southeast to northwest. Select parking areas for the trail are listed below. For a detailed list of parking areas and other waypoints, go to **TrailLink.com™**.

Indicates that at least one accessible parking space is available.

HYATTSVILLE*: Green Meadows, Sligo Pkwy. and Roanoke St. (38.9659, -76.9792).

ADELPHI*: Parklawn Recreation Building, 1601 East–West Hwy. (38.9724, -76.9815).

TAKOMA PARK: Sligo Creek North Neighborhood Park, Sligo Creek Pkwy. and Heather Ave. (38.9799, -76.9946).

TAKOMA PARK*: Sligo Creek Stream Valley Unit #1, Hilltop Road and Mississippi Ave. (38.9871, -77.0053).

SILVER SPRING: Houston–Sligo Creek Park, Sligo Creek Pkwy. and Kennebec Ave. (38.9887, -77.0056).

SILVER SPRING: Sligo Creek Stream Valley Unit #2, Sligo Creek Pkwy., 500 feet west of Piney Branch Road (38.9959, -77.0076).

SILVER SPRING: Dale Drive Neighborhood Park, Dale Dr. and Hartford Ave. (38.9963, -77.0096).

SILVER SPRING*: Sligo Creek Stream Valley Unit #2, 9300 Sligo Creek Pkwy. and Ellsworth Dr. (39.0072, -77.0191).

KEMP MILL*: Sligo–Dennis Ave. Local Park, Sligo Creek Pkwy., 0.1 mile north of Dennis Ave. (39.0260, -77.0292).

KEMP MILL*: Sligo Creek Stream Valley Unit #4, Sligo Creek Pkwy., 0.2 mile south of University Blvd. W./MD 193 (39.0342, -77.0295).

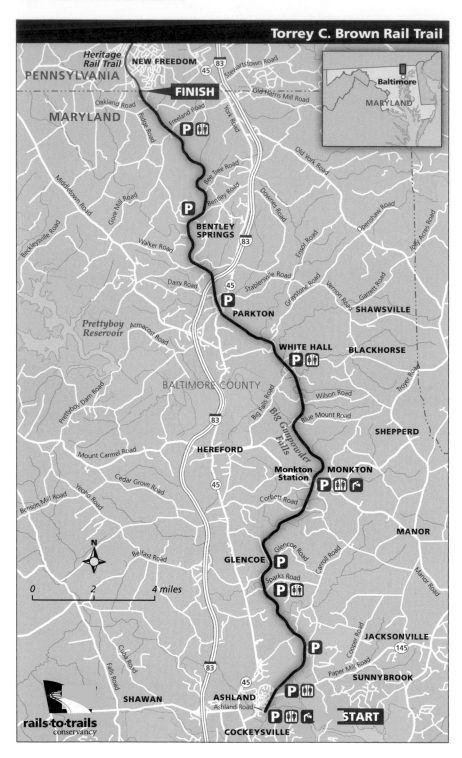

The Torrey C. Brown Rail Trail is a popular destination for outdoor enthusiasts because of its proximity to populous Baltimore and its relatively flat course, which winds along river valleys through the picturesque rolling hills of northern Maryland.

The crushed-stone trail rolls for nearly 20 miles from Cockeysville to the Pennsylvania border, where it connects to the Heritage Rail Trail County Park, which continues for 27 miles to north of York, Pennsylvania. Together, the trails were added to the Rail-Trail Hall of Fame in 2015.

And it's not just bikers, hikers, and equestrians who are drawn to the trail; folks lugging inner tubes use it to escape the muggy Maryland summers by floating the cool waters of Big Gunpowder Falls, which flows along the southern half of the trail.

Katie Harris

This Hall of Fame trail winds through the river valleys of northern Maryland.

County
Baltimore

Endpoints
Ashland Road, 0.2 mile east of MD 145 (Cockeysville, MD); the MD–PA state line at a connection with Heritage Rail Trail County Park (New Freedom, PA)

Mileage
19.7

Type
Rail-Trail

Roughness Index
1

Surface
Crushed Stone, Dirt

The rail corridor of the Northern Central Railway dates back to 1832 and served towns between Baltimore and upstate New York. Some of the original white whistle posts and mileage markers still stand. The railroad ran for 140 years until flooding from Tropical Storm Agnes devastated the railbed in 1972.

After acquiring the rail corridor, the Maryland Department of Natural Resources opened the first 7.2-mile segment from Cockeysville to Monkton in 1984 as part of the Gunpowder Falls State Park. Originally named the Northern Central Rail Trail, the trail was renamed in honor of the agency's former director, Torrey C. Brown, in 2007.

Trail users can learn more railroad history at Monkton Station, which dates to 1898 and today serves as a visitor center and museum. Food and ice cream sales, as well as bike and inner tube rentals, make Monkton a popular stop about 7.2 miles up the trail from Cockeysville. Be sure to park only in designated areas.

The trail passes through several other towns and communities, such as Glencoe, White Hall, Parkton, and Bentley Springs, although these offer little in the way of food or refreshments. If you're traveling through, it's best to carry your own supplies and plan for stops in Monkton and New Freedom (about a mile north of the state line).

The trail starts in the community of Ashland on the outskirts of Cockeysville. The parking lot here can fill up early on summer and fall weekends; a larger lot less than a mile away on Paper Mill Road/MD 145 has more spaces.

About 3.5 miles from Ashland, you'll pass the Sparks Bank Nature Center, which is open during the summer and has interpretive displays on local wildlife. Many bird species populate the forests and fields along the trail, and waterfowl flock to Big Gunpowder Falls.

The trail climbs slightly and is less congested as it heads toward the state line. In New Freedom, rail enthusiasts can board a replica of a Civil War–era train (**northerncentralrailway.com**) to Hanover Junction.

CONTACT: dnr.maryland.gov/publiclands/pages/central/tcb.aspx

PARKING

Parking areas are listed from south to north. Select parking areas for the trail are listed below. For a detailed list of parking areas and other waypoints, go to **TrailLink.com™**. *Indicates that at least one accessible parking space is available.*

COCKEYSVILLE*: 299 Ashland Road, 140 feet east of Stone Row Court (39.4955, -76.6380).

COCKEYSVILLE*: Torrey C. Brown Trail Parking Lot 1, 1302 Paper Mill Road #1300/MD 145 (39.5016, -76.6337).

PHOENIX*: Torrey C. Brown Trail Mile 2 Lot, 14450 Phoenix Road, 300 feet northwest of Carroll Road (39.5191, -76.6192).

SPARKS GLENCOE*: Sparks Bank Nature Center, 1207 Sparks Road, between York Road/ MD 45 and Sparks Station Road (39.5396, -76.6382).

MONKTON*: Monkton Station, Monkton Road/MD 138, between Old Monkton Road and Garfield Ave. (39.5792, -76.6154).

WHITE HALL*: White Hall Trail Parking, Wiseburg Road and School House Road (39.6221, -76.6293).

PARKTON: Frederick Road between Hillcrest Ave. and Hyde Road (39.6408, -76.6595).

BENTLEY SPRINGS*: Bentley Road, 0.6 mile west of Kauffman Road, (39.6750, -76.6705).

FREELAND*: Freeland Trailhead Parking, Freeland Road and Railroad Ave. (39.7058, -76.6830).

Trolley Line #9 Trail

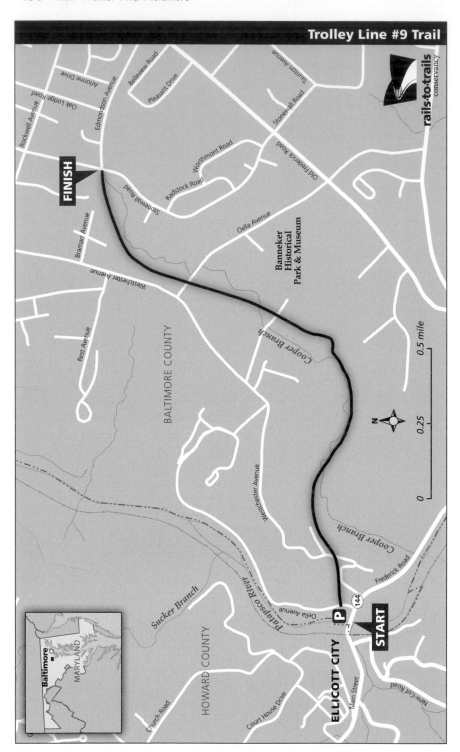

The Trolley Line #9 Trail immerses visitors in a historic working community that sprung up more than 200 years ago in a gorge formed by the Patapsco River near Baltimore. This 1.5-mile segment of an old trolley line begins amidst unadorned brick-and-stone buildings that housed mills and factories. The trail travels through a wooded creek valley and ends in a contemporary suburban neighborhood.

The electric-powered cars of the Catonsville & Ellicott City Electric Railway Co. started carrying commuters and some freight between Ellicott City and Baltimore in the 1890s. The railway endured, under several company names, until the mid-1950s, when it made its last run under the auspices of Baltimore Transit Co.

Pulling into the parking lot in the old mill town of Oella, you'll pass between still-standing stone supports for the long-gone trolley bridge that crossed the river into

County
Baltimore

Endpoints
Oella Ave., just north of Frederick Road/MD 144 (Oella); Edmondson Ave. and Stonewall Road (Catonsville)

Mileage
1.5

Type
Rail-Trail

Roughness Index
1

Surface
Asphalt, Boardwalk

The trail begins as a boardwalk that curves uphill between rocky bluffs.

Ellicott City. These structures are now included on the National Register of Historic Places. Nearby, old buildings house cafés and coffee shops.

The trail begins as a boardwalk that curves uphill between rocky bluffs. The granite from these 100-foot walls had to be hand cut, a time-consuming and dangerous task for 19th-century workers. Trail builders later installed the boardwalk, as the former railbed could get quite muddy.

The trail climbs a moderate grade to a stone arch bridge at 0.4 mile, crosses Cooper Branch, and more or less levels out; the trail crosses another stone arch bridge in half a mile. The rocky stream provides a peaceful soundtrack for your excursion through the woods.

Near the 1-mile mark, a 0.3-mile detour right onto Oella Avenue leads to the Benjamin Banneker Historical Park & Museum (**friendsofbenjamin banneker.com**). You'll find nature trails, archaeological sites, and living-history areas re-creating the Colonial farm life of Benjamin Banneker, an African American astronomer and farmer who died in 1806.

Back on the trolley line, the trail emerges from the woods into a small commercial district with a bakery and then ends at Stonewall Road in 0.4 mile. To explore farther, take a 1.2-mile jaunt on the shoulder or sidewalk along Edmondson Avenue, which brings you to the No. 8 Streetcar Path, a 0.4-mile-long relative of the No. 9.

The return trip includes that downhill through Oella to the river. Now is a good time to try those eateries or take a short stroll across the Frederick Road bridge into old Ellicott City, where you'll find the circa 1930 B&O Ellicott City Station Museum (**rtc.li/ellicott-city-station-museum**), housed in the nation's oldest standing railroad depot.

CONTACT: rtc.li/trolley-line-no-9

PARKING

Indicates that at least one accessible parking space is available.

OELLA*: Oella Ave., 300 feet north of Frederick Ave./MD 144 (39.2685, -76.7934).

The Wayne Gilchrest Trail offers a scenic off-road route across historical Chestertown on the Eastern Shore, connecting Wilmer Park on the Chester River with Washington College on the north side of town. Also known as the Chestertown Rail Trail, the paved path is named for former US Representative Wayne Gilchrest, a noted environmentalist who in 2003 added trail funding to a federal spending bill.

The trail follows the route of the Kent County Railroad, which was opened in 1872. In those days, the trains hauled peaches, apples, and tomatoes to major markets and brought commodities to town. Bought and sold over the years, control of the line fell to the Pennsylvania Railroad in 1900. Passenger service to Chestertown ended in 1949, and freight service ended in 1996. The trail opened on Earth Day in 2012.

Bill Ingersoll/courtesy Town of Chestertown

The paved pathway serves as an important cross-town connector for historic Chestertown.

County
Kent

Endpoints
Wilmer Park on S. Cross St./MD 289, 0.2 mile south of Cannon St. (Chestertown); Manor Ave., 0.1 mile west of Washington Ave./ MD 213 (Chestertown); Gateway Park on High St./MD 20, 0.1 mile east of Flatland Road/MD 514 (Chestertown)

Mileage
2.1

Type
Rail-Trail

Roughness Index
1

Surface
Asphalt

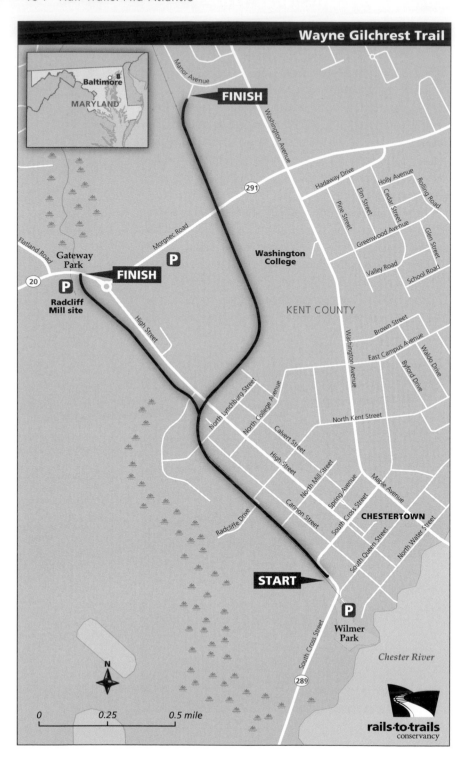

The rail-trail starts in the south near Wilmer Park, an old dockyard on the Chester River. A pavilion overlooks the river, which flows to Chesapeake Bay, and visitors can take a riverfront stroll or relax on benches. Founded in 1706, Chestertown became a wealthy town in Colonial Maryland due to the river trade.

At the trailhead on South Cross Street/MD 289, you'll see a caboose and two vintage passenger cars parked outside an old farm-supply warehouse that now holds offices. Nearby, the trail passes the renovated train depot built by the Pennsylvania Railroad in 1903. Leave the trail here to find the town's touristy business district two blocks up Cross Street.

Back on the trail, you'll come to a junction 0.5 mile past the old depot. To the right, the trail follows the main rail line across High Street and then passes the western edge of the Washington College campus, a private liberal arts college whose founding in 1782 was funded in part by George Washington. In late 2021, an extension was completed, continuing the trail another 0.3 mile to the Foxley Manor residential community; a pedestrian/bicycle signal will be added to the new route at the Morgnec Road/MD 291 crossing in spring 2022. Long-range plans call for extending the trail 3 miles north along the old railbed to the town of Worton.

Taking the left fork back at the junction, the trail follows a spur railbed behind businesses on High Street about 0.6 mile to parking at Gateway Park on High Street/MD 20. Across the street, the still-standing Radcliff Mill site, built in the 1890s, became an important railroad stop for local commerce.

CONTACT: townofchestertown.com/residents-3/parks-and-trails

PARKING

Parking areas are located in Chestertown and are listed from south to north. *Indicates that at least one accessible parking space is available.*

WILMER PARK*: 413 S. Cross St., 0.2 mile south of Cannon St. (39.2057, -76.0666).

GATEWAY PARK*: 872 High St. (39.2190, -76.0814).

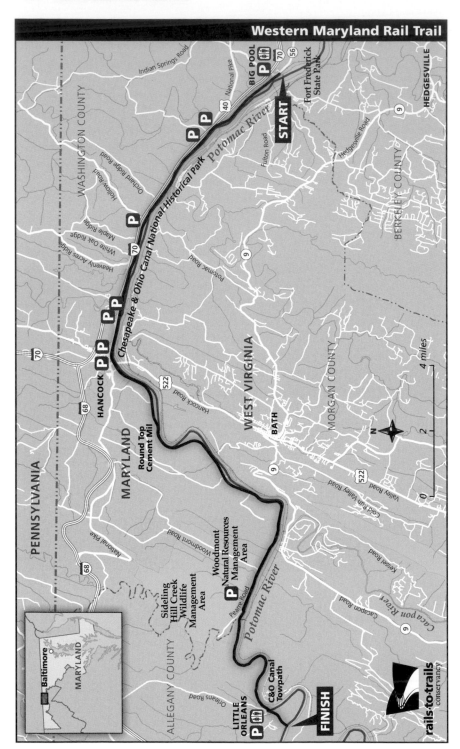

Hugging the picturesque Potomac River and the C&O Canal Towpath (see page 45), the Western Maryland Rail Trail (WMRT) rolls for nearly 28 miles through Maryland's narrow panhandle wedged between Pennsylvania and West Virginia.

The flat route through the remote, wooded river valley set in the Appalachian Mountains passes many historical sites, including the old river town of Hancock. Trail users can either use the campsites and facilities on the close-by C&O Canal Towpath—the popular 185-mile unpaved route between Washington, D.C., and Cumberland—or use the towpath as a return route on out-and-back treks.

The trail follows the corridor of the Western Maryland Railway, which ran from Baltimore into West Virginia coal country. Although construction on the railway

Shortly after beginning in Big Pool, you'll reach this stone underpass.

Counties
Allegany, Washington

Endpoints
Big Pool Road/MD 56, 0.3 mile south of I-70 (Big Pool); C&O Canal Towpath (Little Orleans)

Mileage
27.5

Type
Rail-Trail

Roughness Index
1

Surface
Asphalt, Dirt

started in the 1850s, the segment that later became the WMRT was completed in 1906 and was celebrated for achieving easy grades through challenging mountain terrain. The train was shut down by the 1980s, and the state acquired it in 1990. In Cumberland, the railway lives on as the Western Maryland Scenic Railroad tourist train.

The WMRT starts in the east at Big Pool, about a mile from Fort Frederick State Park, home of a reconstructed stone fort built in 1756 to protect the frontier during the French and Indian War. Heading west toward Hancock, you're free to explore locks and aqueducts on the adjacent canal. Although it's wooded, the trail is never far from I-70 traffic in this segment.

In 11 miles, you'll find a bike shop right at the Hancock trailhead and cafés, museums, and antiques shops nearby. The town, named for a local ferry operator, saw a skirmish during the Civil War when several buildings were shelled by artillery.

A more scenic trail segment rolls west from town as you leave the I-70 traffic behind. There are better views of the Potomac River through the trees, and large rock outcroppings will catch your attention. Three miles from Hancock you'll find the ruins of the Round Top Cement Mill, which dates to the 1830s and was the area's largest employer during the Civil War.

Be on the lookout for deer, wild turkey, and even bears as you pass through the Woodmont Natural Resources Management Area and Sideling Hill Creek Wildlife Management Area. About 14 miles past Hancock, you'll take a 2.3-mile detour onto the dirt C&O Canal Towpath, which bypasses the Indigo Tunnel so as not to disturb the eight species of bats that hibernate there.

Back on the trail, you'll find a grocery in Little Orleans. The trail ends about a mile later just before a dilapidated iron bridge into West Virginia.

CONTACT: dnr.maryland.gov/publiclands/pages/western/wmrt.aspx

Take in this view of the Sideling Hill Creek Aqueduct on the west end of the trail.
TrailLink user pgericson

PARKING

Parking areas are listed from east to west. *Indicates that at least one accessible parking space is available.*

BIG POOL*: Big Pool Station, Big Pool Road/MD 56 at Homestead Dr. (39.6238, -78.0167).

BIG POOL: 0.25 mile south of US 40/National Pike (39.6531, -78.0491). From I-70 eastbound, take Exit 9. Turn right onto US 40, then right again just before the bridge across Licking Creek.

BIG POOL: Mile Marker Lane, parking lot driveway accessed from National Pike/US 40, 0.4 mile east of Pecktonville Road. Parking lot is 0.7 mile down road (39.6572, -78.0556).

HANCOCK: Little Pool Use Area, Hollow Road, 450 feet south of Millstone Road/MD 615 (39.6844, -78.1038).

HANCOCK*: Four Locks Trailhead, parking lot driveway accessed from E. Main St./MD 144 and Ford Dr. Parking lot is 400 feet south down road (39.6941, -78.1538).

HANCOCK*: Hancock Coal Trestle, 273 E. Main St./MD 144 (39.6963, -78.1630).

HANCOCK*: Hancock Station, N. Church St. and W. Main St./MD 144 (39.6985, -78.1780).

HANCOCK: Little Tonoloway, parking lot driveway accessed from Berm Road, 150 feet west of S. Pennsylvania Ave. Parking lot is just across a one-lane bridge (39.6978, -78.1819).

WOODMONT*: Pearre Station, 1641 Pearre Road, between Allegany Line Road and Woodmont Road (39.6368, -78.3237).

LITTLE ORLEANS*: Fifteen Mile Creek, High Germany Road, 0.1 mile south of Orleans Road SE (39.6259, -78.3855). Pass through the one-lane underpass, turn right (south), and cross the one-lane bridge.

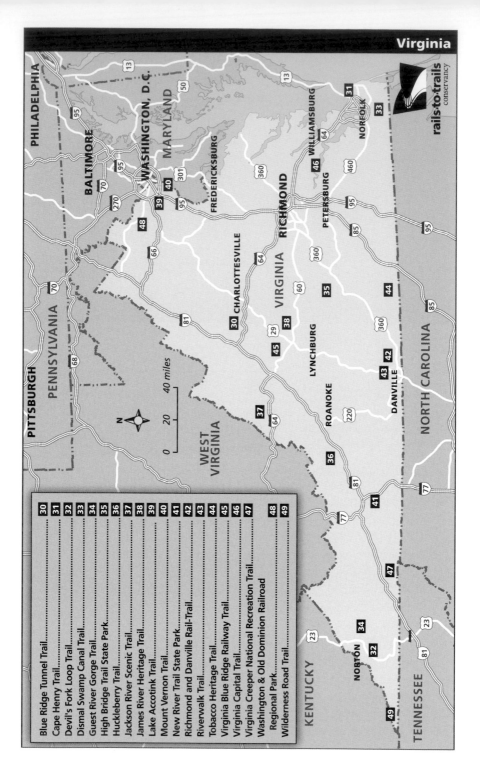

Virginia

Virginia

View bald cypress swamps and salt marshes on the Cape Henry Trail (see page 115).
Tiffany Wu

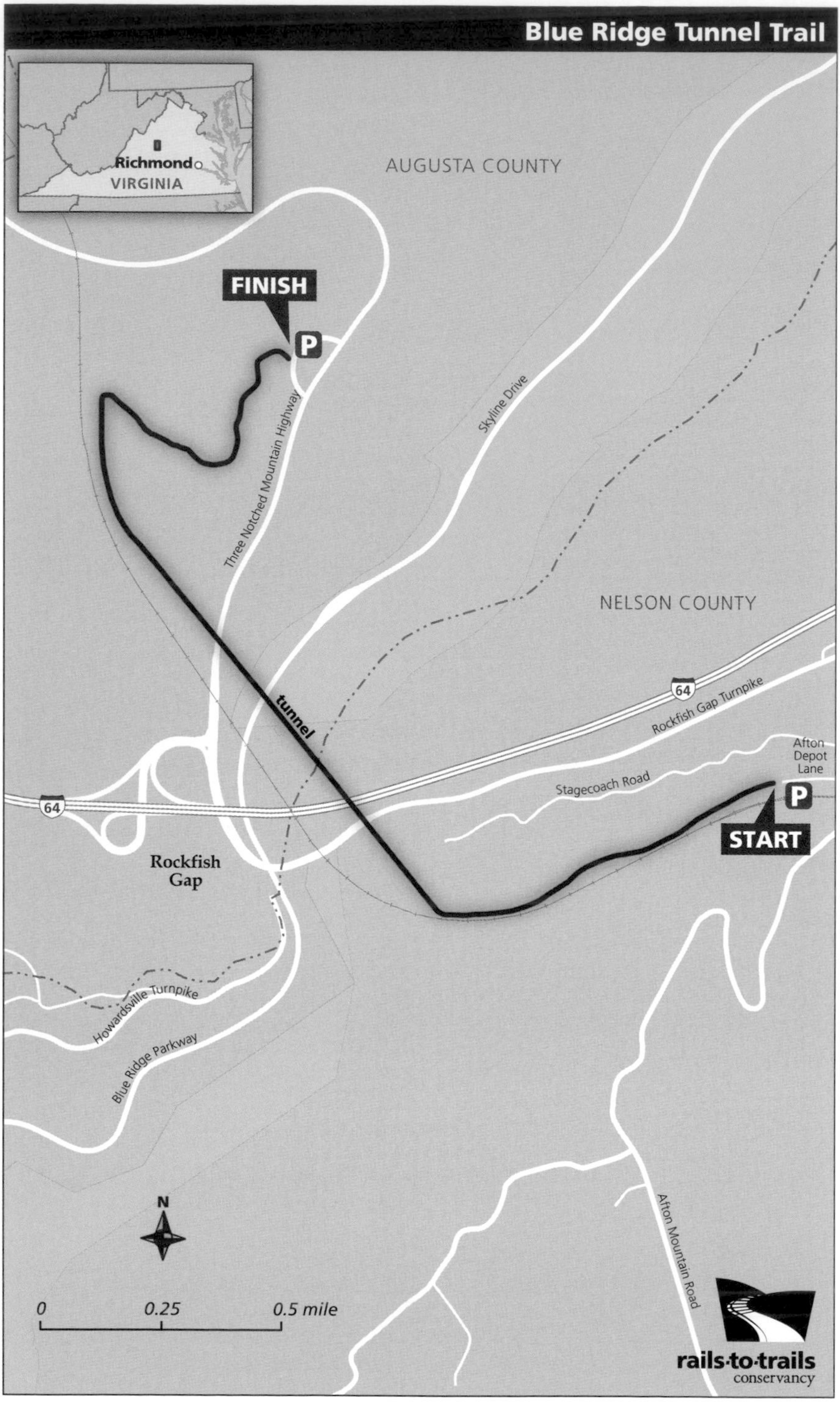

Blue Ridge Tunnel Trail

AUGUSTA COUNTY

Richmond
VIRGINIA

FINISH

Three Notched Mountain Highway

Skyline Drive

NELSON COUNTY

64

Rockfish Gap Turnpike

Afton Depot Lane

Stagecoach Road

tunnel

64

P START

Rockfish Gap

Howardsville Turnpike

Blue Ridge Parkway

Afton Mountain Road

N

0   0.25   0.5 mile

rails·to·trails
conservancy

The impressive Blue Ridge Tunnel, nestled in the Blue Ridge Mountains of central Virginia, was designed by French engineer Claudius Crozet to allow the Blue Ridge Railroad to pass through the mountains to reach the Shenandoah Valley.

The tunnel is located below Rockfish Gap, with the community of Afton on its eastern side and the city of Waynesboro near its western end. A 2.3-mile crushed-stone trail leads to the tunnel from both towns, but we recommend that you start in Afton for a more gradual grade. On the Waynesboro end, the route gets steep, with an average grade of 6.5% and a maximum grade of 19%. Although bikes are permitted on the trail, it's advisable to walk your bike in the tunnel due to foot traffic and the uneven surface of the tunnel floor.

From the Afton trailhead, it's a 0.6-mile hike to the eastern portal. The trail parallels active CSX tracks and

The western tunnel entrance with its elliptical stone portal is more ornate than the eastern end.

Counties
Augusta, Nelson

Endpoints
Afton Depot Lane,
0.1 mile west of Afton
Mountain Road (Afton);
Three Notched Mountain
Highway, 0.7 mile north
of I-64 (Waynesboro)

Mileage
2.3

Type
Rail-Trail

Roughness Index
1–2

Surface
Crushed Stone

113

overlooks Rockfish Valley. Despite the light visible at the end of the tunnel, you should come prepared with a flashlight or headlamp as the tunnel is not lit.

The tunnel itself is stunning. Construction began in 1850 using only hand drills, pickaxes, and black powder. The work, done mostly by Irish laborers and enslaved Black people, was completed in 1858; you can still see the drill holes in the stone. Stretching nearly a mile, it was the longest tunnel in the country at the time and was designated a National Historic Civil Engineering Landmark in 1976. It was abandoned during World War II when a new tunnel was bored to accommodate larger trains. In 2007, CSX Transportation donated the tunnel and trail right-of-way to Nelson County. The trail and tunnel were opened to the public in 2020. As you walk along the trail, look for interpretive signage that details its storied past.

As you pop out of the tunnel at its western entrance, be sure to note the beautiful elliptical stone portal, which contrasts with the rocky entrance of the eastern portal. Beyond the tunnel, the trail becomes a series of steep switchbacks until it reaches the parking lot at its western terminus in Waynesboro. For an easier walk, you may wish to turn around and head back to Afton after experiencing the tunnel.

CONTACT: nelsoncounty.com/blue-ridge-tunnel

PARKING

Parking areas are located at the trailheads on both sides of the mountain. Since the trail is quite popular, trail managers recommend visiting during the week in the morning or late afternoon to avoid the crowds. Please respect the private property around the area and only park in designated spots. *Indicates that at least one accessible parking space is available.*

AFTON*: 215 Afton Depot Lane (38.0333, -78.8421).

WAYNESBORO: 483 Three Notched Mountain Hwy./US 250 (38.0436, -78.8575). Traveling from this end of the trail is more challenging due to steeper grades.

The northern end of the Cape Henry Trail follows a former railroad corridor built to connect the isolated Cape Henry to Norfolk. In 1902, a second rail line to Virginia Beach was developed through Cape Henry, a popular destination. While the vision of a new resort at Cape Henry was promising, and Norfolkians enjoyed spending time on the cape, the rail line ultimately proved more significant for the development of Virginia Beach.

Today, the Cape Henry Trail provides opportunities for recreation, sightseeing, and access to local restaurants and shops around the community through its total 7.5-mile stretch. The first 1.5 miles are within the city, and the remaining 6 miles run through the First Landing State Park, connecting with other recreational trails.

The Cape Henry Trail begins on Jade Street, about 350 feet south of US 60/Shore Drive, in a residential neighborhood. The asphalt portion of the trail is ADA-accessible, but use caution as it crosses several local roads before reaching the First Landing State Park entrance at Kendall Street in 1.5 miles. After continuing for about 1 mile on paved terrain, the trail meets a local road leading to the Trail Center on the left, across from the VA 343 intersection.

County
Virginia Beach

Mileage
7.5

Endpoints
Jade St./US 60, 350 feet south of Shore Dr. (Virginia Beach); 64th St Narrows in First Landing State Park (Virginia Beach)

Type
Rail-Trail

Roughness Index
1–2

Surface
Asphalt, Boardwalk, Crushed Stone, Dirt, Gravel, Sand

Tiffany Wu

Within First Landing State Park, the Cape Henry Trail connects to other recreational trails.

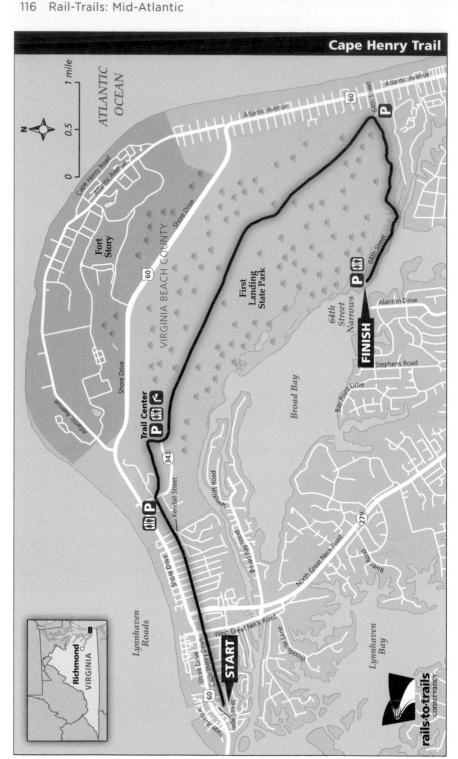

Cape Henry Trail

Wheelchair-accessible parking, picnic tables, drinking fountains, restrooms, and bike racks are available at the Trail Center. Returning to the Cape Henry Trail, the surface shifts to mostly dirt and sand.

In less than a quarter mile, you reach a viewing bridge overlooking the bald cypress swamps. After passing the lookout, the trail contains more bumps and uneven surfaces while still staying at a level grade. Throughout the trail, the conditions are bumpy in certain areas. Tree roots and small depressions could pose problems for smaller-tired bikes and wheelchairs, particularly in muddy conditions after a rainy day. The terrain conditions stay consistent for the next 3.5 miles.

Within the state park, you can experience a variety of ecosystem transitions, from maritime forests to bald cypress swamps and salt marshes. Spread out along the trail are benches and HealthTrek exercise systems that go beyond monkey bars and a pull-up station.

Nearing the southern end of the Cape Henry Trail, you will pass the First Landing State Park 64th Street entrance, which connects to a residential neighborhood with parking options. Past the entrance, the terrain turns sandy with a narrower path, which may prove difficult for bikes and wheelchairs. Ecosystems such as salt marshes and sandy shorelines present opportunities for fishing and osprey sightings. The trail ends at the 64th Street Narrows, which offers additional parking, restrooms, and a boat ramp.

Recent improvements to the Cape Henry Trail within the state park include benches alongside the path and renovated restrooms at the 64th Street Narrows. In the city, the addition of a multiuse path on the Lesner Bridge over Lynnhaven Inlet has improved the active-transportation system around Shore Drive. Future improvements aim to connect neighborhoods south of the trail as well as develop additional pedestrian and bike facilities between Shore Drive and the Cape Henry Trail.

CONTACT: dcr.virginia.gov/state-parks/first-landing and www.vbgov.com/govern mont/departments/parks-recreation/parks-trails/pages/bikeways-trails.aspx

PARKING

Parking areas are located within First Landing State Park in Virginia Beach and are listed from west to east. There is a nominal fee to enter the park. *Indicates that at least one accessible parking space is available.*

Shore Drive Entrance*: Cypress Swamp Dr./VA 343 and Conservation Ct., 0.1 mile south of Shore Dr. (36.9161, -76.0511).

Trail Center*: 2500 Shore Dr. (36.9159, -76.0407).

64th St. Entrance: 64th St., 0.2 mile west of Atlantic Ave./US 60 (36.8899, -75.9920).

The Narrows: 64th St. Narrows, 1.8 mile west of Atlantic Ave./US 60: (36.8907, -76.0172).

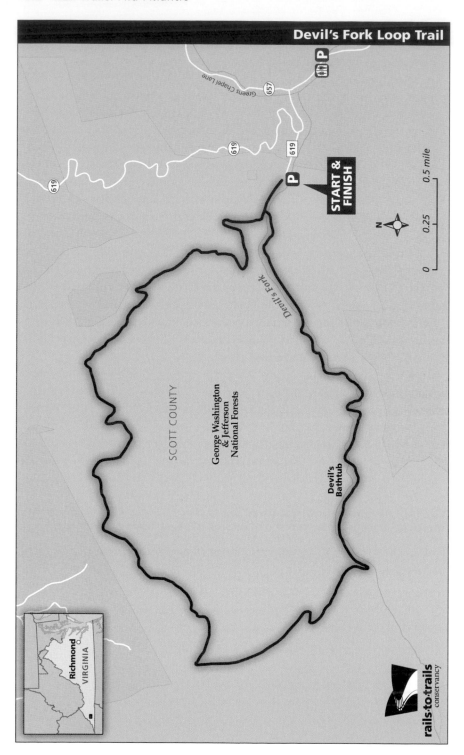

Devil's Fork Loop Trail

The Devil's Fork Loop Trail provides an impressively beautiful route through an old-growth hemlock and rhododendron forest. Amazing rock formations, waterfalls, swimming holes, and mountain views give you plenty to see and do, but keep one eye on the trail, as the going can be rough—while the trail is maintained regularly, excessive use and its remote location have resulted in challenging conditions. The trail follows yellow blazes for its entire 7 miles, but it is often difficult to find the blazes and the path, which in several places scrambles over large rocks or up steep cliff faces.

Heading west from the U.S. Forest Service parking lot, the trail makes its first stream crossing of Devil's Fork in about 0.25 mile. Be prepared to get your feet wet. This,

Devil's Bathtub, the trail's main attraction, is just 1.5 miles from the start.

TrailLink user cearly

County
Scott

Endpoints
Forest Road 619
(Jefferson National
Forest, near Fort
Blackmore)

Mileage
7

Type
Rail-Trail

Roughness Index
3

Surface
Dirt

like many of the trail's water crossings, has very slippery rocks and seasonally changing water levels. After this, the trail breaks in two directions. The less strenuous route is to the left, following the loop clockwise. This also lets you hit the highlights of the trail much sooner.

A 3-mile portion of the trail lies on an old railbed. The railroad was used to transport logs and coal, and an abandoned coal car sits on the trail about halfway up Little Mountain. The corridor is narrower and its grade much steeper than a standard-gauge railway.

The trail's main attraction is Devil's Bathtub (or "the Tub"), located 1.5 miles from the start. The rushing water of Devil's Fork shoots out of the soft sandstone and swirls quickly through this stone luge, plummeting into a beautiful pool of blue-green water.

Approximately 1 mile of the trail is being rerouted between the first stream crossing and the Tub. Once finished, the rerouting project will eliminate six to eight stream crossings, enhance visitor safety and wayfinding, and improve highly degraded trail conditions resulting from overuse. Improvements to the trail surface near the Tub are also being planned.

Another trail highlight, shortly after the Tub, is the 50-foot waterfall at the mouth of Corder Hollow. The trail enters a very different landscape as you leave Devil's Fork and begin hiking along the ridges of several mountains. The forest has little underbrush, and the path can be easily lost.

Your adventure concludes on an old logging road with about a mile of steep switchbacks heading toward the loop's end, where you cross Devil's Fork for the last time. You can continue hiking by taking the 1.8-mile Straight Fork Ridge Trail via the parking lot. The scenery on Straight Fork Ridge is similar to that of the Devil's Fork Loop Trail, but the latter is considered the more interesting of the two trails.

Cautionary Note: This trail is challenging, with multiple unimproved stream crossings that require visitors to wade through water and a 1,200-foot elevation change. There are also no facilities (such as drinking water or restrooms) along the trail, so visitors are encouraged to come prepared, wear sturdy footwear, and check the weather beforehand as the area is subject to flash flooding.

CONTACT: rtc.li/devils-fork-loop

PARKING

Parking areas are listed from west to east.

DUFFIELD: Forest Road 619 (unmarked dirt road, 0.4 mile northwest of abandoned white house) (36.8184, -82.6272).

SCOTT COUNTY: Stony Creek Park (High Knob Road/VA 619, 0.3 mile north of its intersection with VA 653 (36.8148, -82.6152).

Cautionary note: The access road to the U.S. Forest Service's dirt/gravel parking lot serving this trail has private property on both sides, and the owner does not permit parking here. Please be courteous and respectful to all adjacent landowners. Do not park on private property or block local access routes for other visitors and emergency vehicles. Vehicles are occasionally towed on busy days because they have blocked entry/exit.

The road to the parking lot is very rutted and may require a high-clearance vehicle. You will pass the trailhead on your right just before you reach the parking lot; there are also stairs up to the trail from the parking lot. The parking lot can comfortably accommodate no more than seven cars. If you get to the trail and find no parking spots available, additional trail parking can be found at Stony Creek Park, adjacent to VA 619, approximately 0.5 mile from the trailhead. Stony Creek Park officially opened in November 2020 and contains a restroom, Wi-Fi, trout stream access, and a lawn area, in addition to overflow parking for the trail.

The southern leg of the loop follows Devil's Fork through an old-growth forest.   TrailLink user cearly

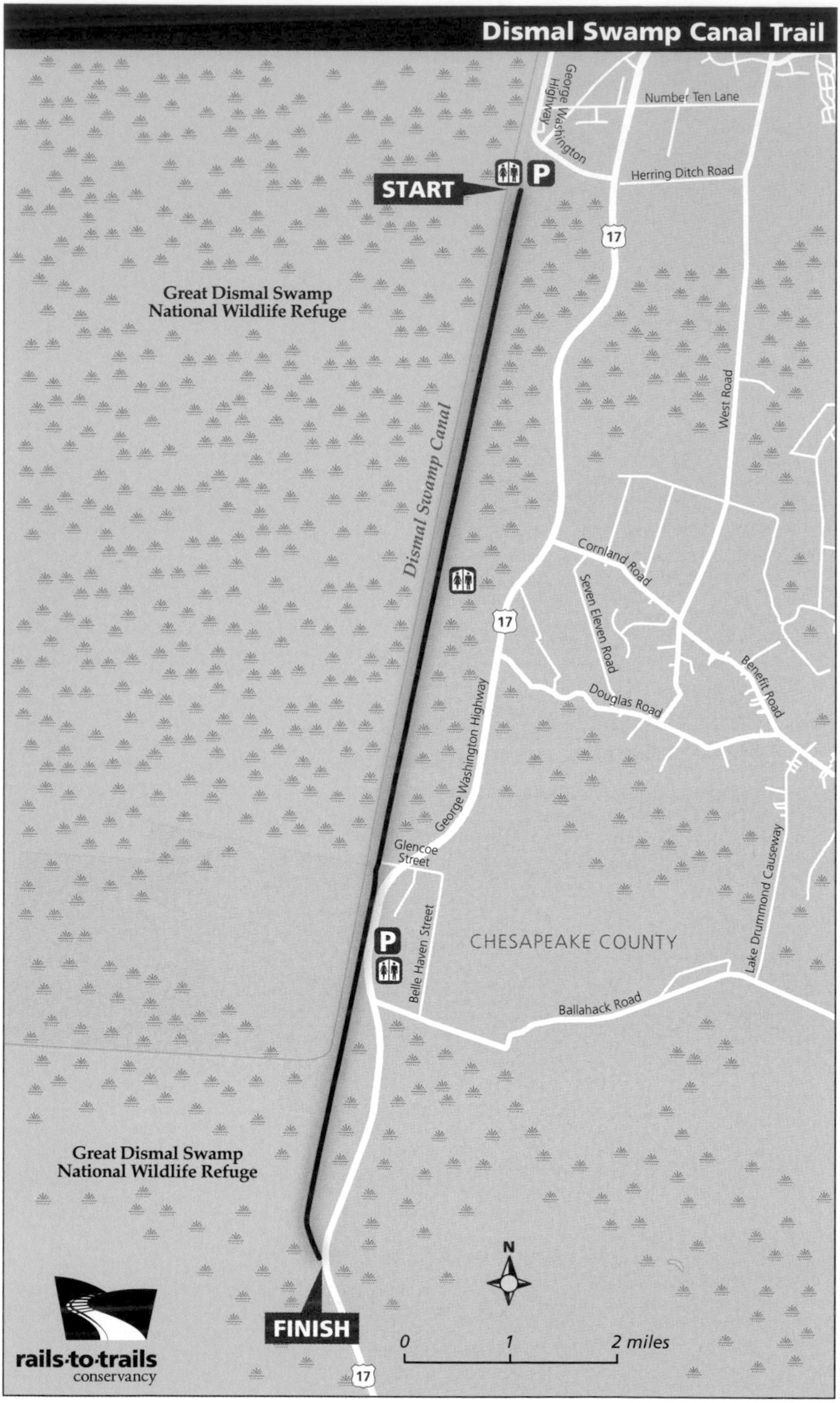

Dismal Swamp Canal Trail

George Washington Highway

Number Ten Lane

Herring Ditch Road

START

P

17

**Great Dismal Swamp
National Wildlife Refuge**

Dismal Swamp Canal

West Road

Cornland Road

Seven Eleven Road

17

Douglas Road

Benefit Road

George Washington Highway

Glencoe
Street

Lake Drummond Causeway

P

Belle Haven Street

CHESAPEAKE COUNTY

Ballahack Road

**Great Dismal Swamp
National Wildlife Refuge**

N

FINISH

rails·to·trails
conservancy

17

0   1   2 miles

17

Formerly part of US 17, the Dismal Swamp Canal Trail offers users a remote experience as it runs alongside the Dismal Swamp Canal and the Great Dismal Swamp National Wildlife Refuge. On this wide, flat, linear trail, you can experience the feeling of standing in the middle of a roadway without needing to worry about passing cars, as gates close the path to vehicular traffic. Horseback riding is allowed along the entire trail.

As you travel along the trail, benches provide places to enjoy the scenery and wildlife and to reflect on the history of the trail and its namesake canal. Interpretive signage explains the location's past as the site of Civil War raids, as well as how the canal was built by the labor of enslaved people and how the surrounding area served as a refuge for runaway slaves as part of the Underground Railroad.

A dock allows for a closer look at the Dismal Swamp Canal, which the trail parallels.

County
Chesapeake

Endpoints
George Washington Hwy. S. and Whedbee Carroll Lane (Chesapeake); 2 miles south of the trail's intersection with Ballahack Road (Chesapeake)

Mileage
8.5

Type
Greenway/Non-Rail-Trail

Roughness Index
1

Surface
Asphalt

TrailLink user OldTerry

A statue of Ches A. Peake (aka Chessie the Bear) welcomes visitors to the northern trailhead of the Dismal Swamp Canal Trail, the recommended starting point for your trip. Signs remind users to be "bear aware" due to the number of bear sightings reported in the area. But bears are not the only wildlife you may see on the trail, as more than 210 bird species have been identified in the Dismal Swamp.

As you head south, the surrounding trees give you the feeling of traveling through a tunnel. Enjoy the unique ecology as you pass markers explaining the history of the trail. At the 3.5-mile marker, you will find bathrooms, picnic benches, a dock, and bike racks. At the dock, you can take a closer look at the color of the Dismal Swamp, which has been dyed by peat, a layer of soil created over thousands of years by the decomposition of fallen twigs and leaves.

Continuing south past the 5-mile marker, you will find additional trail access at Glencoe Street. This is also the site of the Superintendent's House, the last standing vestige of the Dismal Swamp Canal Company and the place where tolls for using the Dismal Swamp Canal were collected. Across the street you will find the future site of a historical village.

After a quarter mile, the trail opens to a field on the left side, and you may start to hear cars traveling along the nearby highway. After the 5.75-mile mark, you will pass a gate, the last parking area for the trail, a boat ramp, and accessible portable toilets. After this point, the trail continues briefly on a road that is open to cars until a gate blocks vehicular traffic just past Ballahack Road.

Past this gate, you will continue straight, with open fields to your left and the Dismal Swamp Canal and trees to your right. The trail ends somewhat abruptly at a turnaround surrounded by trees where a sign lists the rules of the trail. To head back to parking, simply turn around at this point.

CONTACT: tinyurl.com/dismalswamptrail

PARKING

Parking areas are listed from north to south. *Indicates that at least one accessible parking space is available.*

CHESAPEAKE*: 1246 Dismal Swamp Canal Trail, just south of the intersection of George Washington Hwy. and Whedbee Carroll Lane (36.6901, -76.3583).

CHESAPEAKE: 1200 Dismal Swamp Canal Trail (36.6046 -76.3813).

opular with cyclists, hikers, and rock climbers, this trail meanders along 300-million-year-old sandstone cliffs that plunge 400 feet to the pristine waters below. The deep gorge was created as the Guest River—now designated as a state scenic river—eroded a passage through Stone Mountain on its way toward the Clinch River.

The grade and crushed-stone surface of the out-and-back Guest River Gorge Trail make for a comfortable walk or bike ride when heading downhill but a challenge heading uphill. Benches along the route offer more than a place to rest; they also yield stunning views of crystal-clear currents that, when interrupted sporadically by boulders, turn into impressive rapids. Some people enjoy fishing along the trail, although accessing the water can be challenging. There is also no drinking water available along the trail, so bring some with you.

The trail meanders along sandstone cliffs that plunge 400 feet to the Guest River below.

Counties
Scott, Wise

Endpoints
Forest Road 2477, about 4 miles south of Coeburn (George Washington & Jefferson National Forests); the dead end at railroad tracks immediately after crossing the Guest River (George Washington & Jefferson National Forests)

Mileage
5.8

Type
Rail-Trail

Roughness Index
2

Surface
Crushed Stone

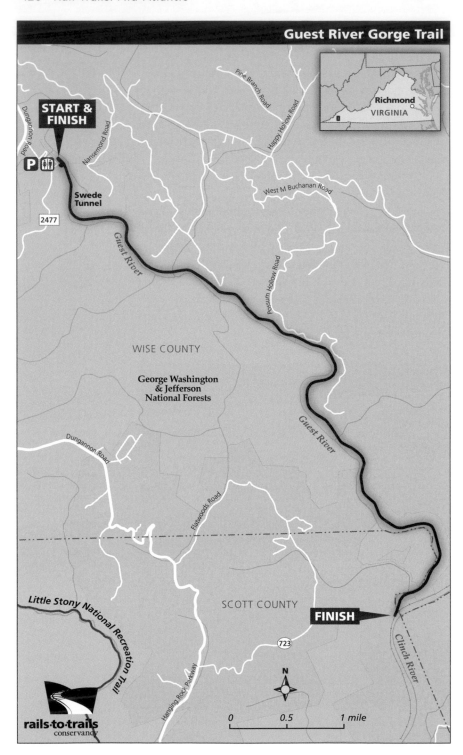

Guest River Gorge Trail

Richmond
VIRGINIA

START &
FINISH

Dungannon Road

Nansemond Road

Pine Branch Road

Happy Hollow Road

West M Buchanan Road

P

Swede
Tunnel

2477

Guest River

Possum Hollow Road

WISE COUNTY

George Washington
& Jefferson
National Forests

Dungannon Road

Guest River

Flatwoods Road

Little Stony National Recreation Trail

SCOTT COUNTY

FINISH

723

Clinch River

Hanging Rock Parkway

N

rails·to·trails
conservancy

0   0.5   1 mile

In addition to spectacular Guest River views to the south, the trail offers a trip through the Swede Tunnel, built in 1922 (and supposedly designed by Swedish engineers). The trail also crosses three bridges that were built over small creeks to replace the trestles once traveled by railcars hauling coal mined nearby. Be sure to look for devil's-walking-stick, a plant native to the southeast and a member of the ginseng family. This tall and spindly plant produces white blooms in July and August.

Near the end, the trail slopes downhill toward a working rail line across the Guest River. Just before this point, you will see a connection to the Heart of Appalachia Bike Route, which stretches another 125 miles to Burke's Garden in Tazewell County, Virginia. Legend has it that Burke's Garden is so beautiful that it was originally sought after as the location for George Washington Vanderbilt's Biltmore Estate, but the people of Burke's Garden refused to sell him any land and thus he built his estate in Asheville, North Carolina, instead.

CONTACT: rtc.li/grg-trail

PARKING

There is only one parking area for the Guest River Gorge Trail. The trailhead is marked with a kiosk at the edge of the paved parking area. *Indicates that at least one accessible parking space is available.*

COEBURN*: Guest River Gorge Trailhead, 1.4 miles northeast of the intersection of Dungannon Road/VA 72 and Forest Road 2477 (36.9234, -82.4517).

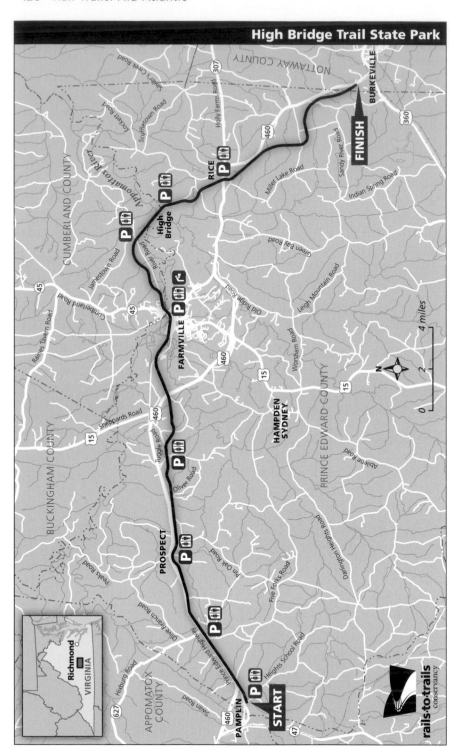

High Bridge Trail State Park

The central feature for which the High Bridge Trail State Park is named is an unforgettable experience, towering 125 feet above the mighty Appomattox River and nearly a half mile (2,422 feet) across it. The bridge's breathtaking view of the surrounding central Virginia countryside, combined with the ease of getting here (the trail is only about an hour's drive from both Lynchburg and Richmond), makes it a must-see destination.

During the Civil War, the bridge—included on the National Register of Historic Places—was a strategic point for both Union and Confederate soldiers; both armies made attempts to destroy it to prevent the other side from crossing the river. About a dozen miles from the west end

The trail's iconic bridge towers 125 feet above the Appomattox River.

Counties
Cumberland, Nottoway, Prince Edward

Endpoints
CR 660, 0.1 mile south of Pamplin Road (Pamplin); the dead end 1.9 mile south of Orchard Road and Johns Lane (near Burkeville)

Mileage
31.4

Type
Rail-Trail

Roughness Index
1

Surface
Crushed Stone

TrailLink user lisa.jarnigan

of the High Bridge Trail is the Appomattox Court House, where General Lee finally surrendered. Several museums and other historical attractions in Appomattox make the town a worthwhile side trip.

If you're looking for a short, easy outing, begin your journey in the charming town of Farmville. From downtown, riders and hikers will only have to go 4.5 miles east to reach the bridge. The route follows the wide, gentle grade of the former South Side Railroad, a spur off the Norfolk Southern Railway. Along the way, look for the railroad's three-digit mile markers dating back to the 1850s; those marked with *N* list the distance from Norfolk, while those labeled with a *W* notified railroad engineers to blow their whistles. For an even shorter excursion, park in the lot at River Road, about a mile from the bridge.

For the more adventurous, the rail-trail extends outward from either end of the bridge, totaling more than 30 miles through woodlands and rural farmland. Starting with the High Bridge as mile marker 0, newer, two-digit mile markers line the trail heading both east and west. In addition to Farmville, the communities of Pamplin, Prospect, and Rice are connected by the trail. The trail's eastern end lies just outside of Burkeville.

The trail's surface of finely crushed limestone is well suited for hybrid and mountain bikes, and horseback riding is also permitted. Restrooms are available en route, but drinking water is available only in downtown Farmville, so be sure to pack some.

CONTACT: dcr.virginia.gov/state-parks/high-bridge-trail

The rail-trail traverses a tree-lined corridor just north of Farmville's downtown.

PARKING

Note for cyclists and equestrians: To access the High Bridge, cyclists might prefer parking at the Rice parking lot, which is 3.2 miles from the bridge and 8.2 miles from Farmville; they might also wish to park at the Main Street plaza parking lot in Farmville, which is 4.5 miles from the bridge. Designated horse trailer parking lots are at Prospect (14.1 miles from the bridge), Osborn Road (3.9 miles from the bridge), and Camp Paradise Road (0.6 mile from the bridge).

A nominal fee is required for trail parking, which can be found at the following locations, listed from west to east. *Indicates that at least one accessible parking space is available.*

PAMPLIN: Heights School Road/County Road (CR) 660, 0.1 mile south of Heights School Road/CR 660 and Pamplin Road/US 460 Bus. (37.2609, -78.6635).

PAMPLIN*: 3443 US 460 (intersection of Sulphur Spring Road and E. Prince Edward Hwy./US 460 in the unincorporated community of Elam) (37.2843, -78.6168).

PROSPECT: Prospect Road, 0.1 mile south of Prince Edward Hwy./US 460 and Glenn Carson Road (37.3021, -78.5574). Designated horse trailer parking.

FARMVILLE*: Tuggle Road/CR 695 and Hardtimes Road/CR 648 (37.3068, -78.4881).

FARMVILLE: N. Main St. and First St. (37.3048, -78.3911).

FARMVILLE*: 555 River Road/CR 600 (37.3240, -78.3369).

RICE*: 1466 Camp Paradise Road (37.3065, -78.3138). Designated horse trailer parking.

RICE*: 642 Rices Depot Road, 0.6 mile south of Prince Edward Hwy./US 460 (37.2699, -78.2940).

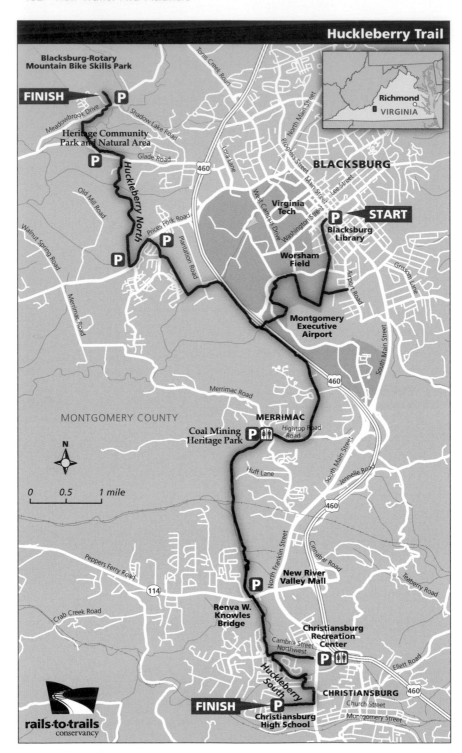

Huckleberry Trail

Blacksburg-Rotary
Mountain Bike Skills Park

FINISH P

Shadow Lake Road

Meadowbrook Drive

Heritage Community
Park and Natural Area

P

Glade Road

Old Mill Road

Huckleberry North

Prices Fork Road

P

P

Walnut Spring Road

P

Plantation Road

Merrimac Road

Tonis Creek Road

North Main Street

Progress Street

460

Iola Lane

BLACKSBURG

West Campus Drive

Virginia
Tech

Main Street

Lee Street

Washington Street

P **START**

Blacksburg
Library

Worsham
Field

Airport Road

Grissom Lane

Montgomery
Executive
Airport

South Main Street

460

Merrimac Road

MONTGOMERY COUNTY

N

MERRIMAC

Coal Mining
Heritage Park

P

Hightop Road
Road

South Main Street

Jennelle Road

0   0.5   1 mile

Huff Lane

460

Peppers Ferry Road

114

Crab Creek Road

North Franklin Street

Cinnabar Road

New River
Valley Mall

Teaberry Road

P

Renva W.
Knowles
Bridge

Christiansburg
Recreation
Center

Cambria Street
Northwest

P

Ellett Road

Huckleberry
South

FINISH P

Christiansburg
High School

CHRISTIANSBURG 460

Church Street

Montgomery Street

Richmond
VIRGINIA

rails·to·trails
conservancy

In the early 1900s, the Virginia Anthracite Coal and Railway Company built a rail line to transport coal from the Merrimac Mines and provide mail and passenger service to Blacksburg. The line was also used by the Corps of Cadets at Virginia Tech, who unofficially renamed the Blacksburg train station Huckleberry Junction because the train often stalled or ran so slowly that the cadets could step off the train and eat from the abundance of huckleberries that grew along the line. Trail users can still find some huckleberry bushes growing along the trail today.

The Huckleberry Trail winds through a mix of urban, agricultural, forested, and wetland landscapes. In 2019, the original trail from Blacksburg south to Christiansburg was expanded to include two additional segments,

Hethwood Pond in Blacksburg is one of many recreational gems along the Huckleberry Trail.

County
Montgomery

Endpoints
Blacksburg Library at Draper Road SW and Clay St. SW (Blacksburg); Gateway Trailhead at Meadowbrook Dr., 0.1 mile west of Shadow Lake Road (Blacksburg); Christiansburg High School at Independence Blvd. NW and Gold Leaf Dr. NW (Christiansburg)

Mileage
15.5

Type
Rail-Trail/Rail-with-Trail

Roughness Index
1

Surface
Asphalt, Boardwalk

TrailLink user tom.joy

133

Huckleberry North and Huckleberry South. The original 8.3-mile Huckleberry Trail starts at the Blacksburg Library, several blocks from the Virginia Tech campus. In the first 2 miles, you may hear a marching band in the distance or notice a game at the nearby Worsham Field. Continuing along this meandering trail, you'll leave the town and enter a rural landscape, passing quiet homes, open fields, and pockets of forests.

After a large tunnel passing under US 460, you'll reach a roundabout. Here you can either turn right to hop on Huckleberry North or turn left to stay on the original Huckleberry Trail heading south. The 5-mile Huckleberry North segment ends at Heritage Community Park and Natural Area, a 169-acre park on the north side of Blacksburg. At the northern end of the park, you'll find both the Gateway Trailhead and the Blacksburg-Rotary Mountain Bike Skills Park.

Continuing south on the original Huckleberry Trail, you'll hit the Coal Mining Heritage Park and Loop Trail at mile 5—just before you reach a railroad bridge over the still-active Norfolk Southern rail line. The park borders the Huckleberry Trail on both sides and contains old mining equipment and interpretive signage.

The trail continues to the west of New River Valley Mall in Christiansburg, running adjacent to the active rail line. Using the Renva W. Knowles Bridge over VA 114, the trail continues behind big-box stores to Cambria Street NW and a trailhead at the Christiansburg Recreation Center.

The Huckleberry South segment picks up at the intersection of Cambria Street NW and Providence Boulevard and winds through residential neighborhoods to the new southern terminus at Christiansburg High School.

Unlike most rail-trails, the Huckleberry Trail is quite hilly. While certain sections of the trail were built on former rail line alignments, the trail also rolls through agricultural fields where the climbs are short but the grades can be as steep as 6%. Where the grades are greater than 5%, turnouts are provided. The Huckleberry Trail connects to a series of natural-surface trail systems, including the McDonald Hollow Trail Network, the Gateway Trail, and the Poverty Creek Trail System.

CONTACT: huckleberrytrail.org

PARKING

Parking areas for the trail are listed from north to south. *Indicates that at least one accessible parking space is available.*

BLACKSBURG: Gateway Trailhead on Meadowbrook Dr., 400 feet southwest of Old Farm Road (37.2450, -80.4597).

BLACKSBURG: Heritage Community Park and Natural Area, 2300 Glade Road (37.2377, -80.4605).

BLACKSBURG: Blacksburg Fire Department Station #2, 2700 Prices Fork Road (37.2185, -80.4550). Limited designated spaces; do not block access to the station.

BLACKSBURG*: Good Shepherd Church-Brethren, 950 Heather Dr. (37.2228, -80.4492). Church-provided parking spaces are in the paved lot adjacent to the trail.

BLACKSBURG*: Huckleberry Trail Lot 001444, Harrell St. and Miller St. SW (37.2250, -80.4136).

BLACKSBURG*: Coal Mining Heritage Park, Hightop Road/VA 808 and Merrimac Road/VA 657 (37.1896, -80.4255).

CHRISTIANSBURG: New River Valley Mall, 782 New River Road (37.1629, -80.4286). Park either on the north side near the entrance of New River Community College, or on the south side near the movie theater.

CHRISTIANSBURG: Christiansburg Recreation Center, 1600 N. Franklin St. (37.1516, -80.4160).

CHRISTIANSBURG: Christiansburg High School, 100 Independence Blvd. NW (37.1457, -80.4179). Parking is unavailable when school is in session.

A 500-foot boardwalk section over wetland is a highlight of the northern section of trail.
TrailLink user tom.joy

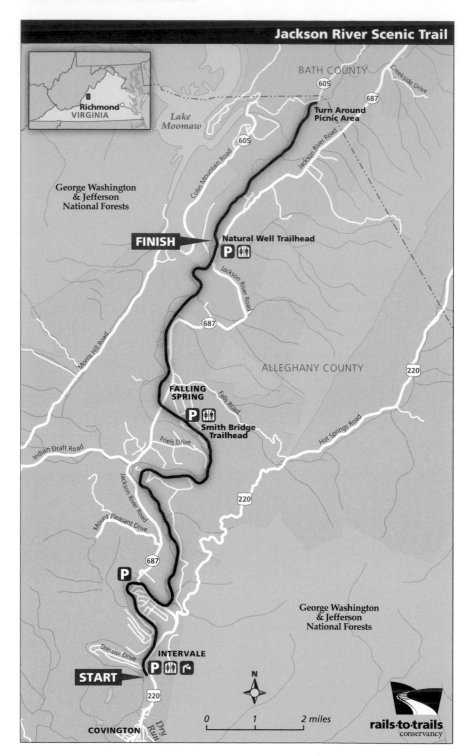

Waterfalls, river views, rugged rock formations, vibrant fall foliage, and delicate flowers in the spring: These are the sights that put the *scenic* in Jackson River Scenic Trail. This serene rail-trail, nestled in the Allegheny Highlands of western Virginia, traces the route of what was once the Hot Springs Branch of the Chesapeake & Ohio Railway. Much of the route is wooded, and you might see deer, rabbits, groundhogs, and other wildlife along the way. In addition to walking and biking, horseback riding is permitted on all sections of the trail.

Jackson River Scenic Trail begins in Intervale, just north of the city of Covington, and heads both north and south. Heading north, the winding trail hugs the curves of its namesake river. Picnic benches along the water allow you to rest and take in the beautiful surroundings. For added adventure, you can kayak or canoe in the river, also

TrailLink user speidel20

This serene rail-trail is nestled in the Allegheny Highlands of western Virginia.

County
Alleghany

Endpoints
Dressler Dr., off Hot Springs Road/US 220 (Intervale); 3 miles north of Jackson River Road/VA 687 at Natural Well Road/VA 638 (Natural Well)

Mileage
14.3

Type
Rail-Trail

Roughness Index
2

Surface
Gravel

known for its excellent trout fishing. You'll find the Smith Bridge trailhead 7.2 miles north of Intervale and in another 6.5 miles reach the Natural Well trailhead, near the Alleghany–Bath county line.

The trail's crushed-gravel surface extends 3 miles north of the Natural Well Trailhead to a dead-end at the Turn Around Picnic Area. A 1.6-mile extension is planned for completion in late 2022 to the new Cedar Creek Trailhead at the trail intersection with VA 605 in Bath County.

If you're returning to the Intervale trailhead at the end of your journey, continue south another 0.6 mile toward Dry Run in Covington, the southern terminus of the trail. Round out your experience with a visit to the C&O Depot in Covington for a peek at the trail's railroad past. The restored 1908 structure now houses the Alleghany Historical Society and its exhibits on the history of the region.

Rail buffs may also want to head 11 miles east of Covington to the town of Clifton Forge, where historical railroad artifacts and equipment are on display at the C&O Railway Heritage Center. Another nearby and worthwhile side trip is the Falling Spring Falls overlook. The roadside attraction is a jaw-dropping 80-foot waterfall on Hot Springs Road/US 220, 8 miles north of Covington and just south of Hot Springs Road/US 220 and Falls Road/VA 640.

CONTACT: jacksonrivertrail.com

PARKING

Parking areas are listed from south to north. *Indicates that at least one accessible parking space is available.*

COVINGTON*: Intervale trailhead, Dressler Dr./VA 778 and Depot Dr. (37.8198, -79.9870).

ALLEGHANY*: Petticoat Junction, Jackson River Road/VA 687 southeast of Mays Lane (37.8405, -79.9888).

HOT SPRINGS*: Smith Bridge trailhead, N. Smith Bridge Road/VA 721 and S. Smith Bridge Road (37.8784, -79.9755).

HOT SPRINGS*: Natural Well trailhead, Natural Well Road/VA 638 and Jackson River Road/VA 687 (37.9195, -79.9658).

The James River Heritage Trail is one of the premier urban trails in the state, passing through lush forest and the heart of historical, industrial downtown Lynchburg. The well-marked 10-mile trail is actually an interconnected system of shorter trails: the Blackwater Creek Trail, Point of Honor Trail, Kemper Station Trail, RiverWalk, and Percival's Island Trail. You can hop on the James River Heritage Trail from many places along its route. Drop by the Lynchburg Visitors Center (216 12th St.) for detailed maps of the trail system.

In October 2020, the City of Lynchburg opened the half-mile Blackwater Creek Trail Extension, which runs from the Ed Page Trailhead to the new westernmost endpoint at Linkhorne Middle School. Included in this extension is the Langhorne Road Trestle, which was converted into a beautiful pedestrian and bike bridge.

From the Ed Page Trailhead, the Blackwater Creek Trail follows an old railroad grade for 3 miles to Jefferson Street in downtown Lynchburg, near where the creek flows into the James River. The trail traverses the Blackwater

Hollins Tunnel spans nearly half a mile but is well lit.

Counties
Amherst, Lynchburg

Endpoints
Linkhorne Middle School (Lynchburg); Civitan Park, 0.6 mile east of Fertilizer Road (Lynchburg); Kemper Street Station at Park Ave. and Kemper St. (Lynchburg)

Mileage
10.1

Type
Rail-Trail/Rail-with-Trail

Roughness Index
1

Surface
Asphalt, Dirt, Wood Chips

TrailLink user wsbridges

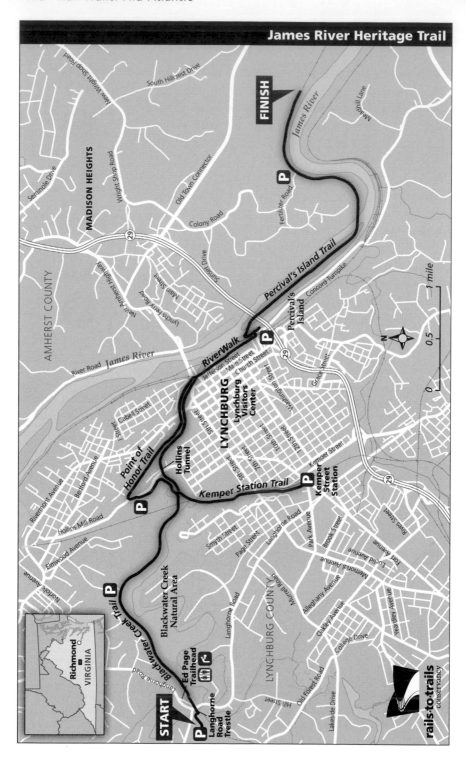

James River Heritage Trail

Creek Natural Area, and a few unpaved (but clearly marked) paths lead into the woods down a steep bank to the creek.

Shortly after you go under a railroad bridge high above you near mile 2.5, the Point of Honor Trail (1.75 miles long) branches off to the left. To the right, you'll find the 1-mile Kemper Station Trail. Approaching the historical Kemper Street Station, the trail features a long uphill grade that can be challenging for cyclists and wheelchair users; backtrack to return to the main trail.

If you continue on the main Blackwater Creek Trail, you'll go through the nearly 0.5-mile Hollins Tunnel, which bends but is well lit. If you take the Point of Honor Trail, you'll cross a spillway. Use caution when water is flowing over the top; if it's too high and fast, cross above at Hollins Mill Road.

At mile 3.5 (4.25 if you take the Point of Honor Trail), the Blackwater Creek Trail meets the RiverWalk, a 1-mile segment along Jefferson Street's sidewalks to Washington Street. At Washington Street, turn left, cross the tracks, and continue on the trail (which becomes Percival's Island Trail). You'll cross a spectacular refurbished railroad bridge onto the island. The trail traverses the mile-long island before crossing a second former rail bridge to the river's eastern shore. Back on the mainland, private property surrounds the trail, and signs warn you to stay on the trail to avoid trespassing.

The James River Heritage Trail continues another 1.25 miles along the river's edge to its eastern endpoint—0.6 mile past the last access point and parking area off Fertilizer Road. When you reach the endpoint, the railroad corridor clearly continues, but the trail becomes a dirt track that eventually crosses the river again after going under US 29, emerging onto VA 726/Mt. Athos Road.

CONTACT: lynchburgparksandrec.com/trails

PARKING

Parking areas are listed from west to east. *Indicates that at least one accessible parking space is available.*

LYNCHBURG*: Linkhorne Middle School, 2525 Linkhorne Dr. (37.4173, -79.1928).
Weekend parking is sunrise–sunset. Parking is unavailable when school is in session.

LYNCHBURG*: Ed Page Trailhead, 1720 Langhorne Road (37.4186, -79.1874).

LYNCHBURG*: Randolph Pl. E. south of Woodland Ave. (37.4264, -79.1726).

LYNCHBURG*: Hollins Mill Park, 521 Hollins Mill Road (37.4238, -79.1594).

LYNCHBURG*: Kemper Street Station, 825 Kemper St. (37.4064, -79.1571).

LYNCHBURG*: Percival's Island Natural Area, 1600 Concord Turnpike (37.4104, -79.1351).

MADISON HEIGHTS: Fertilizer Road/VA 1013 southeast of Carolina Ave. (37.4068, -79.1128).
Access to the parking area requires a significant drive along Fertilizer Road, a bumpy dirt road.

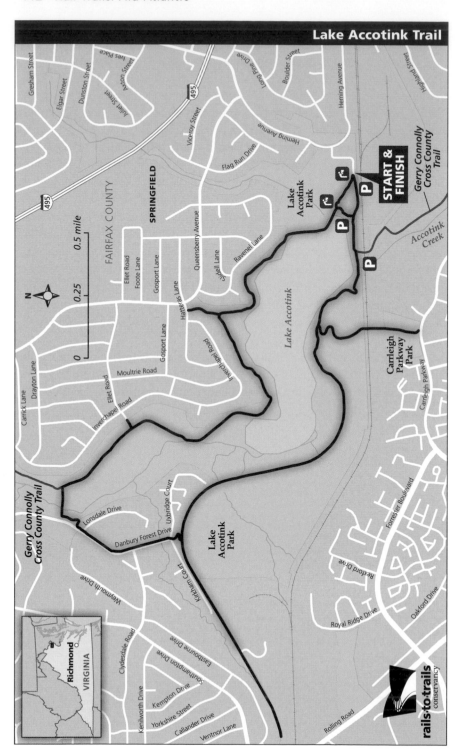

In Northern Virginia's suburban community of Springfield, Lake Accotink Park provides a wilderness escape amid the city surroundings. The 500-acre park features picnic areas, miniature golf, an antique carousel, a 55-acre lake with canoe and kayak rentals, and miles of multiuse trails. The main Lake Accotink Trail follows part of the former railbed of the Orange and Alexandria Railroad, along which soldiers and supplies were transported during the Civil War. Historical markers outline the railroad's history and mark the entry to the park.

On the north side of the lake, as well as downstream from the lake, the trail connects to Fairfax County's 40-mile Gerry Connolly Cross County Trail. South of the lake, between the main trail and the railroad tracks, is an extensive network of singletrack trails popular with bikers and hikers. (Many of these trails feature steep inclines, with some leading off park property, and signage is not

The elevated Virginia Railway Express parallels the trail in Lake Accotink Park.

County
Fairfax

Endpoints
Marina at Lake Accotink Park (Springfield); Rolling Road, between Southampton Dr. and Morrissette Dr. (Springfield)

Mileage
4.5

Type
Rail-Trail

Roughness Index
2

Surface
Asphalt, Dirt, Gravel

143

provided.) Ninety percent of the trail is a mix of gravel and dirt, with patches of asphalt covering the rest. Stretches of the trail featuring asphalt include the northern part of the trail (around Ellet Road) and the southernmost part of the trail heading to Carrleigh Parkway.

At the trail's start, it's impossible to miss the still-operating trestle high above Accotink Creek. The creek's dam, constructed more than 50 years ago, created a popular fishing hole. (Do not attempt to cross during or after heavy rainfall, as this area is susceptible to frequent flooding.) As you leave the picnic and boat-rental area behind on this clockwise route, you'll head up a short, steep hill toward the woods surrounding the lake. (If that seems daunting, do the route in reverse and descend the 60° hill instead.)

The first half of this route hugs the lake's curves as it travels deeper into the small wooded preserve that provides shade and wonderful views of the marsh-land and lake. When you reach the fork in the road at the trail's midpoint, either continue straight for another 0.75-mile jaunt on the rail-trail before it dead-ends at Rolling Road/VA 638 or follow the trail marker indicating a right turn to a 4.5-mile loop back to your starting point. The loop option takes you down a short hill and onto neighborhood sidewalks for three or four blocks and past an elementary school before you return to the park.

On the main route, several stairs lead downhill to a bridge and back to the Lake Accotink Trail, which circles around the other side of the lake to the creek and surrounding marshland. Your round-trip will end with a wonderful view of the antique carousel and geese swimming in the shallow lake waters.

CONTACT: fairfaxcounty.gov/parks/lake-accotink

PARKING

Parking areas are all located within Springfield and are listed from east to west. *Indicates that at least one accessible parking space is available.*

Lake Accotink Heming Ave. Parking Lot*: 5660 Heming Ave. (38.7942, -77.2119).

Lake Accotink Park*: 7500 Accotink Park Road (38.7936, -77.2155).

Lake Accotink Parking*: Accotink Park Road west of Highland St. (38.7922, -77.2173).

The 18-mile Mount Vernon Trail is one of the Washington, D.C., metro area's most popular trails, passing through park sites, yacht clubs, wetlands, neighborhoods, towns, and wooded acres. Just across the Potomac River from D.C. in Virginia, the trail links Theodore Roosevelt Island Park with George Washington's estate in Mount Vernon. The trail follows the course of the Potomac, linking Fairfax County and Alexandria to Arlington County and major Potomac River bridge crossings into the District of Columbia. The trail is also part of the Capital Trails Coalition (**railstotrails.org/ctc**), a Rails-to-Trails Conservancy TrailNation™ project that aims to develop an 800-mile trail network connecting the greater Washington, D.C., metropolitan region.

The winding trail is mostly paved, but some sections are boardwalk. In many places the trail is narrow, and

The Washington Monument and D.C. can be seen across the Potomac River.

TrailLink user ringogarcia1972

Counties
Alexandria, Arlington, Fairfax

Endpoints
US 29 and George Washington Memorial Pkwy. (Rosslyn); Mount Vernon estate at George Washington Memorial Pkwy. (Mount Vernon)

Mileage
18.0

Type
Greenway/Non-Rail-Trail

Roughness Index
1

Surface
Asphalt, Boardwalk

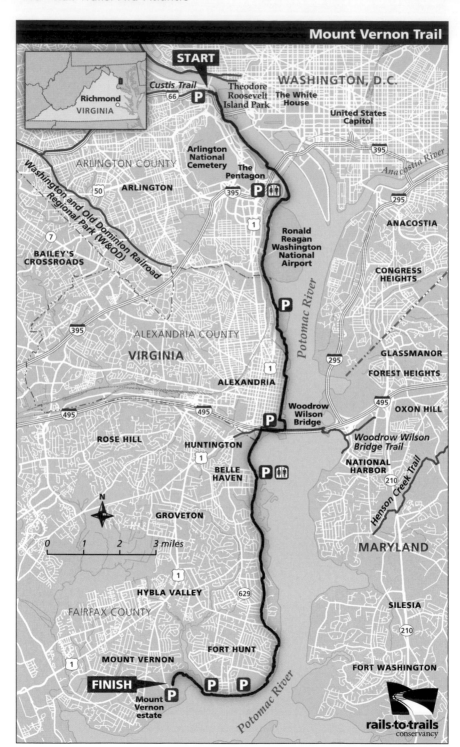

because it is heavily used (especially on weekends), all recreationists—whether on foot or wheels—must use caution when passing others and when entering the trail from any of its many access points. Cyclists must dismount at some of the bridge crossings (there are 38 in total). There are also steep grades in places, as well as areas with sharp turns, and several of the 18 at-grade road crossings have no detectable warnings for visually impaired and blind users.

At the midpoint of the Mount Vernon Trail, navigating Old Town Alexandria can be tricky. You have several all-street routes to choose from. From north to south, one route follows East Abingdon Drive to Bashford Lane to Royal Street. Or you can simply ride along George Washington Memorial Parkway/Washington Street and pick up the trail again south of I-95/I-495 (on the river side of the road). The other route veers to the left (coming from the north) and continues on Union Street. From here, you have easy access to Alexandria's waterfront parks, restaurants, and shops. The marina boardwalk area is lively, with all kinds of entertainment year-round but mainly between Memorial Day and Labor Day. You can return to the trail at the end of Union Street near the townhomes along the river.

Approaching the Woodrow Wilson Bridge (I-95/I-495), you can detour east across the Potomac River on the wide, paved Woodrow Wilson Bridge Trail, which flanks the northern side of the bridge, to reach National Harbor in Maryland. There, you'll find dozens of shops and restaurants, not to mention the occasional waterside entertainment, such as water-ski shows and boating events. Otherwise, continue under the Woodrow Wilson Bridge to take the trail through more parks, marshlands, and neighborhoods.

As you near the Mount Vernon estate, the trail begins a steep climb through the forest, where it ends in the parking lot for the estate grounds. On a hot day, you can slake your thirst at the visitor center and rest in the shade of the trees.

At the northern end of the trail, at the parking lot for Theodore Roosevelt Island Park, you can explore the island park's loop trail via a footbridge over the river or take a pedestrian bridge over the road and pick up the Custis Trail, which leads to the Washington & Old Dominion Trail (see page 173).

You can access the Mount Vernon Trail from numerous places along its route, including Theodore Roosevelt Island Park, Old Town Alexandria, the Mount Vernon estate, and more. The trail is also accessible from Washington's Metro system on the Blue and Orange Lines. The website below has more information, or you can visit the Washington Metropolitan Area Transit Authority's website (**wmata.com**).

CONTACT: nps.gov/gwmp/planyourvisit/mtvernontrail.htm

continued on next page

PARKING

Parking areas are listed from north to south. *Indicates that at least one accessible parking space is available.*

WASHINGTON, D.C.: Theodore Roosevelt Island Park, George Washington Memorial Pkwy. north of Arlington Memorial Bridge (38.8968, -77.0672). This lot is accessible only via northbound GW Pkwy.

ARLINGTON: Gravelly Point, George Washington Memorial Pkwy. north of Airport Access Road (38.8647, -77.0406). This lot is accessible only via northbound GW Pkwy.

ALEXANDRIA: Daingerfield Island, Marina Dr. east of George Washington Memorial Pkwy. (38.8301, -77.0410).

ALEXANDRIA: Jones Point Dr. east of S. Royal St. (38.7934, -77.0411).

ALEXANDRIA*: Bell Haven Park, driveway east of George Washington Memorial Pkwy. (38.7792, -77.0519).

FORT HUNT: Mount Vernon Trail Potomac Overlook, George Washington Memorial Pkwy. and River Farm Dr. (38.7103, -77.0573). The lot is safely accessible only via northbound GW Pkwy.

FORT HUNT*: Riverside Park, Stratford Lane south of George Washington Memorial Pkwy. (38.7109, -77.0725).

MOUNT VERNON*: Mount Vernon estate, 146 George Washington Memorial Pkwy. (38.7127, -77.0858).

Southwest Virginia's New River Trail is one of America's premier rail-trails; the U.S. Department of the Interior designated it an official National Recreation Trail in 2002. The trail is also a linear state park running along the New River through Grayson, Carroll, Wythe, and Pulaski Counties. In 1986, the Norfolk Southern Railway donated the railroad corridor, which originally served the once-expanding iron industry, to the Commonwealth of Virginia.

If you travel from Galax or Fries and head north to Pulaski, the mileage markers count down beginning with P51 at Galax and P45 at Fries (the numbers indicate the distance to Pulaski). Much of the trail is downhill from south to north. Equestrians should note that horseback

One of two tunnels along the rail-trail.

TrailLink user lisa.jarnigan

Counties
Carroll, Grayson,
Pulaski, Wythe

Endpoints
US 221/US 58 and
T. George Vaughan Jr.
Ave. (Galax); W. Main
St. and Riverview Ave.
(Fries); E. Main St./VA 99
and Xaloy Way (Pulaski)

Mileage
57.7

Type
Rail-Trail

Roughness Index
1–2

Surface
Crushed Stone

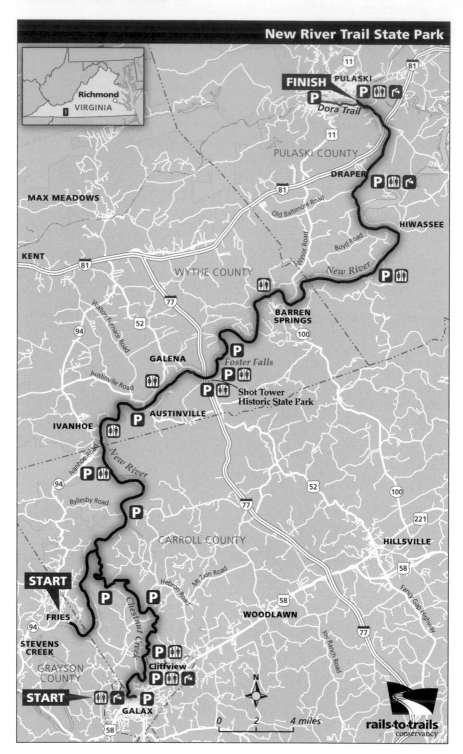

riding is allowed on all sections of the trail except for the first 2.4 miles between Galax and Cliffview. Horse trailer parking is available at the Cliffview parking area and several other parking areas along the trail.

If you start from Pulaski (Dora Junction) and head south, the first 3 miles are uphill, though most won't find it a burdensome climb. A mile or so after Draper (mile marker 6), the trail travels downhill to the impressive 950-foot-long Hiwassee trestle at the river. This 5-mile section features numerous trestles and offers a study in mountain railroading, as the tracks climbed away from Claytor Lake and the river to reach the mainline at Pulaski.

Many visitors choose to begin at Foster Falls (mile marker 24), the New River State Park headquarters, located about midway along the New River Trail. The park's Foster Falls Boat and Bike Livery (116 Orphanage Dr. in Max Meadows) provides shuttle services and rents bikes, canoes, kayaks, and float tubes.

The Galax trailhead, which features an old red caboose, has plenty of parking. From here, you'll follow Chestnut Creek along a 12-mile section leading to Fries Junction. The creek affords rugged scenery from the narrow valley it carved on its way to the river. At mile marker 39, you'll encounter the beautiful Fries Junction trestle spanning the New River. Just across the bridge, you have the option of taking a pleasant excursion to Fries, an 11-mile round-trip. This 5.5-mile spur is included in the trail's total length.

The remaining 39 miles proceed north (downgrade with the river) along the peacefully flowing New River as it runs through Ivanhoe, Austinville, Foster Falls, and Allisonia. The trail is isolated for much of this journey, so if you are on this stretch, be sure to carry all necessary supplies in case of an emergency or quick bike repair.

Along the way, you'll see many railroading highlights, including cavernous tunnels, steep dams, and trestle bridges, as well as the historical Shot Tower, built in 1807. The Galax and Pulaski trailheads have all your post-trail amenities.

CONTACT: dcr.virginia.gov/state-parks/new-river-trail

continued on next page

PARKING

Parking areas are listed from south to north. Note that there is a $7 daily parking fee to access the New River Trail State Park. Select parking areas for the trail are listed below. For a detailed list of parking areas and other waypoints, go to **TrailLink.com™**. *Indicates that at least one accessible parking space is available.*

FRIES*: Fries River Park, 323 Firehouse Dr. (36.7152, -80.9770). Horse trailer parking is available.

GALAX*: Galax Station, E. Stuart Dr./US 221 and T. George Vaughan Jr. Ave. (36.6679, -80.9246).

GALAX*: Cliffview Road/VA 721 and Baldwin Felts Lane (36.6806, -80.9182). Horse trailer parking is available.

GALAX*: Creekview Dr./VA 728, 1.2 miles north of Cliffview Road/VA 721 (36.6951, -80.9165).

IVANHOE*: 400 feet south of Buck Dam Road and Byllesby Road/CR 602 (36.7840, -80.9343).

AUSTINVILLE*: Shot Tower State Park, 176 Orphanage Dr. (36.8698, -80.8705).

GALENA*: Foster Falls Rail Depot, Orphanage Dr. and VA 623 (36.8844, -80.8561).

ALLISONIA: Allisonia Boat Ramp, Julia Simpkins Road and Mabe Hollow Lane (36.9448, -80.7316). Horse trailer parking is available; users must cross Julia Simpkins Road to access the trail.

DRAPER*: Draper Station, Old Baltimore Road/VA 654 and Holbert Ave./County Road 748 (36.9993, -80.7422). Horse trailer parking is available.

DORA JUNCTION: E. Main St./VA 99 at Xaloy Way (37.0457, -80.7497).

PULASKI*: Dora Trail, Pulaski Train Depot, 20 S. Washington Ave. (37.0458, -80.7793).

The Richmond and Danville Rail-Trail follows part of the right-of-way of the old railroad of the same name, an important transportation corridor for the Confederacy during the Civil War. The railroad linked the Confederate capital of Richmond with Southside (the area between the James River and the North Carolina border), where hospitals, prisons, and supply depots were located. Jefferson Davis and the Confederate army took the route of this railroad line when they retreated from Richmond near the end of the war. They also used it to carry war supplies and Union prisoners.

Today, the scenic Richmond and Danville Rail-Trail consists of 5.5 miles of this historic corridor, which eventually became part of the Norfolk Southern Railway system. Also called the Ringgold Rail Trail, the rail-trail opened in January 2001. It travels past farmland and through sparse

TrailLink user sdoyle01

The route winds through southern Virginia countryside east of Danville.

County
Pittsylvania

Endpoints
Ringgold Church Road and Ringgold Depot Road (Ringgold); Kerns Church Road/CR 656 and Railroad Trail/CR 943 (Sutherlin)

Mileage
5.5

Type
Rail-Trail

Roughness Index
2

Surface
Crushed Stone

153

Richmond and Danville Rail-Trail

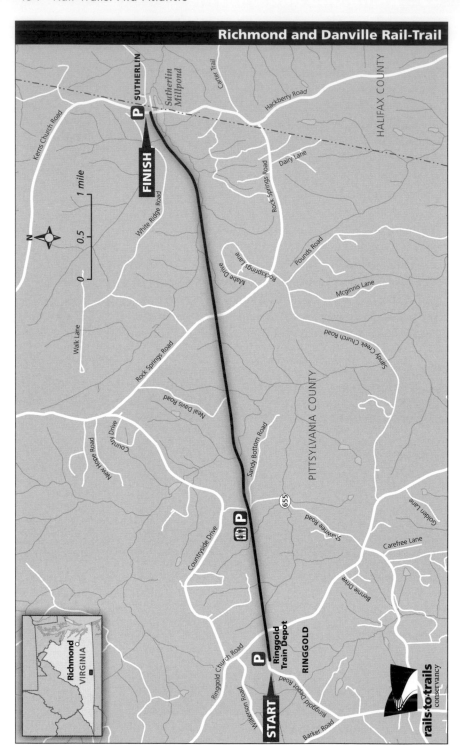

woods, providing a flat route for a walk or bike ride in the rural Virginia countryside on the outskirts of Danville.

Start at the western terminus—the Ringgold Train Depot—and in only 1 mile, you will reach a wetland area for prime waterfowl-watching. At 1.5 miles, you will hit a trailhead at Shawnee Road/County Road 655, where you can find parking and a portable toilet. Continue east another 4 miles to the eastern terminus in Sutherlin. If you are looking for evidence of the trail's railroading past, you'll find a restored railroad depot and an old red caboose at the Sutherlin trailhead.

The ride is comfortable for bicyclists and easy for hikers of all ages; it's also wheelchair-accessible. You can brush up on your Civil War history as well, as plaques along the way detail significant events that happened nearby.

Closure Notice: In October 2018, Hurricane Michael caused a large portion of the trail to wash out and compromised the structural integrity of a stone bridge. The eastern 4 miles of the trail—from the Sutherlin terminus to the Shawnee Road/ County Road 655 trailhead—have since closed to undergo repairs; these are estimated to be completed by the end of 2022. Please check with the trail manager for the latest information on closures and current trail conditions.

CONTACT: **pittsylvaniacountyva.gov/479/ringgold-rail-trail**

PARKING

Parking areas are listed from west to east.

RINGGOLD: 100 Ringgold Depot Road (36.6077, -79.2966).

RINGGOLD: Shawnee Road/CR 655, 300 feet north of Sandy Bottom Road (36.6107, -79.2699).

SUTHERLIN: Kerns Church Road/Hackberry Road, 0.1 mile south of Kerns Mill Road/ VA 688 (36.6245, -79.1997).

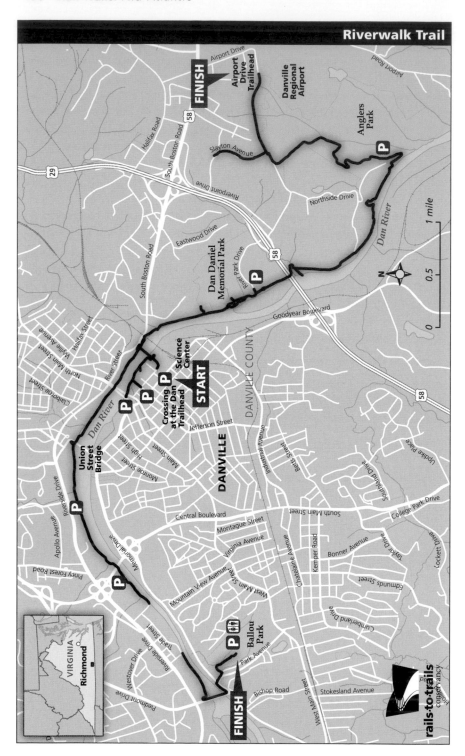

Riverwalk Trail

The nearly 12-mile paved Riverwalk Trail, also called the "Riverwalk on the Dan," is part of Danville's expanding network of trails. This scenic pathway along the Dan River connects industry, beautiful parks, and natural areas.

The Riverwalk Trail travels through some of the most historic Civil War regions of southern Virginia. Throughout the war, Danville functioned as a staging area for many battles. Some of its old tobacco warehouses were turned into prisons, and the city was the last capital of the Confederate States of America after Richmond was captured by the Union army.

The trail's recommended starting point is at the Crossing at the Dan Trailhead in historic downtown Danville, alongside a renovated tobacco warehouse and the active Amtrak station located in the Science Center campus. (The trailhead is located on the north side of the

TrailLink user susiepop66

For most of your journey, you'll have up-close views of the Dan River.

Counties
Danville, Pittsylvania

Endpoints
Ballou Park, 0.4 mile east of Park Ave. at Browder Road (Danville); Stinson Dr. and Airport Road (Danville)

Mileage
11.9

Type
Rail-Trail

Roughness Index
1

Surface
Asphalt, Concrete

parking lot.) From here, you'll cross the Dan River on a restored 1856 railroad bridge. On the other side, you can go east or west. If you turn left (west), the trail follows the river upstream for about a mile until it reaches a beautiful overlook at Union Street Bridge and then continues upstream with access to businesses and restaurants. Parking and restroom facilities are available at Ballou Park, where you can also connect to the 0.75-mile Ballou Park Nature Trail.

The best part of the trail lies to the right, on the eastern side. From here, the riverside trail will take you on an enjoyable trip through the many beautiful parks and natural areas adjacent to the Dan River. You may see a variety of wildlife, including geese, using the trail themselves.

Next, you'll head through Dan Daniel Memorial Park, where a section of trail that was taken out by Hurricane Michael in 2018 has since been repaired. After leaving the park, the trail continues to wind along the river through Anglers Park, where you can access a picnic shelter and tables, a boat ramp, restrooms, parking, and a bike repair station.

At the Anglers Park Trailhead, you have the option to head north on a trail segment leading to Danville Regional Airport. Though the terrain is hilly from here to the airport, it is the most secluded section of the Riverwalk, terminating at the Airport Drive Trailhead. This section of trail connects to the intertwining 25-mile Anglers Ridge singletrack mountain bike trail system.

Stretching stations are available at each major trailhead throughout the trail for your pre- and postworkout stretching.

CONTACT: danvilleva.gov/2035/danville-riverwalk-trail

PARKING

Parking areas are all located within the city of Danville and listed from west to east. *Indicates that at least one accessible parking space is available.*

Ballou Park Shelter 10: 0.4 mile east of Park Ave. at Browder Road (36.5765, -79.4258).

Sandy Creek Trailhead*: Riverside Dr./US 58 Bus. and Mt. Cross Road (36.5902, -79.4165). Access the trail from the northeast corner of the parking lot.

Riverside Drive Trailhead: Riverside Dr./US 58 Bus. and Audubon Dr. (36.5947, -79.4036).

Main Street Plaza*: 111 Main St. (36.5889, -79.3894).

Newtons Landing Trailhead*: 101 Newton St. (36.5873, -79.3854).

Crossing at the Dan Trailhead*: 667 Craghead St. (36.5851, -79.3855).

Dan Daniel Park Trailhead*: River Park Dr., 0.4 mile west of Danville Expy./US 29/58 (36.5746, -79.3739).

Anglers Park*: 0.9 mile south of Northside Dr. and Stinson Dr. (36.5592, -79.3564).

In Southern Virginia, an exciting regional trail project has been taking shape for over a decade. The Tobacco Heritage Trail will one day span 160 miles, connecting the counties of Brunswick, Charlotte, Halifax, Lunenburg, and Mecklenburg. Currently, segments of the planned route—totaling 22.7 miles—are open in all but one of these counties. A portion of the trail is also part of the larger East Coast Greenway, a growing network of multiuse trails connecting 15 states and 450 cities and towns on a 3,000-mile route between Maine and Florida.

Tobacco and cotton made this region prosperous, and the arrival of the railroad here in 1890 transformed the towns along its route from quaint villages to economic hubs. Visitors can now walk, bike, or ride horseback through the old railway corridor, enjoying historical buildings, scenic natural areas, and cultural amenities in

Counties
Brunswick, Halifax, Lunenburg, Mecklenburg

Endpoints
Main segment: South St. and W. Railroad St. (Lawrenceville); High St./ VA 618 and VA 642 (La Crosse)
Other segments: 10th St. between Main St. and Lincoln Ave. (Victoria); 0.8 mile south of the Oral Oaks Road underpass (Victoria); Washington St./VA 92, 0.2 mile south of US 58 (Boydton); Railroad Ave. between Summit Dr. and Edmunds St. (South Boston); 1.6 mile southwest of Lomax Ave. (South Boston); Barnes St. and Pleasant Hill Lane (Kenbridge); 1 block south of S. Decatur St. and E. 6th Ave. (Kenbridge)

Mileage
22.7

Type
Rail-Trail

Roughness Index
1–2

Surface
Asphalt, Crushed Stone

TrailLink user acodispoti

Scenic natural areas abound along this late 19th-century railway corridor in southern Virginia.

159

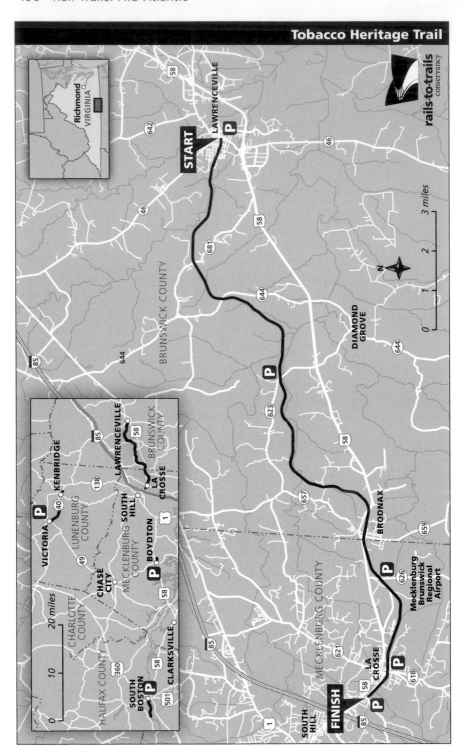

Tobacco Heritage Trail

the area's rural towns. Equestrians will find horse-mounting benches and hitching posts in the stretch between Lawrenceville and Brodnax.

We'll focus this write-up on the longest contiguous segment, a 16.6-mile stretch between Lawrenceville and La Crosse, though four other disconnected sections of the trail are open: 1.8 miles in Victoria, 2.6 miles in South Boston, 1.1 miles in Boydton, and 0.6 mile in Kenbridge. The trail is crushed stone, except a 1.3-mile section in LaCrosse that is paved.

Begin your excursion in central Lawrenceville at the trailhead off South Street; from there, you'll head west on the trail. As you leave town behind, the trail is surrounded by forest and farmlands, setting the tone for most of the journey. Enjoy the quiet and keep your eyes open for interpretative signage about the history of the area. You may even wish to pack a lunch, as there are trailside wooded spots with picnic tables for alfresco dining.

In 7 miles, you'll be rewarded for your efforts with a pretty 300-foot bridge across the Meherrin River. In another 6 miles, you'll reach Brodnax's Main Street. You won't find many restaurants in town, but a gas station just off the trail sells snacks and drinks. As you travel through town, you'll be on quiet Railroad Street; outside of town, you'll be back on trail.

Much of the last leg of the route traverses a lovely tree-lined corridor before you reach trail's end in 3.6 miles. You might catch a glimpse of wild turkey, deer, rabbits, or other wildlife along this stretch. And, as you approach La Crosse's Main Street, keep an eye out for the cherry-red antique caboose.

CONTACT: tobaccoheritagetrail.org

PARKING

Parking areas are listed from east to west. Select parking areas for the trail are listed below. For a detailed list of parking areas and other waypoints, go to **TrailLink.com**™. *Indicates that at least one accessible parking space is available.*

LAWRENCEVILLE: Trailhead parking at South St. and W. Railroad St. (36.7563, -77.8507).

BRODNAX: 3000 Evans Creek Road (36.7355, -77.9593).

BRODNAX: 1950 Regional Airport Road (36.6999, -78.0508).

LA CROSSE*: 115 S. Main St. (36.6967, -78.0937).

LA CROSSE: 239 High St. (36.7029, -78.104) .

VICTORIA*: 1485 Firehouse Road (36.9908, -78.2256).

BOYDTON: 564 Washington St. (36.6693, -78.387).

SOUTH BOSTON: Cotton Mill Park, 196 Railroad Ave. (36.6973, -78.9102).

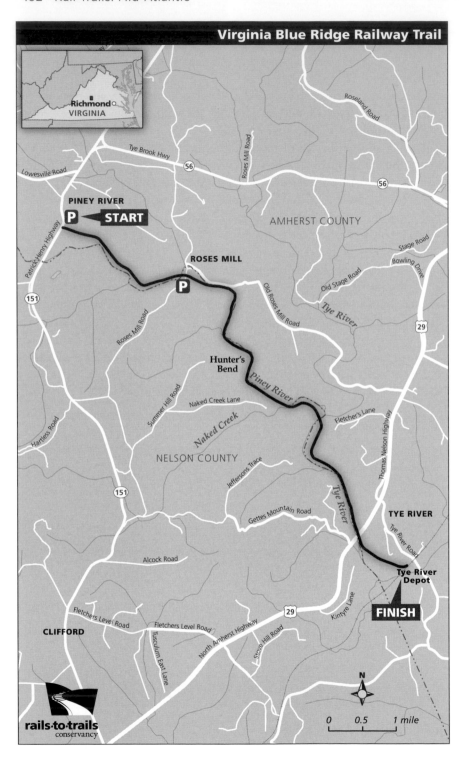

Virginia Blue Ridge Railway Trail

The Virginia Blue Ridge Railway Trail offers a quintessential rail-trail experience in central Virginia, midway between Lynchburg and Charlottesville (less than an hour's drive from each). The trail offers an easy, picturesque route through a beautiful setting with plentiful opportunities to see unique historical sites. Horseback riding is also permitted on the entirety of the trail.

The Piney and Tye Rivers are constant companions, and you'll cross five bridges on the nearly 7-mile route, including a photo-worthy covered bridge at Naked Creek. The railbed on which the rail-trail now rests was originally built in 1915 to haul timber to local mills. Along your journey, you'll see relics of this past, such as railcars and a railroad weighing scale on display.

Begin your journey at the northern trailhead in Piney River, just off VA 151. Here, a renovated depot serves as

The trail is wooded much of the way, offering a cool respite even during the summer months.

Counties
Amherst, Nelson

Endpoints
Patrick Henry Hwy./
VA 151, 0.7 mile south
of Lowesville Road/VA
778 (Piney River); Tye
River Depot (Tye River)

Mileage
6.9

Type
Rail-Trail

Roughness Index
1

Surface
Crushed Stone,
Dirt, Gravel

TrailLink user crichardson2

a visitor center, and a historical railroad park—complete with a refurbished caboose—is ready to explore. As the larger of the two trailheads serving this trail, Piney River also offers ample parking for cars and horse trailers, portable toilets, and a kiosk with nature information for kids.

A second, smaller trailhead is located on Roses Mill Road, 1.7 miles east of Piney River trailhead. Amherst County is in the process of expanding the parking lot here. At Hunter's Bend, 1.9 miles south of the Roses Mill Trailhead, you'll pass a new gazebo. Just 0.5 mile from Hunter's Bend is the Naked Creek bridge. The trail ends at the Tye River Depot, but note that there is no exit at this southern end; you'll need to turn around and head back to Piney River.

The trail is primarily crushed stone and is wooded much of the way, offering a cool respite even during the summer months. White-tailed deer and other wildlife are plentiful, so trail users should wear blaze-orange clothing during the autumn hunting season. The trail also passes through farm country and open fields. Come in the spring to see wildflowers sprinkling color into the lush green backdrop.

CONTACT: countyofamherst.com/department/division.php?structureid=167 and nelsoncounty-va.gov/departments/parks-recreation/hiking

PARKING

Parking areas are listed from northwest to southeast. *Indicates that at least one accessible parking space is available.*

PINEY RIVER*: 3124 Patrick Henry Hwy./VA 151, 0.7 mile south of Lowesville Road (37.7077, -79.0232).

TYE RIVER*: 1434 Roses Mill Road/VA 674, 0.1 mile south of Old Rose Mill Road/VA 665 (37.700, -78.99657).

The Virginia Capital Trail transports visitors through time as it travels nearly 52 miles between the state's early capital at the Jamestown Settlement and its current capital city of Richmond, traversing lands first inhabited by the Powhatan, Chickahominy, and other Native Americans. Along the way, the smooth pathway follows Scenic Route 5, offering access to trailside businesses and views of historical sites, natural areas, rolling countryside, and the James River.

Construction of the trail began in 2005, and it was developed through a public/private partnership formed by the Virginia Department of Transportation and the Virginia Capital Trail Foundation. Today, the route hosts approximately 1.2 million people per year, serving as a popular destination and generating millions of dollars for the region. Plans are underway for additional trail connections along the route.

The western end of the trail is located in downtown Richmond.

Counties
Charles City, City of Richmond, Henrico, James City

Endpoints
200 feet south of Dock St. at S. 17th St. (Richmond); Jamestown Settlement at Jamestown Road and Colonial Pkwy. (Jamestown)

Mileage
51.7

Type
Rail-with-Trail; Greenway/Non-Rail-Trail

Roughness Index
1

Surface
Asphalt, Boardwalk

Mary Ellen Koontz

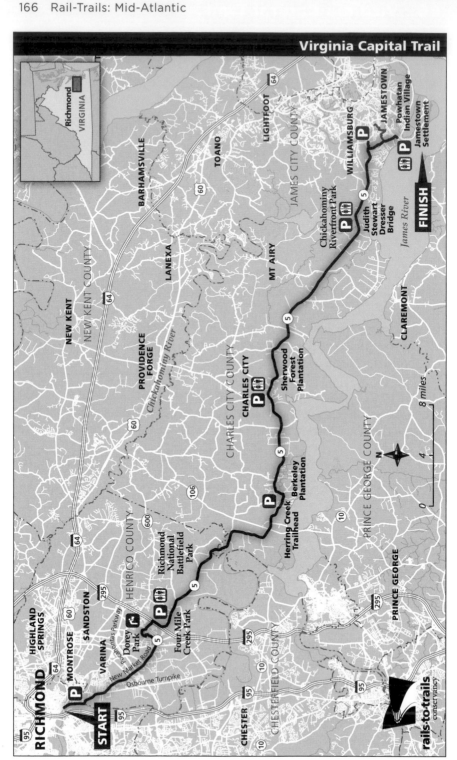

The well-maintained trail is mostly paved, with some short wooden board-walk sections and occasional road crossings, which are marked or signaled. It has seven main sections and is equipped with plenty of amenities, including restrooms, parking, and ample signage, making it easy for visitors to enjoy shorter trips or the trail in its entirety.

If your journey begins in Richmond, you'll commence at Great Shiplock Park, which features a restored lock on a canal that connected the James River with the docks in Richmond. With a rail line overhead and the river on your side, you'll be guided by the sounds of the city as you travel the busiest section of the Richmond Riverfront segment of trail.

In the Varina segment, between mile markers 49 and 50, you will prog-ress up the first and most significant hill—which rewards its conquerors with a sweeping view of Richmond and the James River—before continuing along the Osbourne Turnpike. At mile marker 48, the trail runs parallel to New Market Road and eventually comes to a signaled crossing of the Pocahontas Parkway.

Just before Doran Road, follow signs to Dorey Park. About 1 mile into the park segment, the trail briefly turns west onto the residential Kinvan Road before turning right into Dorey Park. (The next segment of the trail offers little shade, so you may want to refill your water supply here.) As the trail weaves through the park, enjoy the shaded paths and boardwalk. The trail continues under I-295 into Four Mile Creek Park, which has a bike repair station, parking, restrooms, benches, and the beloved "Big Bike" sculpture.

Leaving the park after mile marker 40, the trail reconnects with New Mar-ket Road in the vicinity of the Civil War's Battle of New Market Heights, where African American soldiers made significant contributions to the Union vic-tory. On your way to Herring Creek Trailhead at mile marker 27, you will pass by many fields and several former plantations, including Berkeley Plantation, birthplace of William Henry Harrison, the ninth president of the United States.

Within the Charles City Courthouse segment, the trail will have two brief on-road sections: before and after the courthouse, where a parking area and restrooms are available. The trail transitions to the Sherwood Forest segment as it continues alongside the wooded John Tyler Memorial Parkway, named for the 10th US president, whose home, Sherwood Forest Plantation, is visible from the trail near mile marker 17.

As you approach mile marker 7, the trail crosses the Chickahominy River, for which this segment is named. Standing 50 feet above the river on the Judith Stewart Dresser Memorial Bridge, you will be treated to photo-worthy views of the sparkling waters. The bridge leads to Chickahominy Riverfront Park, which offers parking, restrooms, kayak rentals, campsites, and other attractions.

You will wind through the trail's last few miles in the Greensprings segment, where you will find bike repair tools and exercise stations. At the trail's eastern endpoint is the historic Jamestown Settlement, where parking and restrooms are available; museums and exhibits, including the Powhatan Indian Village, abound nearby. Those seeking refreshment and recreation can enjoy a brewery, beach, and marina.

CONTACT: virginiacapitaltrail.org

PARKING

The parking areas are listed from west (mile marker 51.7) to east (mile marker 0). *Indicates that at least one accessible parking space is available.*

RICHMOND: Great Shiplock Park, 2803 Dock St. (37.5263, -77.4210).

RICHMOND: Four Mile Creek Trailhead, 3256 New Market Road (37.4353, -77.3295).

CHARLES CITY: Herring Creek Trailhead, John Tyler Memorial Hwy. and Herring Creek Road/VA 640 (37.3302, -77.1822).

CHARLES CITY*: Charles City Courthouse, 10780 Courthouse Road (37.3413, -77.0717).

WILLIAMSBURG*: Chickahominy Riverfront Park, 1350 John Tyler Memorial Hwy. (37.2652, -76.87229).

WILLIAMSBURG*: Jamestown High School, 3751 John Tyler Memorial Hwy. (37.2527, -76.7891).

WILLIAMSBURG*: Jamestown Settlement, 2110 Jamestown Road (37.2257, -76.7851).

Inducted into RTC's Rail-Trail Hall of Fame in 2014, the Virginia Creeper National Recreation Trail offers scenic wonders ranging from dense forests, open fields, and lush waterways to railroad relics and delightful small towns. Visitors and residents alike love the length of the trail, its multiple access points, and the wide range of uses; in addition to walking and biking, horseback riding is permitted on the full length of the trail.

There are so many trestles along the route that each is numbered, with an identifying plaque at either end. Originally, there were more than 100 trestles spanning the region's web of picturesque creeks and rivers; 47 remain on the rail-trail today.

Views along this rural southwestern Virginia trail include farms and grazing cattle.

Counties
Grayson, Washington

Endpoints
Green Spring Road and Gibson St. (Abingdon); Dolinger Road, 250 feet east of VA 753/Whitetop Gap Road (Whitetop)

Mileage
34.0

Type
Rail-Trail

Roughness Index
2

Surface
Gravel

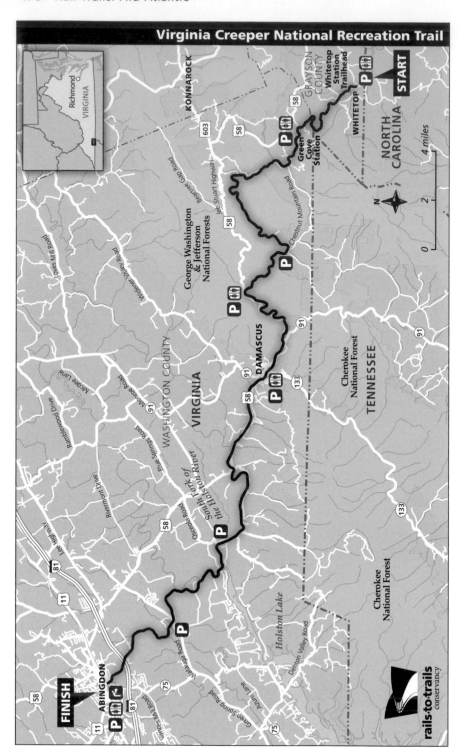

Virginia Creeper National Recreation Trail

Many bike shops in Abingdon (the western terminus) and Damascus (roughly halfway through the trail) offer bike rentals and shuttles to the eastern terminus at the Whitetop Station trailhead (elevation 3,500') at the Virginia–North Carolina border. Most trail users opt for a shuttle from Abingdon or Damascus up to Whitetop Station and then hike or ride back down. Riders can also head to Abingdon directly from Damascus or, for a more challenging route, bike up from Abingdon or Damascus to Whitetop Station.

The first 17-mile stretch heading west from Whitetop to Damascus travels downhill through terrific scenery, from Christmas tree farms and grazing cattle to river views and deep forestland. It includes four access points, some of which are housed in restored railroad depots. Green Cove Station, the oldest station on the trail, was once a post office, general store, and cargo location. Today, it serves as a museum with artifacts on display—including original mailboxes—and frequently features photography exhibits and live music from local groups. The Appalachian Trail weaves on and off the Creeper as well.

Around the midpoint of the Creeper Trail, you'll reach Damascus. If you're continuing to Abingdon, you can enjoy this charming town's restaurants and shops before tackling the rest of the trail. From Damascus to trail's end in Abingdon, the constant downhill is exchanged for a flat grade with gentle rises and descents. It's not strenuous, but it is a change from the first section. This stretch also includes some of the trail's most beautiful river and farmland views.

On a ridgeline high above the South Fork of the Holston River, you'll emerge onto a bridge offering invigorating views of South Holston Lake below. As you continue toward Abingdon, you'll pass through cattle gates marking your entrance to the Creeper's expansive grazing meadows.

About half a mile from Abingdon is a public park with restrooms, picnic areas, and a water fountain. Just across the last bridge, you'll reach the Abingdon trailhead and the Virginia Creeper Trail Welcome Center, open almost daily in season (April–mid-November). Here, you'll find trail merchandise, maps, water, and knowledgeable staff. You also can find several campgrounds nearby, including those operated by the U.S. Forest Service in the Mount Rogers National Recreation Area.

CONTACT: vacreepertrail.org

continued on next page

PARKING

In addition to the parking areas below (listed from east to west), parking is available at various locations in the town of Damascus at bike shops, several small lots, and the town park. Select parking areas for the trail are listed below. For a detailed list of parking areas and other waypoints, go to **TrailLink.com™**.

WHITETOP: Whitetop Station Trailhead, 2146–2084 Whitetop Gap Road (36.59804, -81.6241).

DAMASCUS: Green Cove Station, 41259 Green Cove Road (36.6193, -81.64433).

DAMASCUS: Taylor's Valley Trailhead, Waccamaw Lane and Taylor Valley Road (36.6248, -81.7176).

ABINGDON: Alvarado Station, 21198 Alvarado Road (36.6505, -81.8865).

ABINGDON: Watauga Trailhead on Watauga Road, 2.1 miles southwest of Jeb Stuart Hwy./ US 58 (36.6780, -81.9351).

ABINGDON: Abingdon Terminus, 300 Green Spring Road, mile marker 1, between A St. SE and Gibson St. SE, across from the Virginia Creeper Trail Welcome Center (36.7092, -81.9715).

The Washington and Old Dominion Trail (W&OD), one of suburban Washington, D.C.'s most popular rail-trails, is a fantastic link between the state's rural and historical past and the nation's capital. The trail serves as an important spine in the developing 800-mile Capital Trails Coalition network (**railstotrails.org/ctc**), a Rails-to-Trails Conservancy TrailNation™ project connecting the greater Washington, D.C., metropolitan region. The W&OD was inducted into the national Rail-Trail Hall of Fame in 2008.

The W&OD Railroad was built in 1859, shortly before the Civil War, and went into disuse in 1968. NOVA Parks opened the first few miles of paved trail in Falls Church in 1974 through an agreement with Virginia Electric and Power Company, which owned the right-of-way, and in 1977 began purchasing the land. The trail was completed

Counties
Arlington, Fairfax, Loudoun

Endpoints
Four Mile Run Dr. and Shirlington Road (Arlington); N. 21st St./ VA 690 (Purcellville)

Mileage
45.0

Type
Rail-Trail

Roughness Index
1

Surface
Asphalt, Crushed Stone

Scott Stark

The W&OD begins in the leafy suburbs of northern Virginia.

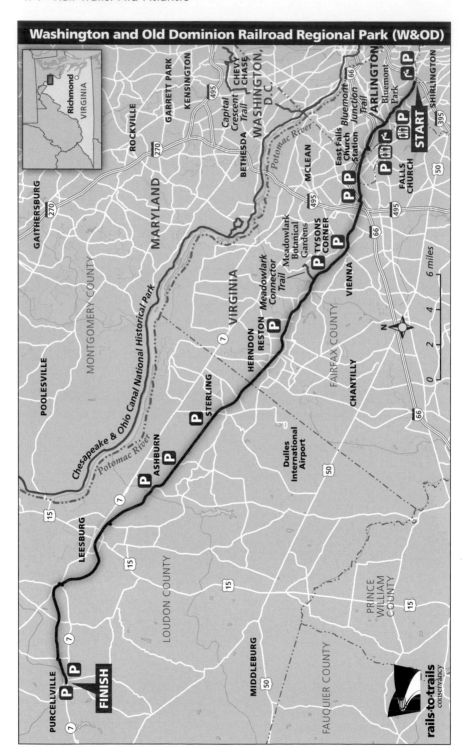

Washington and Old Dominion Railroad Regional Park (W&OD)

in 1988. Today, NOVA Parks maintains the trail with the help of volunteers from Friends of the W&OD.

A crushed-stone trail parallels the paved W&OD for 32 miles and is favored by mountain bikers, equestrians, and joggers. Horses are restricted to this gravel trail, though you'll rarely see one east of Vienna. The trail is exceptionally well marked, with mileposts every 0.5 mile and interpretive signs telling the story of the people and places along the rail line.

The trail's eastern terminus is in the unincorporated community of Shirlington in Arlington, which makes for a nice starting or ending point. From here, the W&OD Trail is urban for a few miles before exchanging the trappings of the city for leafier suburbs. From east to west, the trail gains elevation, albeit gradually. Bluemont Park is one of many picnic areas and parks within the trail's first 10 miles. You'll find water, restrooms, and an old caboose here, as well as a link to the Bluemont Junction Trail, constructed on a former railroad spur.

At 5 miles, the trail provides access to Washington's Metro system on the Orange and Silver Lines via the East Falls Church Station. As you make your way beyond the I-495 Beltway, use caution at all road crossings, especially during rush hour. The path continues through the communities of Vienna—with an old caboose and train depot—and Reston. Both towns offer plenty of shops and restaurants. The suburban neighborhoods surrounding the trail become more wooded, too. For a worthwhile side trip between Vienna and Reston, head onto the mile-long Meadowlark Connector Trail, which leads to the beautiful Meadowlark Botanical Gardens.

The town of Herndon features another caboose and a trailside train depot used as a visitor center. As the trail continues, it passes through Sterling and Ashburn, which features a year-round trailside barbecue restaurant. The historic town of Leesburg is a popular spot for lunch and antiquing. The trail also passes through a nice park. From here, it begins to take on a more rural tone as it continues west.

The final 10 miles from Leesburg to Purcellville travel through the rolling hills of Virginia Piedmont farmland. Horses graze, cornfields flourish, and trail crowds thin out somewhat. The trail ends at the Purcellville Train Depot, which features restaurants and a bike shop.

CONTACT: wodfriends.org and **novaparks.com/parks/washington-and-old -dominion-railroad-regional-park**

continued on next page

PARKING

Parking and trail access are available in dozens of places along the route. The options here are listed from east to west. For more information, visit **wodfriends.org.** Select parking areas for the trail are listed below. For a detailed list of parking areas and other waypoints, go to **TrailLink.com™.** *Indicates that at least one accessible parking space is available.*

ARLINGTON*: Barcroft Community Center, 4200 S. Four Mile Run Dr. (38.8503, -77.1014). The W&OD Trail parallels the north side of S. Four Mile Run Dr.

ARLINGTON*: Bluemont Park, N. Manchester St. and Wilson Blvd. (38.8740, -77.1338).

ARLINGTON*: Bon Air Park, 850 N. Lexington St. (38.8755, -77.1327).

FALLS CHURCH*: Idylwood Park, Virginia Lane, 0.3 mile south of Idylwood Road/VA 695 (38.8914, -77.2120).

VIENNA*: Vienna Community Center, 120 Cherry St. SE (38.9006, -77.2599).

VIENNA*: Vienna Train Station, 231 Dominion Road NE (38.9043, -77.26769).

VIENNA*: Clarks Crossing Park, Clarks Crossing Road, 300 feet west of Batten Hollow Road (38.9209, -77.2856).

RESTON*: Old Reston lot, 1891 Old Reston Ave. (38.9557, -77.3515).

STERLING*: Sterling lot, Pacific Blvd., 0.7 mile north of Waxpool Road/VA 625 (39.0146, -77.4375).

ASHBURN*: Ashburn Road/VA 641, 250 feet south of Stubble Road (39.0441, -77.4871).

ASHBURN*: Jackpit Lane, 400 feet south of Builders Lane (39.0648, -77.5108).

PURCELLVILLE*: Purcellville Train Station, N. 23rd St. and N. 21st St. (39.1383, -77.7160). Additional 2-hour limited parking is available across the street.

PURCELLVILLE*: North Hatcher lot, N. Hatcher Ave./VA 611, 150 feet south of E. Loudoun Valley Dr. (39.1386, -77.7130).

History runs deep along the Wilderness Road Trail, which roughly follows a trail forged by Daniel Boone in April 1775. The trail later became a route on the Louisville & Nashville Railroad before finally being converted to a rail-trail. Stretching from a national historical park to a state park, the Wilderness Road Trail is a registered stop on the Virginia Birding and Wildlife Trail. Horseback riders are allowed on all sections of the trail.

Cumberland Gap National Historical Park is technically the western endpoint of the Wilderness Road Trail, but users are strongly advised to start 2 miles into this trail, at the Gibson Place Park & Ride, as a change of ownership has left the westernmost section unmaintained. (Users who want to experience the national park can park at the Wilderness Road Trail's western terminus and head west on the Colson Trail, which turns into the 1.6-mile Boone Trail and connects to a larger trail system through the Cumberland Gap.)

The rail-trail is screened by trees that buffer the noise of paralleling US 58.

TrailLink user kerr37938

County
Lee

Endpoints
Wilderness Road/
US 58 (TN–VA state line) in Cumberland Gap National Historical Park (Cumberland Gap); Wilderness Road/US 58 at VA 684 (3.4 miles west of Ewing)

Mileage
6.5–8.5

Type
Rail-Trail

Roughness Index
2

Surface
Crushed Stone

177

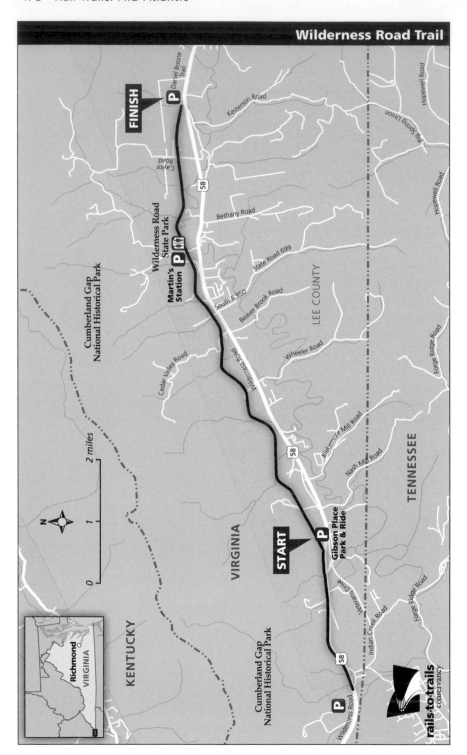

To begin your journey on the 6.5 usable miles of the Wilderness Road Trail, head east from the Park & Ride. From here, the trail retreats into a quiet, scenic area behind a veil of trees that buffers the noise of US 58, which parallels the trail. The route meanders through picturesque farmland, complete with bright-white fences and grazing cattle, and is dotted with quaint homes, barns, and silos. The impressive Cumberland Mountain serves as a backdrop to this idyllic landscape.

On the eastern end of the trail, you'll find yourself in Wilderness Road State Park, open daily, 8 a.m.–sunset. There is a fee to enter the park, which offers three hiking trails, a brown and rainbow trout fishing area, a nature center (open Memorial Day–Labor Day, Thursday–Sunday), and a visitor center (open daily, March 15–Dec. 31, 8 a.m.–4:30 p.m.) that houses a frontier museum and gift shop.

Wilderness Road State Park's Historic Martin's Station (open May 1–Oct. 31, Wednesday–Sunday, 10 a.m.–5 p.m.) is an outdoor living-history museum depicting frontier life in Virginia. Users can also enjoy the park's picnic shelters, 100-seat amphitheater, ADA-certified playground, sand volleyball court, and horseshoe pits. Primitive camping for groups also is available.

CONTACT: dcr.virginia.gov/state-parks/wilderness-road

PARKING

Parking areas are listed from west to east. *Indicates that at least one accessible parking space is available.*

EWING*: Wilderness Road Campground and Picnic Area entrance, Cumberland Gap National Park, 854 National Park Road (36.6026, -83.6311). There is no entrance fee for the park.

EWING*: Gibson Place Park & Ride, 3707 Wilderness Road Trail/Daniel Boone Trail/US 58, 0.1 mile west of Cross Winds Dr. (36.6060, -83.5932).

EWING*: Wilderness Road State Park, Elydale Road, 0.2 mile north of Wilderness Road/Daniel Boone Trail/US 58 (36.6314, -83.5263). There is a $5/day parking fee for the park; self-pay parking information is available at the contact station.

EWING*: US 58 and County Road 684 Park & Ride, north side of Wilderness Road/US 58/Daniel Boone Trail, 0.3 mile west of CR 684 (36.6326, -83.4893).

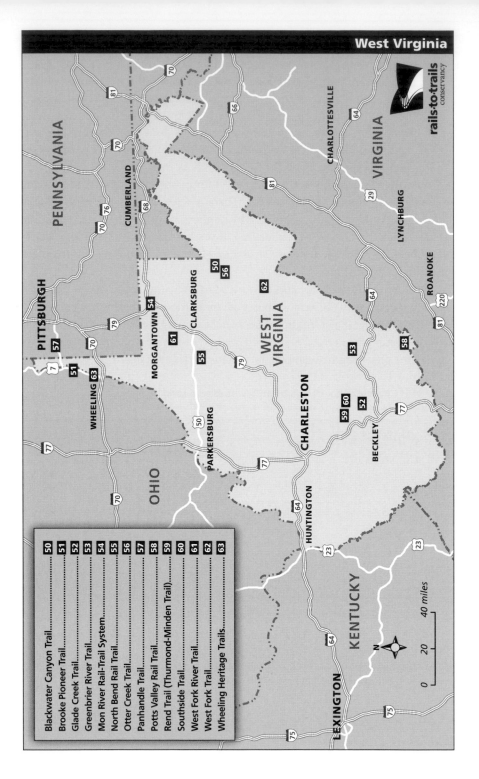

rails·to·trails
conservancy

West Virginia

The Deckers Creek Trail runs between Morgantown and Reedsville (see page 197).
Paul Poling/courtesy of Mon River Trails Conservancy

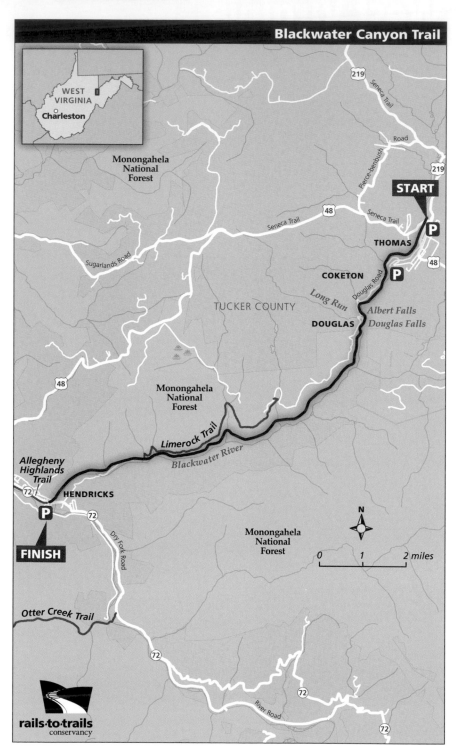

Blackwater Canyon Trail

WEST VIRGINIA
○ Charleston

219
Seneca Trail

Monongahela
National
Forest

Pierce-benbush Road

219

START

48

Seneca Trail

Seneca Trail

P

THOMAS

48

Sugarlands Road

Seneca Trail

COKETON

P

Long Run

Douglas Road

DOUGLAS

Albert Falls

Douglas Falls

48

TUCKER COUNTY

Monongahela
National
Forest

Limerock Trail

Allegheny
Highlands
Trail

72

Blackwater River

HENDRICKS

72

P

FINISH

Dry Fork Road

Monongahela
National
Forest

N

0   1   2 miles

Otter Creek Trail

72

72

River Road

72

rails·to·trails
conservancy

The Blackwater Canyon Trail follows one of the most challenging and picturesque segments of the former West Virginia Central & Pittsburgh Railway. On its 10.7-mile run deep through the Monongahela National Forest in eastern West Virginia, the rough dirt trail passes waterfalls and relics of the railroad and coal industries.

The trail has a steeper than normal grade; in the 1880s, the railroad builders who laid track across the route through the Allegheny Mountains couldn't avoid the forested canyon up the Blackwater River and its North Fork. The uphill grade between Hendricks and Thomas, which climbs 1,200 feet, required trains hauling coal to put on extra locomotives.

Today's visitors can arrange for a shuttle to Thomas to take a one-way downhill ride or choose to steadily climb from Hendricks and coast downhill on the return. The trail surface is rough, so hiking shoes are recommended for hikers, and wide tires are recommended for cyclists.

Located near the top of the grade in the north, Thomas was a bustling center for the coal mines that sprang up

The trail runs deep through West Virginia's Monongahela National Forest.

TrailLink user commanderbk55

County
Tucker

Endpoints
0.2 mile north of the intersection of US 48 and US 219/Seneca Trail (Thomas); Main St./ WV 72 and Third St. (Hendricks)

Mileage
10.7

Type
Rail-Trail

Roughness Index
2–3

Surface
Dirt, Gravel

nearby and shipped their product via the railroad. Today, many brick buildings from that era house boutiques and antiques stores.

Technically, the trail begins in Thomas, 0.3 mile north of the dam on the North Fork of the Blackwater River, which is near the intersection of US 48 and US 219. Visitors can park in the lot at East Avenue/WV 32, located about 0.3 mile south, and take a short walkway to the trail, or they can use a small lot about a mile south on Douglas Road.

The trail is marred by potholes and ruts from the Douglas Road lot to Douglas Falls, about 1.2 miles downstream. Remains of beehive coke ovens that purified coal are visible along the trail just south of Thomas. More than 600 coke ovens operated in this area, known as Coketon. Interpretive signs posted by Friends of Blackwater mark the sites of old train depots, locomotive round-houses, and machine shops along the route.

The roaring river at the base of the canyon provides a steady soundtrack to the journey, as do the waterfalls that are occasionally visible along the way. One of the first is Albert Falls, about a mile past the coke ovens. In another half mile, after crossing a trestle over Long Run, you can hear Douglas Falls cascading 35 feet into a pool below. A path leads to an overlook. Plans are in the works to build a pedestrian suspension bridge across North Fork here to connect with a trail heading east to Blackwater Falls State Park near Davis.

The trail becomes narrower as you head south along the main stem of the Blackwater River, a destination for experienced kayakers. The junction with Limerock Trail appears about 5.6 miles past Douglas Falls. The overgrown hiking trail heads uphill for 4 miles to a Forest Service road on the canyon rim.

Several endangered species, including the West Virginia flying squirrel, the Indiana bat, and the Cheat Mountain salamander, make their home in the canyon. The habitat surrounding the trail is vital to the survival of these species, so it is important to stay on the trail.

The trail widens again as you head another 2.2 miles to the trailhead in Hendricks. Crossing WV 72 in town, you'll meet the Allegheny Highlands Trail, a crushed rock and asphalt rail-trail that heads southwest for 26 miles to Elkins.

CONTACT: fs.usda.gov/attmain/mnf or saveblackwater.org

PARKING

Parking areas are listed from east to west.

THOMAS: 172 East Ave./US 48/WV 32 between the north and south intersections of Spruce St./US 48/WV 32 (39.1497, -79.4984).

THOMAS: Douglas Road/CR 27 and Rail Falls Road/CR 27/3 (39.1386, -79.5110).

HENDRICKS: Second St., 130 feet south of Main St./WV 72 (39.0747, -79.6322).

The Brooke Pioneer Trail rolls along the woodsy eastern bank of the Ohio River, a waterway that once carried early settlers' flatboats to lands in the west. The northern section of the trail, closed for several years for construction of the Wellsburg Bridge spanning the river, is scheduled to reopen in late 2022. The trail provides access to the bridge's shared-used path that will carry walkers and bicyclists westward into Ohio.

The paved trail runs for 6.7 miles between the southern city limits of historic Wellsburg and the Ohio County line at Short Creek, where it meets the Wheeling Heritage Trails. Both trails are paved and provide 18 miles of scenic walking or bicycling along the river.

Interpretive signs along the trail describe its origins as a southern spur of the Pittsburgh, Cincinnati, Chicago and St. Louis (PCC & StL) Railroad, which was commonly

County
Brooke

Endpoints
Wellsburg Yankee Trail at Charles St. and Second St. (Wellsburg); Wheeling Heritage Trails at Warwood Ave./WV 2 and Stone Shannon Road (Short Creek)

Mileage
6.7

Type
Rail-Trail

Roughness Index
1

Surface
Asphalt

Courtesy of Brooke Pioneer Trail Association

Rolling along the woodsy Ohio River, the trail is tucked away from WV 2.

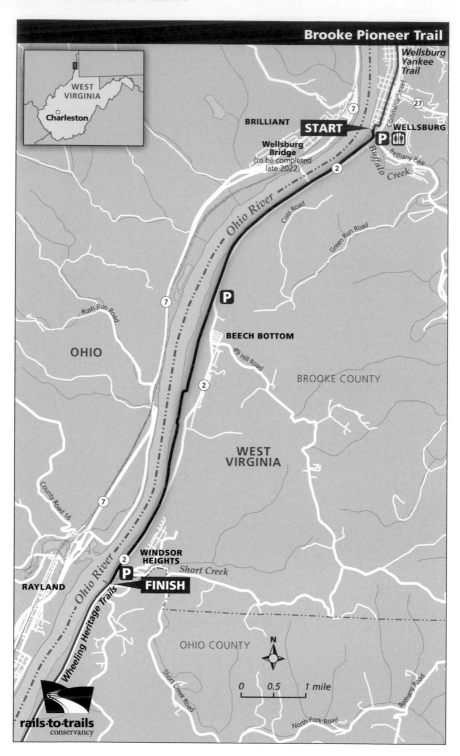

Brooke Pioneer Trail

WEST VIRGINIA

Charleston

Wellsburg Yankee Trail

BRILLIANT

START

WELLSBURG

Wellsburg Bridge (to be completed late 2022)

Ohio River

Coss Road

Green Run Road

Buffalo Creek

Bethany Pike

Rush Run Road

OHIO

BEECH BOTTOM

#9 Hill Road

BROOKE COUNTY

WEST VIRGINIA

County Road 16

WINDSOR HEIGHTS

Short Creek

RAYLAND

Ohio River

Wheeling Heritage Trails

FINISH

OHIO COUNTY

Short Creek Road

North Fork Road

Bethany Road

0   0.5   1 mile

N

rails·to·trails
conservancy

called the Panhandle Railroad. The corridor between Weirton and Benwood opened in 1878, carrying passengers until 1951 and freight until 1981. Crews pulled the track in 1987, and a decade passed before trail construction began.

The northern end of the trail begins at the southern limits of Wellsburg and the terminus of the 2.2-mile Wellsburg Yankee Trail that passes through downtown. Continuing south from Wellsburg, you'll cross Buffalo Creek on a restored railroad trestle paralleling WV 2.

In about a mile, you'll come to the Wellsburg Bridge, scheduled to open in fall 2022 (see closure notice below). The bridge's shared-use path provides a unique opportunity for walkers and bicyclists, as there is no other shared-use path on an Ohio River bridge between Pittsburgh and Cincinnati—a distance of 322 miles.

The trail is wedged between WV 2 and the Ohio River for its entire length. The mostly wooded corridor obscures the view of both the road and the river, though occasional openings reveal vistas of the powerful river and the hilly western shore. The woods are home to deer, groundhogs, and other critters.

History buffs will be interested to learn that human habitation along the river dates back thousands of years. Scientists excavating an earthen mound in the town of Beech Bottom, about 3.5 miles south of Wellsburg, found artifacts dating to 400 BC. The town was also home to a fort that guarded the frontier during the Revolutionary War.

Those looking for reminders of the area's industrial past won't be disappointed. The trail skirts the edge of a handful of manufacturing properties between Wellsburg and Windsor Heights. Among them is the former site of the Windsor Power Plant—a onetime electricity generator for the region—and its company town of 100 homes, all of which are gone today. On the opposite shore, the large cooling tower and smokestack of Ohio's Cardinal Power Plant interrupt the views of the rolling wooded landscape.

The trail ends at a pedestrian bridge over Short Creek and seamlessly continues south as the Wheeling Heritage Trails (see page 227).

Closure Notice: As of March 2021, portions of the northern end of the trail south of Wellsburg are closed due to the construction of a new bridge across the Ohio River that will include a shared-use path for walkers and bicyclists. The trail will be subject to continuous closures during the project, which is slated for completion in late 2022; check with the trail manager for up-to-date information. The southern end of the trail remains open.

CONTACT: facebook.com/groups/brookepioneertrail

continued on next page

PARKING

Parking areas are listed from north to south.

WELLSBURG: WV 2, about 300 feet north of Williams Lane (40.2627, -80.6159).

BEECH BOTTOM: WV 2 and Carolina Ave. (40.2356, -80.6519).

SHORT CREEK: Ironmen Park, west side of WV 2 at Short Creek Road/CR 2/2 (40.1861, -80.6744).

The paved pathway connects the communities of Wellsburg and Windsor Heights.

Courtesy of Brooke Pioneer Trail Association

The Glade Creek Trail in the New River Gorge National Park and Preserve offers visitors many opportunities to cool off on hot summer days in the swimming holes along the cascading stream.

The trail follows a former narrow-gauge railroad that served lumber camps and sawmills that have disappeared since the 1930s. Visitors walking through the luxurious second-growth forest might find it hard to believe, but logging companies had once scoured the landscape clean. The forest is protected today within the boundaries of the New River Gorge, which became a national park in 2021. Fifty-three miles of the New River Gorge were designated for protection as a national river in 1978.

Starting at the Glade Creek campground fronting the New River, you're at the former townsite of Hamlet. The logging camp was linked to the town of Glade across the river by a bridge that has since been torn down, leaving only the concrete pilings. Moss-covered foundations of the sawmill and other buildings remain in the forest.

The first 0.25 mile of trail is wheelchair-accessible, including a platform for catch-and-release fishing from a

County
Raleigh

Endpoints
Glade Creek Campground/Glade Creek Road, 5.6 miles east of WV 41/Stanaford Road (Beaver); Scott Branch Road/CR 22 about 0.3 mile southwest of US 64 (Crow)

Mileage
5.8

Type
Rail-Trail

Roughness Index
1–2

Surface
Dirt, Gravel

The forested trail begins at the Glade Creek campground.

TrailLink user yonkk

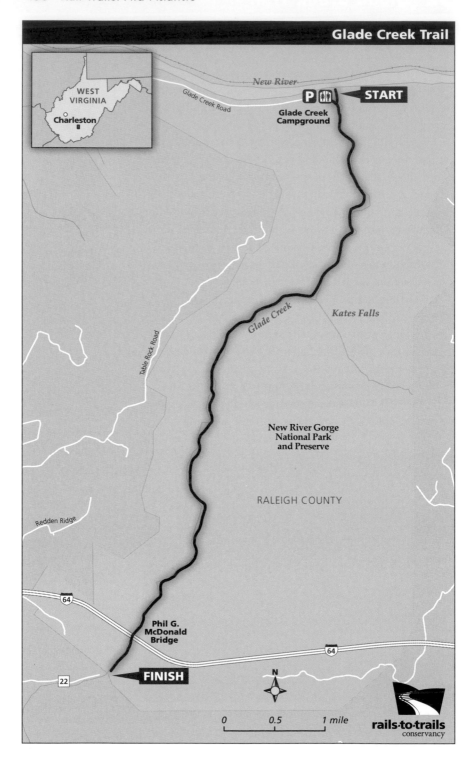

Glade Creek Trail

New River

WEST VIRGINIA

Charleston

Glade Creek Road

Glade Creek Campground

START

Glade Creek

Kates Falls

Table Rock Road

New River Gorge
National Park
and Preserve

RALEIGH COUNTY

Redden Ridge

64

Phil G.
McDonald
Bridge

64

22

FINISH

N

0   0.5   1 mile

rails·to·trails
conservancy

bridge spanning Glade Creek. The trailhead, trail segment, picnic area, camping area, and parking site were improved to meet ADA standards by Boy Scout volunteers in 2013.

Beyond that short stretch, you'll find that the lower half of the trail is narrow and sometimes strewn with rocks and tree branches. This is also where you'll find the best swimming holes, such as a picturesque one at the base of a waterfall about a mile from the trailhead.

The trail continues its moderate uphill grade to a bridge at the 3-mile mark, where it becomes wider and better maintained. In another 1.5 miles, a steep side trail heads uphill 0.2 mile to Kates Falls. A washout at the junction of the two trails makes this section impassable during high water.

In about a mile, the trail passes beneath the Phil G. McDonald Bridge on I-64. Soaring 700 feet overhead, the bridge is the highest in the interstate highway system and among the top 10 in the United States.

The trail ends just ahead at a trailhead on Forest Road 22. Park rangers strongly discourage parking here, as a four-wheel-drive, high-clearance vehicle is required for the steep, twisty, muddy road that serves the trailhead.

As always in the park, keep your eyes open for birds and animals you might encounter. Hawks fly across the area during fall migration, and other birds that spend most of their lives in the tropics come here to breed.

CONTACT: nps.gov/neri/planyourvisit/glade-creek-trails.htm and nps.gov/neri

PARKING

Indicates that at least one accessible parking space is available.

BEAVER*: Glade Creek Campground, Glade Creek Road, 5.6 miles east of WV 41/Stanaford Road (37.8286, -81.0125).

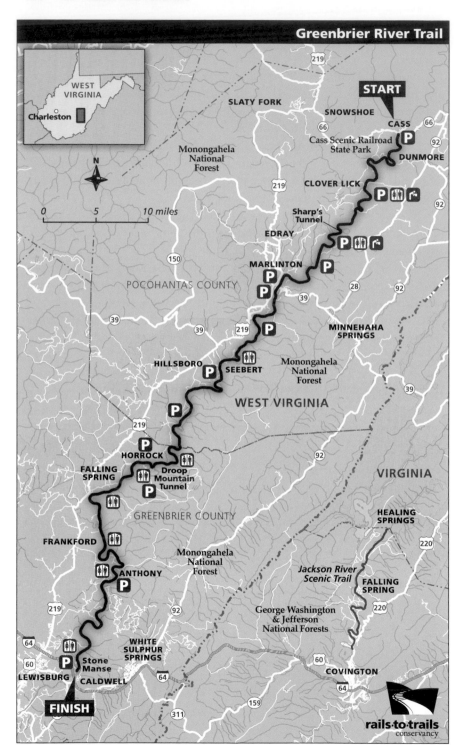

The Greenbrier River Trail is arguably West Virginia's premier rail-trail, running for 78 miles past remote small towns and through lush forests along the banks of the longest undammed river in the eastern United States. The trail's accolades include induction into the Rail-Trail Hall of Fame, as well as recognition as a National Recreation Trail and one of 52 Millennium Legacy Trails in the United States.

The longest rail-trail in the state, the crushed-stone route crosses 35 bridges and passes through two tunnels as it follows the meandering Greenbrier River downstream from the Cass Scenic Railroad State Park to Caldwell. Maintained by the state parks department and the non-profit Greenbrier River Trail Association, the trail uses the former corridor of the Chesapeake and Ohio Railway (C&O), which hauled coal and lumber out of the mountains from the early 1900s until the 1970s.

Counties
Greenbrier, Pocahontas

Endpoints
Deer Creek Road, 350 feet south of Back Mountain Road/WV 66 at Cass Scenic Railroad State Park (Cass); Stone House Road/CR 38 and Mountain View Farm Dr. (North Caldwell)

Mileage
78

Type
Rail-Trail

Roughness Index
2

Surface
Asphalt, Crushed Stone

Marlinton, the largest town on the trail, hosts a circa 1901 C&O railroad depot.

193

Thru-travelers will find few services along the route and are encouraged to carry their own food and water. Check the trail association's website (**green brierrivertrail.com**) for information on bike rentals and shuttles. Drinking water is available at the beginning and end of the trail, at trailside parks, and at mileposts 9.5, 28.5, 63.8, and 69.6. A dozen campsites are available along the river, and accommodations are also available off-route in the town of Marlinton and in Watoga State Park. The lack of cell service on parts of the trail—because of a quiet zone created for a nearby radio telescope—compounds the feeling of remoteness here in the midst of the Appalachian Mountains.

The mileposts start at the southern end of the trail in Caldwell, but you can take advantage of a gentle downhill slope by following the river downstream from the northern end at Cass Scenic Railroad State Park. Created as a company town for a giant lumber mill operation, Cass now serves as the base of operations for steam locomotives that run tourists to nearby mountain destinations.

Heading south for 9 miles, the first town you will pass is Clover Lick, which houses a restored railroad depot built in 1900 that once served the booming logging industry. The trail continues its serpentine route for 6 miles to the 500-foot-long Sharps Tunnel and a trestle that crosses the river.

Another 9 miles takes you to a nearly 4-mile stretch of paved trail through Marlinton, the largest town on the trail and the first settlement in the Greenbrier Valley, in 1749. The circa 1901 C&O railroad depot now houses the Pocahontas County Artists Co-op, where you can find trail information. Several cafés, grocery stores, bike shops, and overnight accommodations are available in town. Hungry trail users can also partake in the celebrated annual Roadkill Cookoff in the fall.

Autumn is a popular season for leaf-peepers to visit the trail as the hardwoods splash the mountainsides in yellows and reds. Trail users can stumble upon deer, groundhogs, bears, and snakes during much of the year.

Eight miles south of Marlinton, you'll cross the river on another old trestle, and in 2 more miles, you'll arrive in Seebert, which boasts a well-known ice-cream stop. Over the next 15 miles, most towns are little more than names on a map, but another remnant of the railroad era emerges at the 402-foot-long Droop Mountain tunnel just before Horrock.

The trail ends about 28 miles farther south at milepost 3 in North Caldwell. Three-tenths of a mile north on Stone House Road, you'll find a historic home called the Stone Manse, dating from 1796. The trailhead is located just outside Lewisburg, which has a variety of shops, restaurants, and lodging.

CONTACT: wvstateparks.com/park/greenbrier-river-trail

PARKING

Parking areas are listed from north to south. Select parking areas for the trail are listed below. For a detailed list of parking areas and other waypoints, go to **TrailLink.com™**. *Indicates that at least one accessible parking space is available.*

CASS*: Deer Creek Road, 500 feet south of Black Mountain Road/CR 66 (38.3921, -79.9224).

CLOVER LICK*: Clover Lick Depot, Edray Road/CR 1 and Laurel Run Road/CR 1/4 (38.3312, -79.9706).

MARLINTON: C&O Railroad Depot, Ninth St. between Third Ave. and Fourth Ave. (38.2217, -80.0943).

MARLINTON: Stillwell Park, Municipal Park Road, about 0.2 mile northwest of Stillwell Road/CR 39/2 and U.S. Forest Service Road 304 (38.2116, -80.0994).

SEEBERT: Seebert River Road/CR 27/3, 0.2 mile south of Seebert Lane Road/CR 27/6 (38.1267, -80.1753).

HORROCK: Rorer Road/CR 7/2, 0.3 mile east of Rorer Island Crossing (38.0250, -80.2764).

CALDWELL: Mountain View Farm Dr. and Stone House Road/CR 38 (37.7934, -80.3807).

The trail traces the wooded banks of the longest undammed river in the eastern United States.
TrailLink user lisa.jarnigan

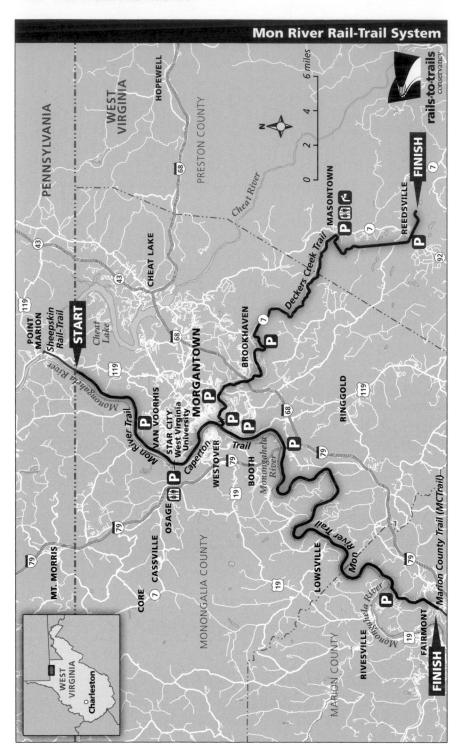

Three trails comprise the Mon River Rail-Trail System—the Mon River Trail, Caperton Trail, and Deckers Creek Trail, which radiate from Morgantown for 48 miles through former Allegheny Plateau coalfields in north-central West Virginia.

Inducted into the Rail-Trail Hall of Fame in 2020, the trails roll past bustling urban settings, remote rural areas, and rusting remnants of the industrial past. Officials credit the rail-trail with boosting tourism, giving locals a recreational outlet, helping to transform Morgantown's riverfront into an attractive destination, and building support for the restoration of polluted Deckers Creek.

Two of the trails—the Mon River Trail and Caperton Trail—trace the Monongahela River for 29 miles, from the West Virginia–Pennsylvania state line through Morgantown to Prickett's Fort State Park. The 19-mile Deckers Creek Trail runs along a creek of the same name between Morgantown and Reedsville.

Counties
Marion (WV),
Monongalia (WV),
Preston (WV)

Endpoints
Sheepskin Rail-Trail at the WV–PA state line; MCTrail at Pricketts Fort State Park (Fairmont); Caperton Trail at Hazel Ruby McQuain Riverfront Park, Garrett St. and Sturgiss St. (Morgantown); Morgan Mine Road, 0.3 mile south of Cedar Meadows Cir. (Reedsville)

Mileage
48.5

Type
Rail-Trail

Roughness Index
1

Surface
Asphalt, Crushed Stone

In Morgantown, the Caperton Trail bridge crosses the mouth of Deckers Creek.

Courtesy Rails-to-Trails Conservancy

The Mon River and Caperton Trails follow the route of the Fairmont, Morgantown and Pittsburgh Railroad, opened in 1894. Later acquired by the Baltimore and Ohio Railroad (B&O), the route—known as the Pittsburgh Division or Sheepskin Line—hauled coal to Pittsburgh. The Deckers Creek Trail got its start as the Morgantown and Kingwood Railroad in the early 20th century but later became part of the B&O. After both merged into CSX Transportation, they were shut down due to dwindling traffic in the 1990s.

Starting at the 1.7-mile Sheepskin Rail-Trail's southern terminus at the Pennsylvania border, the compacted-stone Mon River Trail runs south along the wooded riverbank of the Monongahela River for 6.3 miles to Star City, where it meets the Caperton Trail.

The only trail in the system that's entirely paved, the 5.7-mile Caperton Trail passes the Edith Barill Riverfront Park in Star City, West Virginia University's Core Arboretum in Morgantown, and the outdoor amphitheater at Hazel Ruby McQuain Riverfront Park, next to the restored B&O train depot.

The Decker Creek Trail forks left just after the riverfront park at 3.7 miles, following the Monongahela River tributary on a steady climb into the Allegheny foothills. The first 2.5 miles are paved; the rest is crushed gravel. In a few miles it enters a rocky gorge where the creek noisily rushes over rapids and waterfalls. At Masontown, a restored 1907 coal company building provides restrooms and drinking fountains. The grade flattens, and woods give way to pastures and farmland around Reedsville.

Back in Morgantown, the right fork of the trail network follows the Caperton Trail another 1.5 miles to the southern section of the Mon River Trail. The crushed-stone trail follows the serpentine route of the Monongehela River for 17.3 miles to Prickett's Fort State Park, a reconstructed frontier stronghold built in 1774.

The trail meets the Marion County Trail (MCTrail), which follows Prickett Creek another 2.4 miles to Fairmont.

The trail system is part of the Parkersburg to Pittsburgh Corridor, a 240-mile corridor being developed by the Industrial Heartland Trails Coalition (**railstotrails.org/ihtc**), a Rails-to-Trails Conservancy TrailNation™ project to create a 1,500-mile trail network through Pennsylvania, West Virginia, Ohio, and New York.

Other trails on this corridor route include the North Bend Rail Trail (see page 201), Harrison North Rail-Trail, West Fork River Trail (see page 221), and MCTrail in West Virginia and the Sheepskin Trail in Pennsylvania.

CONTACT: montrails.org

PARKING

Parking areas are listed from north to south. Select parking areas for the trail are listed below. For a detailed list of parking areas and other waypoints, go to **TrailLink.com**™. *Indicates that at least one accessible parking space is available.*

Mon River Trail

VAN VOORHIS: Van Voorhis Trailhead additional parking, dead end of Van Voorhis Road (39.6835, -79.9567).

VAN VOORHIS*: Van Voorhis Trailhead, Van Voorhis Road and Boston St. (39.6830, -79.9551).

FAIRMONT*: Prickett's Fort State Park, 88 State Park Road (39.5177, -80.0949).

Caperton Trail

STAR CITY: Edith Barill Riverfront Park, Leeway St. and Frontier St. (39.6596, -79.9913).

MORGANTOWN*: Hazel Ruby McQuain Riverfront Park, 124 Garrett St. (near University Ave.) (39.6289, -79.9600). Metered.

MORGANTOWN*: Mountaineer Heritage Park, Don Knotts Blvd./US 119, 0.3 mile south of Waterfront Pl. (39.6210, -79.9665).

Deckers Creek Trail

MORGANTOWN: Hazel Ruby McQuain Riverfront Park, Moore St., 1 block west of University Ave. (39.6298, -79.9592). Free 2-hour parking for trail use.

MORGANTOWN*: Hazel Ruby McQuain Riverfront Park, 124 Garrett St. (near University Ave.) (39.6289, -79.9600). Metered.

MORGANTOWN: Marilla Park, 799 E. Brockway Ave. (39.6280, -79.9389).

MELLONS CHAPEL: Mellon Chapel Trailhead, Breakiron Hill Road/CR 7/22, 260 feet east of Beulah Road (39.6013, -79.8941).

MASONTOWN: Masontown Trailhead, Sand Bank Road and Bridgeway St. (39.5544, -79.8026)

REEDSVILLE: Reedsville Trailhead, S. Robert Stone Way/CR 92, 1 block southeast of Fleetwood Dr. (39.5059, -79.8034).

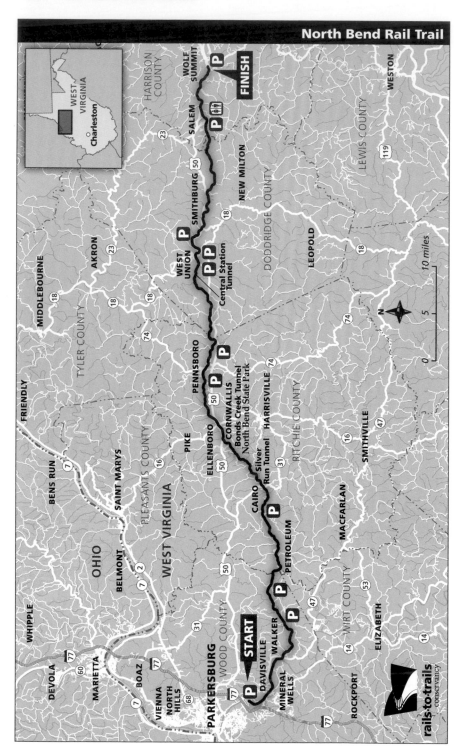

History beckons around every rocky bend and in every chilly tunnel on the North Bend Rail Trail, which follows an old railroad corridor through hill and hollow in northern West Virginia. The second-longest in the state—behind the Greenbrier River Trail (see page 193)—the 72-mile trail closed for more than a year for the installation of fiber-optic cable. It was scheduled for a full reopening in 2022, with an improved 10-foot-wide surface of crushed stone and a 0.8-mile section of wheelchair-accessible pavement through West Union. At press time, only the westernmost 20 miles of the trail had reopened. Visit West Virginia State Parks' official website (**wvstateparks.com/park/north-bend-rail-trail**) for current closures. And because wet weather–related issues such as washouts and landslides can affect the trail's surface at any time, cyclists are advised to use 1- to 1.5-inch or wider tires.

The rail-trail carries travelers down a corridor built for the Baltimore and Ohio Railroad (B&O) between 1853 and 1857. Known as the Parkersburg Branch, it carried Federal troops during the Civil War and served a string of

Counties
Doddridge, Harrison, Ritchie, Wood

Endpoints
Happy Valley Road/ CR 47/26 and Catalino Dr. (Cedar Grove); School St. and Wilsonburg Road/ Old US 50/CR 11 (Wolf Summit)

Mileage
72

Type
Rail-Trail

Roughness Index
2

Surface
Asphalt, Crushed Stone

From the west end of the trail in Parkersburg, the rail-trail rolls through rural countryside.

TrailLink user rob412

towns between Parkersburg and Clarksburg as it became the system's mainline to St. Louis. After more than 120 years, passenger operations ceased in 1971. The dwindling freight business was handled by CSX Transportation, which sold the corridor to the state in the 1980s. Work on the trail started in the 1990s.

Of the original 13 tunnels the builders bored through the rugged Allegheny Plateau to shorten the route, 10 are still passable today. Visitors in the summer will feel a blast of cool, moist air at the stone-block tunnel portals—quite a change from the smoke, cinders, and heat that filled the tunnels as 19th-century locomotives passed through. Some are long enough inside to require a flashlight.

At 2,207 feet long, the Central Station Tunnel, located at milepost 49.5 near West Union, is the longest on the trail and played a role in a 1915 train robbery that netted some $1 million in today's value. The Silver Run Tunnel (1,376 feet long), at milepost 22.8 between Cairo and Petroleum, is reputed to be haunted. Tunnel No. 13, the Bonds Creek Tunnel near Cornwallis, was the site of a deadly train crash in 1956 when a westbound train emerged onto the scene of a fresh avalanche and plummeted into the creek below.

Other man-made features of the trail include the 36 bridges and trestles that visitors cross. The longest bridge spans Middle Island Creek on the east side of West Union. Old, refurbished B&O depots are still standing in Pennsboro, Smithton, and Salem. These towns and others along the route offer dining and refreshment to travelers, as well as marble and hand-blown-glass factories, arts-and-crafts markets, fairs, festivals, and veterans memorials.

A major attraction along the trail is North Bend State Park, located slightly off-trail between Cairo and Ellenboro. Here you'll find more than a dozen miles of trails, camping, showers, and the only indoor lodging along the trail. Free camping is allowed anywhere on the rail-trail, and several campsites with fire rings and pit toilets are available along its length.

Be prepared for long stretches through rural areas (without services), where you'll see deer in forest clearings, beaver lodges in ponds, and perhaps a black bear or two. The edges of farmland also provide habitat for bird-watching.

While most of the trail traffic is locally generated, a growing number of travelers are including the trail on longer excursions. The North Bend Rail Trail is on the 6,800-mile, coast-to-coast American Discovery Trail (**discoverytrail.org**). It is also part of the Parkersburg to Pittsburgh Corridor, a 240-mile corridor being developed by the Industrial Heartland Trails Coalition (**railstotrails.org/ihtc**), a Rails-to-Trails Conservancy TrailNation™ project to create a 1,500-mile trail network through Pennsylvania, West Virginia, Ohio, and New York.

While the trail is managed by West Virginia State Parks, the North Bend Rails-to-Trails Foundation is responsible for raising public interest for the trail as well as organizing many ongoing activities. One of the most popular is the evening Luminary Walk, for which 1.5 miles of the rail-trail, from North Bend State Park to Tunnel 13, is lit with luminaries. Check the foundation's Facebook page (**facebook.com/northbendrailtrail**) for details and dates.

CONTACT: wvstateparks.com/park/north-bend-rail-trail

PARKING

Parking areas are listed from west to east. Select parking areas for the trail are listed below. For a detailed list of parking areas and other waypoints, go to **TrailLink.com™**. *Indicates that at least one accessible parking space is available.*

PARKERSBURG: Happy Valley Road/CR 47/26 and Catalino Drive (39.2234, -81.5125).

PENNSBORO: Pennsboro Depot, Broadway St./WV 74 between Collins Ave. and Kimball Ave. (39.2848, -80.9687).

WEST UNION: Railroad St. and W. Main St. (39.2955, -80.7763).

WEST UNION: West Union City Park, across bridge on WV 18, 0.3 mile west of US 50 (39.2905, -80.7712).

SMITHBURG: Smithbury St./CR 50/9 and Smithton Road/CR 50/30 (39.2889, -80.7344).

SALEM: Salem Depot, E. Main St./CR 50/28 and Railroad St. (39.2823, -80.5581). Note that Railroad St., which provides access to the trailhead, is unmarked.

SALEM: South St./WV 29 and Mechanic St. (39.2814, -80.5551).

WOLF SUMMIT: Wilsonburg Road/CR 11 and School St. (39.2803, -80.4626).

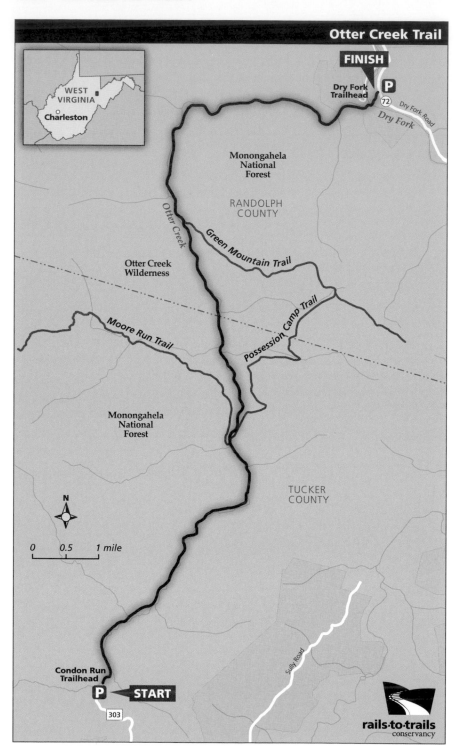

The Monongahela National Forest's Otter Wilderness covers 20,000 acres in a bowl formed by Shavers and McGowan Mountains east of Elkins and south of Parsons. Because it is wilderness, bicycles are prohibited.

There are 45 miles of trails in the Otter Creek Wilderness, and the Otter Creek Trail connects with seven of them. These trails have intentionally been kept very primitive, so there are no signs or blazes, although potentially confusing sections are marked with stone cairns. Trail maintenance is kept to a minimum, so fallen trees remain where they land and water drains onto the trails, which can be muddy and overgrown. All stream crossings are by foot, except for the suspension bridge over Dry Fork at the northern trailhead. The trail is not recommended for wheelchair use.

Brooke Andrew/courtesy of the U.S. Forest Service

The trail follows Otter Creek downstream through national forest.

Counties
Randolph, Tucker

Endpoints
Condon Run Trailhead
on Forest Road 303,
0.6 mile north of Stuart
Memorial Dr./Forest
Road 91 (Condon);
Dry Fork Trailhead on
Dry Fork Road/WV 72,
4.5 miles south of
US 48 (Parsons)

Mileage
11.8

Type
Rail-Trail

Roughness Index
3

Surface
Dirt

The whole area was clear-cut from 1897 to 1914 by the Otter Creek Boom and Lumber Co. The Otter Creek Trail follows a railroad corridor used to haul that timber to sawmills. The rails were later removed, but you'll likely see sections of railroad ties buried in the dirt. The forest has been healing since 1975, when Congress designated the area a US wilderness.

The trail roughly follows the course of Otter Creek downstream in a northward then eastward direction from Condor Run Trailhead in the south to Dry Fork Trailhead in the north. It descends about 1,600 feet along the 11.8-mile path. The trail is popular for day hikes from either trailhead or for backpacking to campsites off the trail.

Black bear, white-tailed deer, wild turkey, grouse, rabbit, and several types of squirrels inhabit these woods. Spruce are common at higher elevations, trending to black cherry and birch downhill. Apple trees are common around old logging camps.

Horseback riders are warned not to use the segment of the Otter Creek Trail between the Moore Run Trail and Green Mountain Trail; the trail is narrow through here with a steep drop. Equestrians should instead take the Possession Camp Trail to bridge the gap.

CONTACT: fs.usda.gov/recarea/mnf/recarea/?recid=12369

PARKING

Parking areas are listed from south to north.

BOWDEN: Condon Run Trailhead at end of FR 303, 0.6 mile north of Stuart Memorial Dr./ Forest Road 91 (38.9412, -79.6687).

PARSONS: Dry Fork Trailhead on Dry Fork Road/WV 72, 4.5 miles south of US 48 (39.0456, -79.6068).

The Panhandle Trail offers the most direct and scenic route for self-propelled travel between the Northern Panhandle of West Virginia and the suburbs of Pittsburgh, Pennsylvania. Although the trail follows an old railroad grade through the hilly terrain, there was only so much the railroad builders could do to flatten the route across the Allegheny Plateau. Expect a steady climb to Bulger, the high point on the rural journey.

This route was made famous by the merger of several railroads in the 1860s to create the Pittsburgh, Cincinnati, Chicago and St. Louis Railroad (PCC & StL), also referred to simply as the Panhandle Railroad. It was named for the sliver of northern West Virginia it crossed. The Pennsylvania Railroad leased the route in the 1920s, and the line later became part of the Penn Central and Conrail systems until it fell into disuse in 1991.

The Panhandle Trail crosses under a railroad trestle for the Montour Trail near McDonald.

Counties
Brooke (WV), Hancock (WV), Allegheny (PA), Washington (PA)

Endpoints
1.1 mile west of McColl Road and Three Arches Road (Colliers, WV); Walkers Mill Road/ PA 3028 and Scott Alley (Walkers Mill, PA)

Mileage
29.2

Type
Rail-Trail

Roughness Index
1–2

Surface
Asphalt, Crushed Stone

207

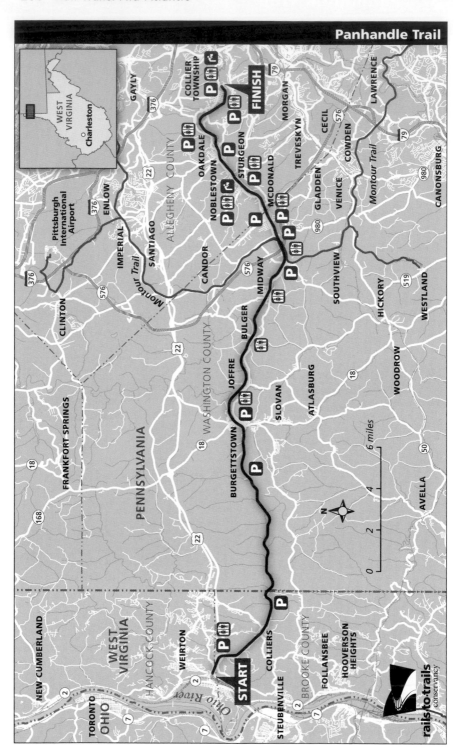

The 29-mile trail is maintained by several communities and organizations along its route. It is part of the 3,700-mile Great American Rail-Trail®, a cross-country route that will connect Washington, D.C., and Washington State, and is a segment of the 1,500-mile trail network through Pennsylvania, West Virginia, Ohio, and New York being developed by the Industrial Heartland Trails Coalition. Both are Rails-to-Trails Conservancy TrailNation™ projects.

The Panhandle Trail starts in Weirton, which borders both Ohio and Pennsylvania in West Virginia's narrow Northern Panhandle. It makes a steady 16-mile climb through hardwood forests to Bulger, where it begins its descent to Collier Township in the western suburbs of Pittsburgh. The 17-mile center segment through Washington County is paved. The Panhandle Trail crosses the 61.5-mile Montour Trail, which links to the 150-mile Great Allegheny Passage (**gaptrail.org**; see page 51) and the 184.5-mile C&O Canal Towpath (page 45) for an off-road connection to Washington, D.C. Horseback riding is allowed in the corridor in Pennsylvania but not on the trail itself.

Beginning at the trailhead on McColl Road in the onetime steel mill town of Weirton, the crushed rock trail heads west to a dead end in about a mile. Heading east, you'll follow Harmon Creek, with its wildflowers and flowering shrubs, through the small community of Colliers, to the Pennsylvania state line in 4 miles. The trail continues on a grade for 7 miles to Burgettstown, the first burg with services for hungry or thirsty travelers.

After a short descent, you'll continue at a steady grade for 4.5 miles to the high point in Bulger. In 2 miles the trail arrives in Midway, so named because it is the railroad's halfway point between Pittsburgh and Steubenville, Ohio.

In 2 miles, travelers can hook up to the north–south Montour Trail via a mile-long connector trail. In 0.5 mile, the Panhandle Trail passes beneath the Montour Trail's 1913 railroad trestle, which also crosses Robinson Run.

More services are available in a mile in McDonald, home of the McDonald Trail Station, a history center at the South McDonald Street (Railroad Street) trailhead. It's open weekends April–October. The substantial brick buildings in McDonald are evidence of the oil boom that struck in the late 1800s; coal is still mined, and coal piles can be seen.

Over the next 3.5 miles, the trail passes through Sturgeon, Noblestown, and Oakdale. All have food, refreshments, and trailhead picnic tables (some covered).

You'll cross Robinson Run six times over the next 3.7 miles before the trail's end at Walkers Mill Road in Collier Township. A pedestrian bridge 0.6 mile before the end crosses Robinson Run to Fossil Cliff, where rock hounds can search for fossilized fern leaves.

CONTACT: panhandletrail.org or wvrailtrails.org/rail-trail/panhandle-rail-trail

continued on next page

PARKING

Parking areas are listed from west to east. Select parking areas for the trail are listed below. For a detailed list of parking areas and other waypoints, go to **TrailLink.com**™. *Indicates that at least one accessible parking space is available.*

WEIRTON, WV: McColl Road, 0.2 mile north of Harmon Creek Road (40.3938, -80.5691).

BURGETTSTOWN, PA: 1802 N. Main St., Whitaker Ave. and N. Main St. (40.3866, -80.3908).

MCDONALD, PA: Noblestown Road and Johns Ave. (40.3588, -80.2612).

MCDONALD, PA*: Trail Station, 151 S. McDonald St., between Johns Ave. and E. Ohara St. (40.3670, -80.2347).

STURGEON, PA*: Station St. between Main St. and McVey St. Ext. (40.3790, -80.2134).

NOBLESTOWN, PA*: 1788 Mill St., 365 feet south of Noblestown Road (40.3899, -80.1983).

OAKDALE, PA: Union Ave./PA 978 and Seminary Ave. (40.3969, -80.1847).

OAKDALE, PA*: 1115 Gregg Station Road, 0.2 mile east of Noblestown Road (40.4063, -80.1651).

CARNEGIE, PA*: 49 Walkers Mill Road/PA 3028, 0.1 mile south of Noblestown Road (40.3961, -80.1314).

Nestled in a remote mountain valley deep in the Appalachians, the Potts Valley Rail Trail skirts a wilderness area and farmland as it rolls through forests for 4.5 miles in the southern part of the state just east of the Continental Divide.

The trail is partly built upon the former corridor of the Norfolk and Western Railway. Called the Potts Valley Branch, the line opened in 1909 to haul iron ore from local mines and virgin timber cut from the mountainsides. By 1932, those industries had fallen into decline, and rail operations ended, allowing the valley to return to its agricultural pursuits. The trail opened in 2010.

About 3.5 miles of the trail run just outside the border of the Mountain Lake Wilderness in the George Washington & Jefferson National Forests. Most of the remainder uses a right-of-way through private property. Along the

Spencer Riddle

Nestled in a valley of the Appalachians, the trail skirts a wilderness area and farmland.

County
Monroe

Endpoints
Waiteville Road/CR 17, 0.2 mile east of WV–VA state line (Waiteville); Rays Siding Road/ CR 15/5, 0.7 mile east of Waiteville Road/CR 17 (Waiteville)

Mileage
4.5

Type
Rail-Trail

Roughness Index
2–3

Surface
Dirt, Grass

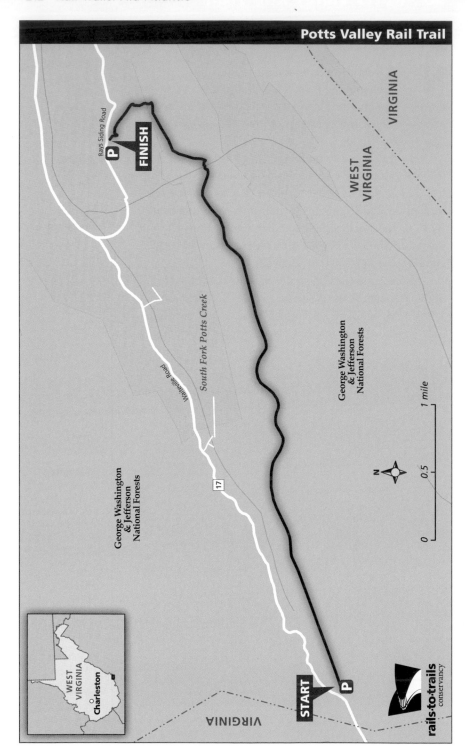

trail, you will find interpretive signs about Potts Valley's history, as well as benches where you can rest and enjoy the forest's solitude and views from overlooks.

The southwest trailhead on Waiteville Road/CR 17 lies a few hundred yards from the Eastern Continental Divide and 0.2 mile from the Virginia state line. Mountain ridges on each side of the valley trail reach elevations of 3,700–4,100 feet, and the trail runs slightly uphill from the South Fork of Potts Creek, a brook trout stream. The trail traverses a forest of mixed pine and hardwood, with rhododendron in the understory.

The trail on the railroad grade slopes gently downhill from the Waiteville Road trailhead. Short side trails lead to culverts carved by stone masons to drain the streams that frequently cross the path of the railbed.

At about 3.5 miles, you'll arrive at the site of the former trestle across Crosier Creek that once soared 98 feet over the creek on a 600-foot-long bridge. This marks the end of the railroad grade. Taking the switchbacks down to the creek, you'll have to cross on stepping-stones near the century-old bridge supports. Expect to get your shoes wet if the creek is high.

You'll follow singletrack through the woods for about another mile to the northwest trailhead on Rays Siding Road, which was formerly the railroad's route downhill on an S curve. A short section crosses private land; be sure to stay on the trail. A bench just before the trailhead overlooks a pastoral view, complete with a red barn in the distance.

From here, mountain bikers often loop back to the southwest trailhead via a 4.2-mile on-road route by taking Rays Siding Road/CR 15/5 to a left onto Waiteville Road/CR 17. A right turn onto Waiteville Road would lead you to the former depot (now a private business), located at the intersection with Bert Williams Road/CR 15/3, in 1.4 miles.

CONTACT: fs.usda.gov/main/gwj/maps-pubs

PARKING

Parking areas are listed from west to east.

WAITEVILLE: Waiteville Road/CR 17, 1.5 miles east of N. Fork Mountain Road /VA 613 (37.4472, -80.4939).

WAITEVILLE: Rays Siding Road/CR 15/5, 0.7 mile east of Waiteville Road/CR 17 (37.4673, -80.4344).

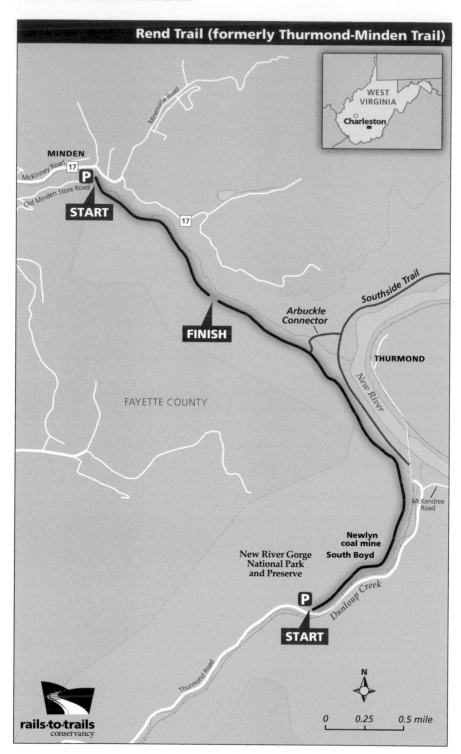

Rend Trail (formerly Thurmond-Minden Trail)

WEST VIRGINIA

Charleston

MINERSVILLE ROAD

MINDEN

McKinney Road

Old Minden Store Road

17

P

START

17

Southside Trail

Arbuckle Connector

FINISH

THURMOND

New River

FAYETTE COUNTY

McKendree Road

Newlyn coal mine

New River Gorge National Park and Preserve

South Boyd

Dunloup Creek

P

START

Thurmond Road

N

rails·to·trails
conservancy

0   0.25   0.5 mile

Five old railroad trestles serve as scenic attractions on this dirt trail in the New River Gorge National Park, although one of those trestles has been closed for safety concerns, splitting the trail into two shorter segments of 1.97 miles and 1.2 miles.

The Rend Trail traces the Chesapeake and Ohio Railway's Arbuckle Branch, which, beginning in 1906, served the coal mines that dotted the now-forested landscape in southern West Virginia. Although the railroad pulled out years ago, you can still see evidence of tracks in the forest, as well as remains of coal mines and coke ovens along the route.

The longest stretch of open trail starts at the Thurmond Trailhead on Thurmond Road/County Route 25 near Dunloup Creek. You can find remains of the Newlyn coal mine in the vicinity as well as overgrown foundations of South Boyd.

County
Fayette

Endpoints
CR 25/Thurmond Road, 1.1 mile southwest of McKendree Road/CR 25 (Thurmond); Minden Ave. and Thurmond Road (Minden)

Mileage
3.2

Type
Rail-Trail

Roughness Index
2–3

Surface
Dirt, Gravel

The trail winds through a forested landscape.

Jay Bridges

In about a mile, find an overlook with views across the New River to the old railroad boomtown of Thurmond. Created along with the railroad in the 1870s, the town flourished in the early 1900s with two hotels, two banks, a movie theater, and other businesses, as well as a depot and other structures to serve steam trains. Its decline started with the Great Depression in the 1930s, when the population numbered nearly 500 residents.

Today, the National Park Service owns most of the town, which recorded just seven residents in the latest census. The park restored the depot, which is open as a visitor center during the summer, and has stabilized other buildings. It is still served by Amtrak and is reachable via County Route 25/Thurmond Road.

Continuing on the Rend Trail, you'll pass the third trestle about 1.8 miles from the trailhead. Close by, the 0.3-mile Arbuckle Connector heads to the right down a short, steep, rocky slope to the Southside Trail (see page 217).

This southern segment of the Rend Trail comes to a dead end at a trestle. In 2014, structural engineers determined that the supports were rotting and that the bridge could fall at any time. The park has no timetable to repair the trestle as of 2022.

To visit the northern segment of the trail, use the trailhead at Minden, itself an old coal mining town where several old coal camp houses are still inhabited. The trail crosses one trestle and then ends before the second one in about 1.2 miles.

CONTACT: nps.gov/neri/planyourvisit/bicycling.htm or nps.gov/neri

---

PARKING

Parking areas are listed from south to north. *Indicates that at least one accessible parking space is available. Please note that the trail itself is not recommended for wheelchair use.*

THURMOND (Southern Segment)*: Thurmond Trailhead, Thurmond Road/CR 25, 1.1 mile west of McKendree Road/CR 25 (37.9434, -81.0884).

MINDEN (Northern Segment): Minden Ave. and Thurmond Road (37.9759, -81.1089).

As it weaves past long-abandoned mining towns, the Southside Trail (formerly the Brooklyn to Southside Junction Trail) in the New River Gorge National Park and Preserve tells the story of "King Coal" through the crumbling ruins at coal mine sites, relics of the railroad era, and a cemetery for mine disaster victims.

The trail runs nearly 7 miles within sight and earshot of the New River, a popular whitewater rafting destination preserved as a national river in 1978 and protected as the centerpiece of a 53-mile-long national park since 2021. The trail follows a segment of the Chesapeake and Ohio Railway, which began serving the area in the late 1800s.

A forest of oak trees, rhododendrons, and evergreens envelops travelers alongside the river. Among the most popular of the area's many trails, the Southside Trail is

TrailLink user gus76

A forest of oak trees, rhododendrons, and evergreens envelops travelers alongside the river.

County
Fayette

Endpoints
Cunard River Access Road, 1.7 miles east of Brooklyn Loop/CR 9/14 (Brooklyn); railroad tracks 0.8 mile southwest of Arbuckle Connector trail (Thurmond)

Mileage
6.9

Type
Rail-Trail

Roughness Index
2

Surface
Ballast, Dirt, Gravel

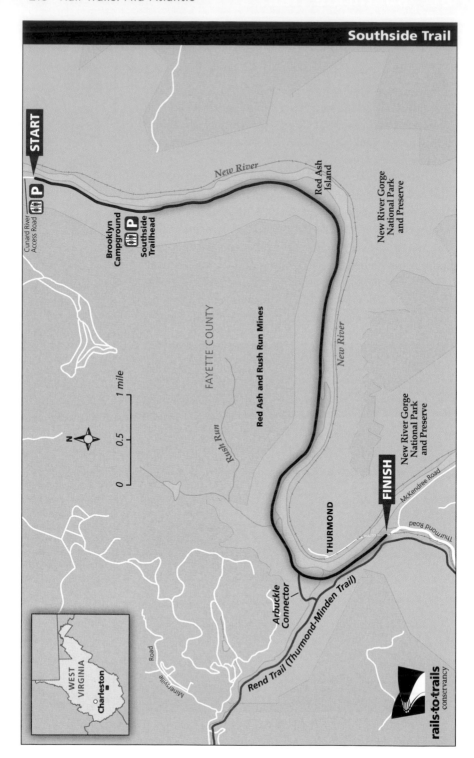

START

Cunard River
Access Road

Brooklyn
Campground

Southside
Trailhead

New River

Red Ash
Island

New River Gorge
National Park
and Preserve

FAYETTE COUNTY

Rush Run

Red Ash and Rush Run Mines

New River

New River Gorge
National Park
and Preserve

FINISH

McKendree Road

Thurmond Road

THURMOND

Arbuckle
Connector

Rend Trail (Thurmond-Minden Trail)

Minersville Road

N

0   0.5   1 mile

WEST
VIRGINIA

Charleston

rails·to·trails
conservancy

particularly attractive to mountain bikers, who enjoy the rough riding provided by exposed railroad ties along its route.

From the Cunard River Access in Brooklyn, the trail shares a road heading south for 1 mile to a parking area at the Brooklyn Campground and Southside Trailhead. Listen for the exuberant screams of whitewater rafters on what's considered one of the finest whitewater rivers in the eastern United States.

About 1.2 miles past the campground, you'll pass a small stream on the left that marks an off-trail low-water crossing to Red Ash Island. Up on a high point on the island you'll find an overgrown cemetery for miners killed in disasters at the nearby Red Ash and Rush Run mines in 1900 and 1905. Most of the burials are simply marked by blank headstones.

Continuing up the trail about 2.8 miles past the campground, you'll pass remains of the Red Ash mine and then the Rush Run mine. Stone and cement foundations are scattered through the woods, as are the remains of coke ovens where coal was purified for industrial and home use.

A trail junction for the Arbuckle Connector appears 5.1 miles past the campground. In 0.3 mile it connects to the Rend Trail (see page 215), which features several trestles and views of the New River and the old railroad boomtown of Thurmond on its southern segment.

The Southside Trail continues another 0.8 mile to a dead end at an active railroad line that runs along Thurmond Road, across the river from the historic Thurmond railroad yard. A legal (and safe) crossing here is currently not available. According to the National Park Service, negotiations are underway, but in the interim, please respect this private property and keep clear of the tracks.

CONTACT: nps.gov/neri/planyourvisit/thurmond-and-cunard-area-trails.htm or nps.gov/neri

PARKING

Parking areas are listed from north to south.

FAYETTEVILLE: Cunard River Access, Cunard River Access Road, 1.7 miles east of Brooklyn Loop/CR 9/14 (37.9985, -81.0229).

FAYETTEVILLE: Brooklyn Campground, 1 mile south of Cunard River Access (37.9841, -81.0281).

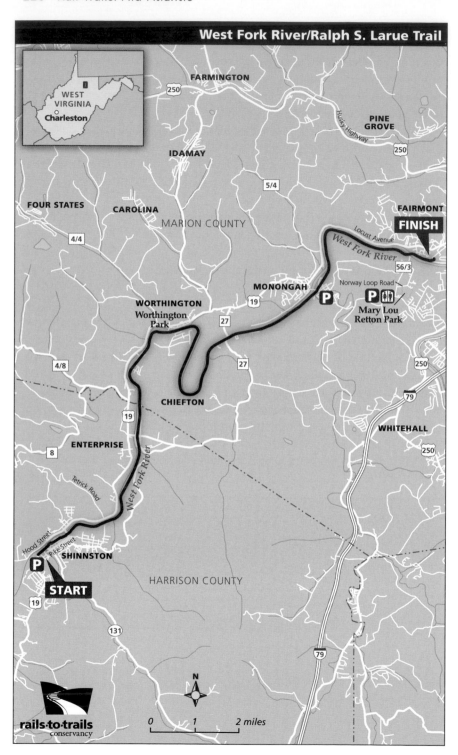

West Fork River/Ralph S. Larue Trail

Many of the Mountain State's rail-trails are known for their long grades up mountain valleys, but the West Fork River/Ralph S. Larue Trail is not one of them. The 14-mile trail follows the slow-flowing West Fork River in northern West Virginia and gains only a few feet between Shinnston and Fairmont.

The Baltimore and Ohio Railroad (B&O) acquired the corridor along the West Fork River in 1860 but waited until the 1890s to lay track. By then, coal companies had opened mines throughout the river valley, and populations soared in the small river towns. The railroad served those miners and hauled the coal to markets. The Marion County Parks and Recreation Commission gained the property in 1995 and opened the trail in 1997, due in

The trail follows the serpentine river through a sylvan setting.

Photo by TrailLink user vdeal

Counties
Harrison, Marion

Endpoints
S. Pike St./US 19 near
Lynn St. (Shinnston);
east end of pedestrian
bridge, 0.2 mile east of
Norway Road (Fairmont)

Mileage
14

Type
Rail-Trail

Roughness Index
1

Surface
Asphalt, Crushed Stone

large part to efforts by commission director Ralph S. Larue, for whom the trail is named. The trail is also a segment of the 1,500-mile trail network through Pennsylvania, West Virginia, Ohio, and New York that is being developed by the Industrial Heartland Trails Coalition (**railstotrails.org/ihtc**), a Rails-to-Trails Conservancy TrailNation™ project.

Visitors to the trail will find that the western 3.5-mile section in Harrison County is hard-packed crushed limestone, while the remainder in Marion County is paved. Horseback riding is allowed only in Marion County, and dogs must be leashed the entire length. The trail follows the serpentine river, which might be partly obscured by vegetation in the summer. Deer and smaller mammals are often seen along the path, and it's not uncommon for a raucous gaggle of geese to wander up from the river.

Starting in Shinnston, the trail is sandwiched between US 19 and the river and crosses a few residential streets before reaching the woods flanking the river in less than a mile. About 0.7 mile south of the trailhead on Pike Street, town founder Levi Shinn's log cabin, dating to the 1770s, still stands (not part of this route). Always a center of commerce, the town's economy grew with the coal boom. In 1944, it was devastated by the loss of 66 residents in a tornado.

Along the trail, you will see many historical markers, such as the Enterprise Coal Mine and coke ovens in about 3 miles, and will pass through Worthington Park, a favorite local fishing spot. As the river swings south just beyond the park, you'll see a dam used by a mill across the river, as well as abutments for a railroad bridge that served a mine.

The trail heads south for 1.4 miles through Chiefton, at one time a bustling coal mine company town, before swinging north and east to Monongah, where, in 1907, an explosion killed 361 miners in the worst mining disaster in the nation's history. A commemorative statue of a miner's widow holding her child stands on Main Avenue at Bridge Street, two blocks from the trailhead.

The trail continues another 2.8 miles to its terminus just past the refurbished B&O bridge spanning the river into Fairmont, the county seat. Because the continuation of the trail past the bridge is not on public land, trail users starting from the east should park in Monongah or about 0.6 mile south of the eastern terminus at Mary Lou Retton Park, named for the locally born and raised Olympic gold-medalist. Note that the route to the trail is on a narrow road with a climb. To reach the trail from the parking lot at the park, head west on Norway Loop Road for 0.2 mile; then turn right on CR 56/3 and go 0.6 mile. After the road curves left, look for the spur entrance to the trail on the right in about 180 feet.

For further exploration, the MCTrail (Marion County Trail) begins on the northeast side of Fairmont and runs for 2.5 miles (including a 1,200-foot-long tunnel) to the southern section of the Mon River Trail, which is part of the Mon River Rail-Trail System (see page 197) and heads 18 miles north to Morgantown.

CONTACT: mcparc.com/rail-trails.html

PARKING

Parking areas are listed from west to east.

SHINNSTON: Sue Ann Miller Trailhead, S. Pike St./US 19 and Lynn St. (39.3938, -80.3065).

WORTHINGTON: Sunrise St. and Pike St. (39.4418, -80.2750).

WORTHINGTON: Worthington Park, Meadowridge Road/CR 90, about 0.1 mile south of Freedom Hwy./US 19 (39.4501, -80.2650).

EVERSON: Everson St./CR 27 and Everson Road (39.4485, -80.2450).

MONONGAH: Bridge St. and Riverview Ave. (39.4610, -80.2146).

FAIRMONT: Mary Lou Retton Park, Norway Loop Road at Olympic Lane, 0.8 mile south of trail via Norway Loop Road and CR 56/3 (39.4621, -80.1852).

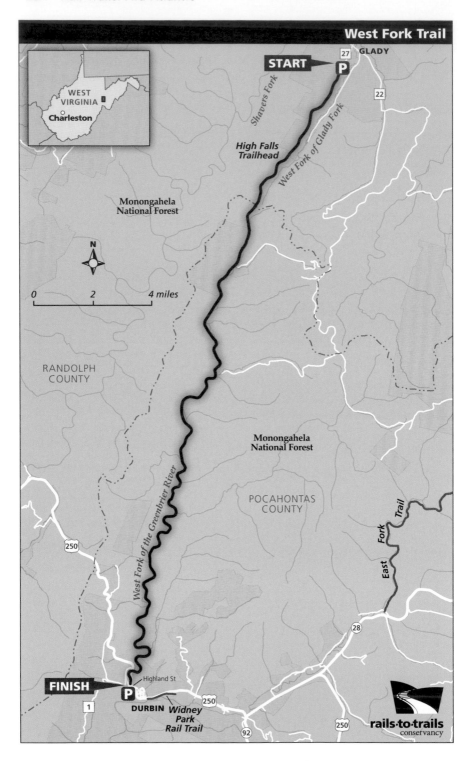

The West Fork Trail snakes its way through remote mountain valleys for 22 miles in the Monongahela National Forest. The soothing gurgle of the river complements the trail's serene environment of thick forests, trailside displays of wildflowers in the spring and summer, and dazzling colors in the fall.

The trail can be a little rocky with ballast left over from the railroad days—despite the fact that U.S. Forest Service crews perform maintenance on the trail a couple of times every summer—and a mountain bike or bike with wide tires is recommended for bicyclists. Trail users should be sure to carry food and water, as there are no towns or facilities between Glady and Durbin. The trail is not recommended for wheelchair use.

The route was constructed by the Coal and Iron Railway to haul away the region's coal and timber. Opened in 1903, it connected with the Chesapeake & Ohio Railway

Hugging the riverbank, the trail winds through the Monongahela National Forest.

Counties
Pocahontas, Randolph

Endpoints
0.5 mile south of Bemis Road/CR 22 on Glady Road/CR 27 (Glady), Highland St. and US 250 (Durbin)

Mileage
22

Type
Rail-Trail

Roughness Index
2

Surface
Ballast, Crushed Stone, Grass

Courtesy of Elkins-Randolph County Tourism

225

in Durbin at the southern end of today's trail. In 1905, the Western Maryland Railway took control of the route, and in the 1980s it was taken over by the U.S. Forest Service.

Starting in the small town of Glady, you'll travel south along a slope overlooking the West Fork of Glady Fork, a tributary of the Cheat River. Clearings in groves of conifers (the town is named for these glades) reveal views of the nearby mountains.

In about 3.5 miles, you'll meet the High Falls Trail, which takes a 6-mile round-trip (not part of this route) to a swimming hole and horseshoe-shaped waterfall on Shavers Fork. Near the falls, you can walk along the tracks of a tourist train that stops here.

In a couple more miles, the West Fork Trail picks up the West Fork of the Greenbrier River, which you'll follow on a slightly downhill, serpentine route to Durbin. The trail traces the meandering river, which makes sweeping turns through a tight valley amid steep hillsides. The West Fork is well known for its brook trout, and you're bound to see anglers along the way.

The trail ends in Durbin, the century-old railroad stop that today is home to the Durbin & Greenbrier Valley Railroad, which hauls tourists in vintage rolling stock behind steam-belching locomotives to several mountain destinations. You'll also find a café and grocery store in town, as well as the 1-mile Widney Park Rail Trail, which connects a campground near the train station with a park.

About 15 miles south of Durbin is Cass, another tourist railroad town and the northern point of the state's longest rail-trail, the 78-mile Greenbrier River Trail (see page 193).

CONTACT: rtc.li/west-fork-trail

PARKING

Parking areas are listed from north to south.

GLADY: West Fork Trail, 0.3 mile south of Glady Road/CR 27 (38.7888, -79.7249).

DURBIN: Highland St./CR 250/17 and US 250/WV 92 (38.5502, -79.8311).

The Wheeling Heritage Trails are known locally as two trails—the Ohio River Trail and the Wheeling Creek Trail—that run along the old railbeds of two railroads that served the transportation network for this onetime manufacturing center. Together, these paved, flat trails offer a total of 16.5 miles of off-road pleasure. Dozens of interpretive signs along the way treat visitors to self-guided tours featuring area attractions such as historical factory sites on Wheeling's waterfront.

The Ohio River Trail section is the longest, running for 11.3 miles along the eastern shore of the Ohio River, from 48th and Water Streets in South Wheeling to the

County
Ohio

Endpoints
48th St. and Water St. (Wheeling); Brooke Pioneer Trail at Warwood Ave./WV 2 and Stone Shannon Road (Short Creek); Water St. and 14th St. (Wheeling); Community St. and Angle Ave. (Elm Grove)

Mileage
16.5

Type
Rail-Trail

Roughness Index
1

Surface
Asphalt

Interpretive signs treat visitors to self-guided tours of attractions on Wheeling's waterfront.

TrailLink user wvmtsl

227

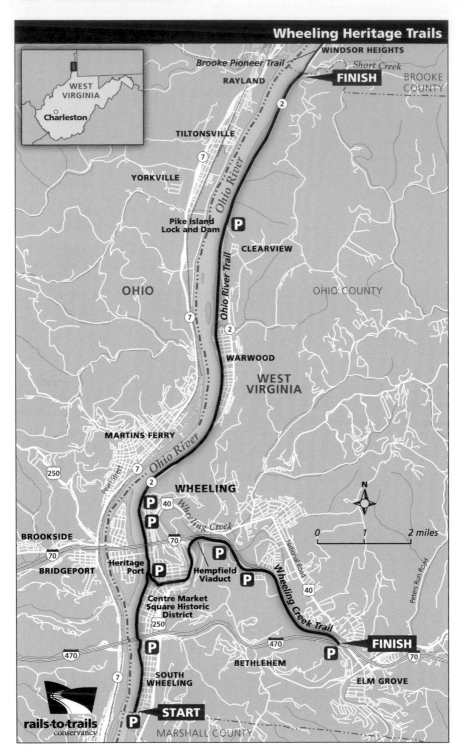

Wheeling Heritage Trails

WINDSOR HEIGHTS

Brooke Pioneer Trail

RAYLAND

Short Creek

FINISH

BROOKE COUNTY

WEST VIRGINIA

Charleston

TILTONSVILLE

YORKVILLE

Pike Island Lock and Dam

CLEARVIEW

Ohio River

Ohio River Trail

OHIO

OHIO COUNTY

WARWOOD

WEST VIRGINIA

MARTINS FERRY

Ohio River

250

Pearl Street

WHEELING

Wheeling Creek

40

BROOKSIDE

70

70

BRIDGEPORT

Heritage Port

Hempfield Viaduct

National Road

Wheeling Creek Trail

40

Centre Market Square Historic District

250

470

FINISH

470

70

BETHLEHEM

ELM GROVE

Peters Run Road

SOUTH WHEELING

START

MARSHALL COUNTY

N

0   1   2 miles

rails·to·trails
conservancy

Short Creek bridge in the north. Here, it connects seamlessly to the 6.7-mile Brooke Pioneer Trail (see page 185), which continues north to Wellsburg.

This rail corridor dates to the 1870s, when the Pittsburgh, Cincinnati, Chicago and St. Louis (PCC & StL) Railroad, known as the Panhandle Railroad, opened a southern spur from Weirton to Benwood, just south of Wheeling.

Beginning at the southern end, the Ohio River Trail rolls through Wheeling's historic industrial waterfront. One of the first sites you'll pass is the former home of the Mail Pouch tobacco company, whose advertising can still be seen fading on thousands of barns throughout the Mid-Atlantic states and the Midwest. Then there's the sprawling Centre Market Square Historic District, followed by Heritage Port, a 3-acre riverfront park that's used for concerts and public celebrations.

The trail passes under the striking Wheeling Suspension Bridge, a National Historic Landmark, and then I-70 as it leaves town and wends north past the Pike Island Lock and Dam in Clearview. You'll likely see barges heading up and down the river and can watch them progress through the locks. From Clearview, the Ohio River Trail continues along Warwood Avenue/WV 2 to its terminus at Short Creek, where Warwood Avenue intersects Stone Shannon Road.

The other Wheeling Heritage Trail, the Wheeling Creek Trail, intersects the Ohio River Trail at the south end of Heritage Port. Following city streets for 0.7 mile, it picks up the corridor of a former Baltimore and Ohio Railroad line, called The Pike, that ran from Wheeling to Washington, Pennsylvania, where it connected to a Pittsburgh-bound line.

Considered less urban than its counterpart, the 5-mile Wheeling Creek Trail climbs gently to the scenic Hempfield Viaduct, which was built in 1857 and carries the trail across Wheeling Creek on a high stone-arch bridge. It immediately enters the 470-foot-long Hempfield Tunnel, rebuilt in 1904, which is dimly lit and rumored to be haunted.

The trail emerges near I-70, which it follows until its terminus at Wheeling Skate Park at Community Street near Wheeling Creek in Elm Grove.

Closure Notice: Construction on adjacent highways in Elm Grove may require trail closures in this section through the first half of 2022. Check with the trail manager for the current status.

CONTACT: wheelingwv.gov/departments/parks-recreation/heritage-trail

continued on next page

PARKING

All parking waypoints listed below are located in Wheeling. *Indicates that at least one accessible parking space is available.*

Ohio River Trail (South to North)

Water St. and 48th St.: (40.0333, -80.7289).

Ballfields at 35th St.*: Between Market St. and Chapline St. (40.0478, -80.7270).

Intermodal Parking Garage: 1401 Main St. (at 14th St.) (40.0649, -80.7234).

5th St. 450 feet west of Main St. (40.0781, -80.7268).

E. First St. and West St.: (40.0832, -80.7263).

Pike Island Dam: 3667 Warwood Ave. (40.1475, -80.7006).

Wheeling Creek Trail (West to East)

Intermodal Parking Garage: 1401 Main St. (at 14th St.) (40.0649, -80.7234).

1010 Rock Point Road: 0.4 mile northwest of Dorman Road (40.0722, -80.7001).

1099 Mount DeChantal Road (at Armory Dr.): (40.0663, -80.6938).

Wheeling Skate Park*: Community St. and Angle Ave. (40.0486, -80.6660).

Blackwater Canyon Trail (see page 183)

TrailLink user tkessel11

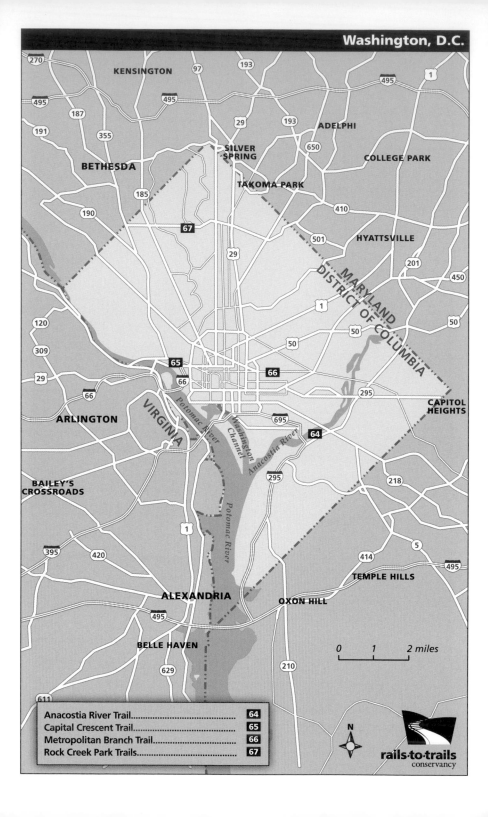

Washington, D.C.

KENSINGTON
ADELPHI
COLLEGE PARK
BETHESDA
SILVER SPRING
TAKOMA PARK
HYATTSVILLE
MARYLAND
DISTRICT OF COLUMBIA
CAPITOL HEIGHTS
ARLINGTON
VIRGINIA
Potomac River
Washington Channel
Anacostia River
BAILEY'S CROSSROADS
Potomac River
TEMPLE HILLS
ALEXANDRIA
OXON HILL
BELLE HAVEN

0   1   2 miles

Anacostia River Trail **64**
Capital Crescent Trail **65**
Metropolitan Branch Trail **66**
Rock Creek Park Trails **67**

N

rails·to·trails
conservancy

A paved trail winds through D.C.'s Rock Creek Park (see page 245), which spans more than 1,700 acres.
Khuyen Dinh

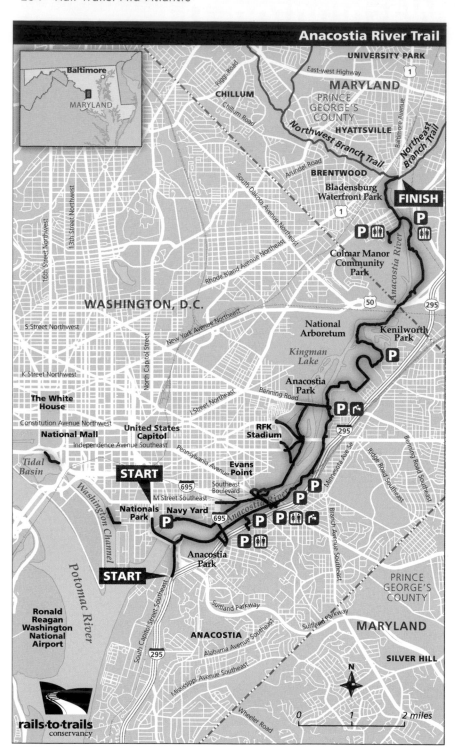

Winding along its eponymous river, the Anacostia River Trail (also known as the Anacostia Riverwalk) is a gem of a trail in southeast Washington, D.C.—a vital recreation and active-transportation amenity for residents and tourists alike. Providing a paved surface across its entirety, the trail occupies riverside, wooded natural areas, marshland, urban development, parks, and sports fields. To date, 12 of what will ultimately be 20 miles of trail are open.

Not a rail-trail, the Anacostia River Trail follows the topography of the land, resulting in gentle hills and graceful turns as it weaves alongside what was once a polluted and impaired river (remediation efforts are underway). Visitors will now find a well-designed and scenic trail that intersects the urban and natural landscapes.

The Anacostia River Trail provides a standout trail experience in the region as part of a trail and bikeway system with access to Washington, D.C., and connections to the Northwest Branch Trail (see page 83) and the Northeast Branch Trail (see page 79) in Maryland. The three trails also comprise a key section of the developing 800-mile Capital Trails Coalition network (**railstotrails.org/ctc**), a

Counties
Prince George's (MD); Washington, D.C.

Endpoints
Nationals Park at S. Capitol St. SE and O St. SW or S. Capitol St. SE and Defense Blvd. (Washington, D.C.); Northwest Branch Trail/Northeast Branch Trail/Bladensburg Waterfront Park at Charles Armentrout Dr. and 42nd Pl. (Hyattsville)

Mileage
12 (round-trip)

Type
Greenway/Non-Rail-Trail

Roughness Index
1

Surface
Asphalt

Winding along the Anacostia River, the trail provides access to many amenities in southeast D.C.

TrailLink user caughtmyeyeimages

Rails-to-Trails Conservancy TrailNation™ project that aims to connect the Washington, D.C., metropolitan region by multiuse trail.

At the southern end, trail users can begin on the east or west side of the river. On the east bank, the trail begins at South Capitol Street Southeast. Expect an immersive nature experience, including access points to tidal marsh, great wildlife-viewing opportunities, and a boardwalk built over the river as you pass under US 50/New York Avenue Northeast.

Heading north along the Anacostia Park waterfront, you'll pass amenities such as two recreation centers; multiple playgrounds, including a pirate ship–themed playground with an adult fitness station; a roller-skating pavilion; and numerous sports fields.

If beginning on the west bank, start at Nationals Park on South Capitol Street Southwest. From here, head north along the river through D.C.'s historic Navy Yard and past Evans Point and RFK Stadium, once a major sports venue that, at press time, was scheduled to be demolished in 2022. At The Fields at RFK Campus, you can also access the Kingman and Heritage Island State Conservation Area to the east by way of a connecting spur. Upon crossing the river at Benning Road, the Anacostia River Trail reunites with itself at the northern end of Anacostia Park.

The trail's most recently constructed section, through the beautiful Kenilworth Park & Aquatic Gardens, managed by the National Park Service, was completed in 2016 and abuts the border between Maryland and Washington, D.C. From the gardens, you'll cross eastward on a segment paralleling Benning Road and then loop northward on a twisting path to Bladensburg, Maryland. *Note:* There is a 0.2-mile section in Brentwood, Maryland, that departs Colmar Manor Community Park to meet the main trail on the west side of the Anacostia River. This section leaving the park is on a steep incline.

Detailed signage helps trail users orient themselves at trail and street intersections throughout. While the route largely consists of dedicated trail, short sections merge with multiuse sidewalks across roadway bridges and along marina frontage. Additionally, a short section of the west-bank segment just east of I-695 places trail users along Water Street—a wide, low-speed, low-use side street in front of a row of small marinas—for just under 0.3 mile.

There are also two short, incomplete sections of trail along the Washington Channel, the first between P Street and Water Street and the second along the east side of the Tidal Basin between Maine Avenue Southwest and Independence Avenue Southwest. When fully built out, the Anacostia River Trail will connect to the Tidal Basin (famous for its cherry blossoms in the spring), the National Arboretum, and the National Mall.

CONTACT: pgparks.com

PARKING

Parking areas are listed from south to north. *Indicates that at least one accessible parking space is available.*

WASHINGTON, D.C.*: The Yards Park (west side of river), 4th St. SE and Water St. SE (38.8735, -76.9999).

WASHINGTON, D.C.: Anacostia Park (east side of river):

Recreation Center* (waterfront parking): 1800 Anacostia Dr. (38.8735, -76.9818).

Pirate Ship Playground* (waterfront parking): Anacostia Dr. and Nicholson St. SE (38.8752, -76.9771).

Roller Skating Pavilion* (waterfront parking): 1500 Anacostia Dr. (38.8788, -76.9707).

Anacostia Boat Ramp (waterfront parking): 1500 Anacostia Dr. (38.8801, -76.9699).

Anacostia Park Ballfields (street parking on east side of park): 350 Anacostia Ave. NE (38.8961, -76.9599).

WASHINGTON, D.C.: Kenilworth Parkside Recreation, 4010 Anacostia Ave. NE, intersection of Anacostia Ave. NE and 42nd St. NE (38.9070, -76.9441). Trail access is located one block west via Anacostia Ave.

COLMAR MANOR, MD: Colmar Manor Community Park, 0.8 mile along access road from park entrance by baseball field (38.9294, -76.9445); very steep grade as you enter the trail.

BLADENSBURG, MD*: Bladensburg Waterfront Park, 4601 Annapolis Road (38.9363, -76.9385), east side of park along road.

Capital Crescent Trail

SOUTH KENSINGTON

495

FINISH

Ray's Meadow
Local Park

Georgia Avenue

Talbot Avenue
Lanier Drive

495

Brockville Road

Wiltonsville Road

**SILVER
SPRING**

*on-road
detour*

Jones Bridge Road

East-West Highway

**WASHINGTON,
D.C.**

Rockville Pike

*under
construction*

Meadowbrook
Local Park

MARYLAND

16th Street Northwest

BETHESDA

P

**CHEVY
CHASE**

Wise Road
Northwest

Bradley Road

Connecticut Avenue

**MONTGOMERY
COUNTY**

P

Bradley Lane

Oregon Avenue Northwest

**Rock
Creek
Park**

Norwood
Local Park

River Road

Little Falls Parkway

*Rock
Creek
Park
Trails*

SOMERSET

River Road

Massachusetts Avenue

Military Road Northwest

Nebraska Avenue Northwest

Broad Branch Road Northwest

Beach Drive Northwest

Chesapeake & Ohio
Canal National
Historical Park

**Little Falls
Stream
Valley Park**

**Rock
Creek
Park**

Connecticut Avenue Northwest

**Dalecarlia
Tunnel**

*Dalecarlia
Reservoir*

WASHINGTON, D.C.

Massachusetts Avenue Northwest

Wisconsin Avenue Northwest

Potomac River

Loughboro Road Northwest

MacArthur Boulevard Northwest

Hohal Road Northwest

**Smithsonian's
National Zoo**

16th Street Northwest

**Glover
Archbold
Park**

**US Naval
Observatory**

*Rock
Creek
Park
Trails*

N

**Fletcher's
Boathouse**

P

U Street Northwe

0   0.5   1 mile

Canal Road Northwest

**Foundry
Branch
Valley
Park**

**Georgetown
University**

R Street Northwest

M Street Northwest

GEORGETOWN

K Street Northwest

Potomac River

VIRGINIA

P

**FOGGY
BOTTOM**

**The White
House**

Virginia Avenue Northwest

rails-to-trails
conservancy

66

*Mount
Vernon
Trail*

START

Forming an emerald arc around the northern and western borders of the District of Columbia, the Capital Crescent Trail, also known as the Georgetown Branch Trail, connects Washington to its Maryland suburbs. The pathway is so lushly wooded that, at times, you might forget that the thrum of the nation's capital lies just over the trees. But a glance over your shoulder while traveling along the Potomac River provides a nice view of the Washington Monument and a reminder of the city's closeness.

D.C.'s Georgetown neighborhood is where 7 miles of paved trail begin, just a few blocks from the prestigious John F. Kennedy Center for the Performing Arts and the infamous Watergate complex. It quickly heads into leafy surroundings on its way north to Maryland and the

TrailLink user carl.graziano

Look for the trail's Dalecarlia Tunnel, spanning 340 feet, near the D.C.–Maryland border.

Counties
Montgomery (MD),
Washington, D.C.

Endpoints
30th St. NW and K St.
NW (Washington, D.C.);
Lanier Dr. and Talbot Ave.
(Silver Spring, MD)

Mileage
7.8 (with an additional
4.9 miles on-road)

Type
Rail-Trail

Roughness Index
1

Surface
Asphalt, Crushed Stone

239

popular dining and shopping area of Bethesda. From there, it will eventually continue as a paved trail adjacent to the Purple Line light-rail system, going another 4 miles into downtown Silver Spring with a future connection to the Metropolitan Branch Trail (see page 243).

The trail offers a near-perfect blend of community connector and recreational asset. Its first few miles are nestled within a national historical park, tucked between the Potomac River and the scenic C&O Canal. The canal's towpath (see page 45) closely parallels the Capital Crescent Trail for a few miles before eventually continuing northwest on a winding journey of nearly 185 miles to Cumberland, Maryland. Both trails are part of the developing 800-mile Capital Trails Coalition network (**railstotrails.org/ctc**), a Rails-to-Trails Conservancy TrailNation™ project that aims to connect the Washington, D.C., metropolitan region by multiuse trail.

A meeting point for the two trails at Fletcher's Cove—which has been in operation since the 1850s—is a favorite spot of locals. An adjacent stone house overlooking the trail is the oldest structure on the canal, and a rental shop offers canoes, kayaks, rowboats, and even hydro bikes for a water's-eye view of the landscape. Note that there's an almost continuous slight uphill grade from Fletcher's Cove continuing north to downtown Bethesda.

Like anything in Washington, the trail has a rich and colorful history. It traces the route of the former Georgetown Branch of the Baltimore and Ohio Railroad, which opened in 1910. The line hauled freight for 75 years, including the coal that provided electricity for Georgetown's streetcars and powered the steam plant that warmed federal buildings like the White House. Limestone for the construction of the Lincoln Memorial was also ferried on the tracks.

Some of the trail's best features are nods to its railroad past. Near the D.C.–Maryland border, the trail goes through the Dalecarlia Tunnel. The 340-foot-long brick structure is especially welcome as a cool respite on hot summer days. Be sure to look for the unusual person-size cutouts in the tunnel's sides, used if a pedestrian needed to get out of the way of a passing train.

The trail is also part of Rails-to-Trails Conservancy's Great American Rail-Trail® (**greatamericanrailtrail.org**), which spans the United States between Washington, D.C., and Washington State.

Detour Notice: *As of September 2017, the Capital Crescent Trail east of downtown Bethesda was closed due to the construction of the Purple Line light-rail system. It is estimated that the reopening of the CCT from Bethesda to Silver Spring as a paved trail adjacent to the Purple Line will happen in 2025 or 2026. An on-road detour has been designated around the closure; a map of the route is available on the website for the Purple Line project (*__purplelinemd.com/cctrail__*).*

*Note: The detour involves busy Jones Bridge Road, which doesn't have a shoulder or a marked bike lane. Trail users can find lower-stress alternatives to the official detour on the Washington Area Bicyclist Association website (***waba.org***).*

CONTACT: cctrail.org and rtc.li/montgomery-parks-capital-crescent-trail

PARKING

Parking areas are listed from south to north. *Indicates that at least one accessible parking space is available.*

WASHINGTON, D.C.: Fletcher's Cove, 4940 Canal Road NW (38.9192, -77.1010). Parking is accessible only from northbound Canal Road NW or Reservoir Road NW. Note that traffic on Canal Road NW is one-way inbound during morning rush hour and one-way outbound during evening rush hour. The trail properly begins 3 miles east in the Georgetown neighborhood of Washington, D.C., but this is the first opportunity for free trailside parking.

BETHESDA: Little Falls Park, Little Falls Pkwy. and Arlington Road (38.9746, -77.1022).

BETHESDA*: Bethesda Elm Street Garage, 4841 Bethesda Ave. (38.9809, -77.0977). Paid parking. The trail is one block east of this Montgomery County–managed garage.

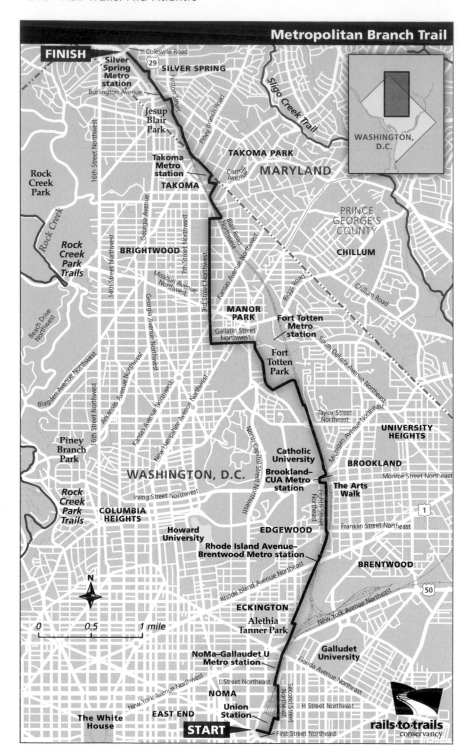

Metropolitan Branch Trail

FINISH

Silver Spring Metro station

SILVER SPRING

Colesville Road 29

Burlington Avenue

Fenton Street

Piney Branch Road

Sligo Creek Trail

Jesup Blair Park

Takoma Metro station

TAKOMA PARK

Carroll Avenue

MARYLAND

TAKOMA

WASHINGTON, D.C.

Rock Creek Park

16th Street Northwest

Georgia Avenue

7th Street Northwest

Blair Road Northwest

PRINCE GEORGE'S COUNTY

Rock Creek Park Trails

BRIGHTWOOD

14th Street Northwest

3rd Street Northwest

Kansas Avenue Northwest

Missouri Avenue Northwest

CHILLUM

Rock Creek

Beach Drive Northwest

Georgia Avenue Northwest

MANOR PARK

Gallatin Street Northwest

Fort Totten Metro station

Riggs Road

Chillum Road

South Dakota Avenue Northeast

Fort Totten Park

Blagden Avenue Northwest

16th Street Northwest

Arkansas Avenue Northwest

Kansas Avenue Northwest

New Hampshire Avenue Northwest

Taylor Street Northeast

Michigan Avenue Northeast

UNIVERSITY HEIGHTS

Piney Branch Park

Catholic University

BROOKLAND

Monroe Street Northeast

Rock Creek Park Trails

WASHINGTON, D.C.

Irving Street Northwest

North Capitol Street Northwest

Brookland–CUA Metro station

Eighth Street Northeast

The Arts Walk

1

COLUMBIA HEIGHTS

Howard University

EDGEWOOD

Franklin Street Northeast

N

Rhode Island Avenue–Brentwood Metro station

BRENTWOOD

Rhode Island Avenue Northeast

New York Avenue Northeast

50

0 0.5 1 mile

ECKINGTON

Alethia Tanner Park

NoMa–Gallaudet U Metro station

Galludet University

Florida Avenue Northeast

New York Avenue Northwest

L Street Northeast

NOMA

Second Street Northeast

H Street Northeast

The White House

EAST END

Union Station

START

First Street Northeast

rails-to-trails
conservancy

The Metropolitan Branch Trail (MBT)—a former piece of the Baltimore and Ohio Railroad (B&O)—serves as a heartbeat of the capital, serving thousands of commuters and recreational trail users as it connects some of the city's most historic and burgeoning neighborhoods. It will eventually comprise 8 miles of trail or separated walking and bicycling facilities, from Washington, D.C.'s Union Station to Silver Spring, Maryland. The trail is also a key segment of the developing 800-mile Capital Trails Coalition network (**railstotrails.org/ctc**), a Rails-to-Trails Conservancy TrailNation™ project that aims to connect the Washington, D.C., metropolitan region by multiuse trail.

Following the route of the B&O's Metropolitan Branch line, the MBT, also called the Met Branch Trail, is a busy, urban rail-with-trail that is adjacent to Metro's Red Line, MARC commuter service, CSX freight trains, and Amtrak. Currently, the trail stretches for about 4 miles between Union Station and Fort Totten, with most of the remaining 4 miles to Silver Spring being a signed, on-street bike route or side paths.

While most of the trails in D.C. are flanked by foliage and water, the MBT features vibrant artwork and a series of

Counties
Washington, D.C.;
Montgomery (MD)

Endpoints
Union Station at First St.
NE and Union Station
Dr. NE (Washington,
D.C.); Silver Spring Metro
Station, Colesville Road
between East-West Hwy.
and Second Ave. (Silver
Spring, MD)

Mileage
4 (eventually 8)

Type
Rail-Trail/Rail-with-Trail/
Greenway

Roughness Index
1

Surface
Asphalt

This urban trail connects some of the city's most historic and burgeoning neighborhoods.

243

revolving murals and provides safe off-road access to community destinations, business areas, and residential areas for thousands of residents and visitors.

Beginning at Union Station at First Street Northeast, the on-road trail heads east then north along a wide side path along Second Street Northeast. At L Street, it heads west under railroad tracks and becomes an off-road pathway for 1.5 miles, to Franklin Street in Edgewood. On this section of trail, you can link to many Northeast D.C. neighborhoods, including NoMa, Eckington, Edgewood, and Brookland, via grade-separated crossings of Rhode Island, New York, and Florida Avenues.

Just after crossing under New York Avenue, you'll find Alethia Tanner Park on your left. The park was completed in 2020 and includes a playground, a dog park, plaza areas, and gardens.

In Edgewood, at US 1/Rhode Island Avenue, you'll come to a pedestrian bridge leading over the highway and active railroad tracks to the Rhode Island Ave–Brentwood Metro station (Red Line). Completed in 2014, the pedestrian bridge was a major milestone in the trail's development, enabling hundreds of people to cross safely over the tracks to the Metro station daily.

Continuing north from Franklin Street, the trail is routed on Eighth Street Northeast for just under 0.5 mile to Monroe Street Northeast and the Edgewood Arts Building in an area known as The Arts Walk. Here, you'll find galleries, studios, and Monroe Street Market, which offers an eclectic array of eateries and a few shops.

You'll head one block west on Monroe, one block north on Seventh Street Northeast, and one block east on Michigan Avenue Northeast before being routed north and along a side path on John McCormack Road near Catholic University. From here, the MBT follows a signed on-street bike route to Takoma Park, where a small section of off-road trail crosses the border between D.C. and Maryland. The trail ends at the Silver Spring Metro station on Colesville Road.

Construction and planning to fill in multiple sections of on-road trail and build new sections of off-road trail, and to create a direct connection with an extended Capital Crescent Trail (see page 239) in Silver Spring, are in progress. For more information, go to **rtc.li/ctc-met-branch-plans.**

CONTACT: metbranchtrail.com

PARKING

While there is not dedicated parking for the trail, the trail is accessible via Metro at the following stations: Union, NoMa–Gallaudet U, Rhode Island Ave–Brentwood, Brookland–CUA, Fort Totten, and Takoma. The trail is also accessible via Amtrak and MARC at Union Station in Washington, D.C.

Located in the northwestern neighborhoods of Washington, D.C., Rock Creek Park serves as a lush natural oasis spanning more than 1,700 acres in the bustling heart of the nation's capital. Established in 1890, it has the distinction of being the oldest and largest urban park in the national-park system. The park offers a variety of trails, consisting of a mix of dirt-surfaced paths for hikers, runners, and equestrians, as well as paved paths for bicyclists, wheelchair users, inline skaters, and walkers. We'll focus this excursion on two paved, multiuse trail sections within the park.

For a quick sampler of the park experience (3.2 miles of traveling), begin at the Rock Creek Park Nature Center and Planetarium—the only planetarium in the national-park system. Open Wednesday–Sunday, 9 a.m.–5 p.m., the center offers educational exhibits and a bird observation

County
Washington, D.C.

Endpoints
Rock Creek Park Nature Center and Planetarium (Washington, D.C.); Oregon Ave. and Chestnut St./Wise Road (Washington, D.C.); Rock Creek Park's Picnic Grove 2, south of Broad Branch Road NW and Beach Dr. NW (Washington, D.C.); Rock Creek and Potomac Parkway NW, 0.4 mile northwest of the Lincoln Memorial (Washington, D.C.)

Mileage
8.5 (paved, multiuse)

Type
Greenway/Non-Rail-Trail

Roughness Index
1

Surface
Asphalt, Dirt

Rock Creek Park serves as a natural oasis in the bustling heart of the nation's capital.

245

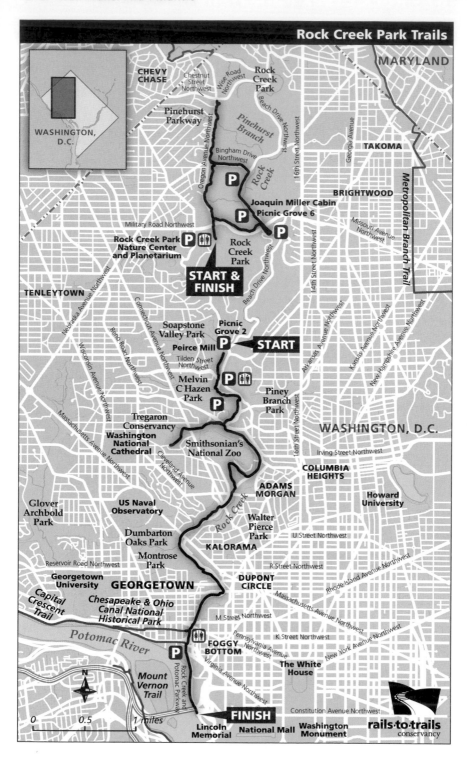

Rock Creek Park Trails

MARYLAND

CHEVY CHASE
Chestnut Street Northwest
Wise Road Northwest
Rock Creek Park
Pinehurst Parkway
Pinehurst Branch
Bingham Drive Northwest
Beach Drive Northwest
16th Street Northwest
Georgia Avenue
TAKOMA

WASHINGTON, D.C.

Oregon Avenue Northwest
Rock Creek

BRIGHTWOOD

Metropolitan Branch Trail

Joaquin Miller Cabin
Picnic Grove 6

Military Road Northwest

Rock Creek Park Nature Center and Planetarium

Rock Creek Park

START & FINISH

Beach Drive Northwest

14th Street Northwest

Missouri Avenue Northwest

TENLEYTOWN

Nebraska Avenue Northwest
Reno Road Northwest
Connecticut Avenue Northwest
Wisconsin Avenue Northwest

Soapstone Valley Park
Peirce Mill
Tilden Street Northwest

Picnic Grove 2

START

Melvin C Hazen Park

Piney Branch Park

Arkansas Avenue Northwest
Kansas Avenue Northwest
New Hampshire Avenue Northwest

Tregaron Conservancy
Washington National Cathedral

Cleveland Avenue Northwest

Smithsonian's National Zoo

WASHINGTON, D.C.

16th Street Northwest

Irving Street Northwest

COLUMBIA HEIGHTS

Massachusetts Avenue Northwest

ADAMS MORGAN

Howard University

Glover Archbold Park

US Naval Observatory

Rock Creek

Walter Pierce Park

U Street Northwest

Dumbarton Oaks Park

KALORAMA

Montrose Park

Reservoir Road Northwest

R Street Northwest

Rhode Island Avenue Northwest

Georgetown University   GEORGETOWN

Capital Crescent Trail

Chesapeake & Ohio Canal National Historical Park

DUPONT CIRCLE

Massachusetts Avenue Northwest

M Street Northwest

Pennsylvania Avenue Northwest

K Street Northwest

New York Avenue Northwest

Potomac River

FOGGY BOTTOM

Virginia Avenue Northwest

The White House

N

Mount Vernon Trail

Rock Creek and Potomac Parkway

Constitution Avenue Northwest

0   0.5   1 miles

FINISH

Lincoln Memorial   National Mall   Washington Monument

rails·to·trails
conservancy

deck and has access to plentiful parking, restrooms, and drinking water. (*Equestrians, take note:* The nature center is just north of the park's Horse Center, which offers trail rides and riding lessons.) Pick up the paved trail just west of the nature center, and head north.

In a mere 0.1 mile, you'll cross Military Road Northwest; although it's a major thoroughfare, there are walking signals and a well-marked crosswalk. Continuing north, you'll be paralleling Oregon Avenue Northwest through a residential area, pleasantly separated from the roadway by a row of trees. In 0.7 mile, you'll reach Bingham Drive Northwest. From here, you can either continue north another 0.7 mile—almost to the Maryland border—under shady tree canopy to trail's end at the intersection of Oregon Avenue and Chestnut Street/Wise Road, crossing pretty Pinehurst Branch about halfway up, or turn right at Bingham Drive Northwest—staying on the pathway paralleling the north side of the road—to loop back to your starting point at the nature center.

If you choose the loop, you'll parallel Bingham Drive Northwest heading east for 0.3 mile before reaching a T-junction with Beach Drive Northwest. Turn right, and parallel Beach Drive as you head south. You'll soon pass a large parking lot at Picnic Grove 7. In another 0.3 mile, you'll see Joaquin Miller Cabin, a 19th-century log cabin built by the noted American poet. Restrooms are available across Beach Drive from the cabin, and Picnic Grove 6 is 500 feet south. Shortly thereafter, you'll reach the underpass for Military Road Northwest; stay on the paved path and follow signs for the nature center, which is less than a mile farther on. The route back will take you over Rock Creek on the Joyce Road bridge and under Military Road a second time. Note that the route from Military Road back to the nature center has a steep grade.

For another fun adventure in the park, begin at Peirce Mill, a still-operational gristmill from the 1820s, and head south 4.6 miles to the vibrant Georgetown neighborhood. From the Peirce Mill visitor center (open limited hours, primarily on weekends), the trail meanders south through the park's woodlands and along Rock Creek, the park's namesake. In 1.3 miles, you'll reach the entrance to the Smithsonian's National Zoo; this free attraction is home to 1,500 animals and is definitely worth a side trip. South of the zoo, you'll have an iconic view of two historical bridges arching overhead: the William Howard Taft Bridge (Connecticut Avenue) and the Charles C. Glover Memorial Bridge (Massachusetts Avenue). Use caution at the Shoreham Drive crosswalk between the two bridges as it's unsignaled. Winding southward, you'll have roadway on one side and lush parkland on the other.

Just after the Pennsylvania Avenue underpass, don't miss the opportunity to connect to the epic Chesapeake & Ohio Canal Towpath (see page 45), which follows a northwest course 184.5 miles to Cumberland, Maryland. Look for the narrow brick pathway heading west along the C&O Canal. A scant 0.1 mile farther south, you'll head under the Whitehurst Freeway; nearby, you can hop on the Capital Crescent Trail (see page 239), which heads north to Bethesda and Silver Spring. All three trails are part of the developing 800-mile Capital Trails Coalition network (**railstotrails.org/ctc**), a Rails-to-Trails Conservancy TrailNation™ project that aims to connect the greater Washington, D.C., metropolitan area.

The trail ends less than a mile farther south, a short distance from the Lincoln Memorial and the National Mall. This final tip of the trail is part of Rails-to-Trails Conservancy's Great American Rail-Trail® (**greatamericanrailtrail.org**), which spans the United States between Washington, D.C., and Washington State.

Closure Notice: The District Department of Transportation and the National Park Service are working on a construction project that began in March 2021 and will affect much of the southern segment of the trail (between M Street and Broad Branch Road NW) until the project's estimated completion in spring 2023. During this time, sections of the trail may be subject to closures and/or detours; please visit **rock-creek-trail-dcgis.hub.arcgis.com** *for the latest information.*

CONTACT: nps.gov/rocr

PARKING

Parking areas are located within Washington, D.C., and are listed from north to south. Select parking areas for the trail are listed below. For a detailed list of parking areas and other waypoints, go to **TrailLink.com**™. *Indicates that at least one accessible parking space is available.*

Picnic Grove 7*: Beach Dr. NW, 0.6 mile north of Joyce Road NW (38.9675, -77.04709).

Picnic Grove 6*: Beach Dr. NW, 0.3 mile north of Joyce Road NW (38.9631, -77.04513).

Rock Creek Park Nature Center and Planetarium*: 5200 Glover Road NW (38.9597, -77.0516).

Peirce Mill Visitor Center*: 2401 Tilden St. NW (38.9404, -77.0520). Note that parking for the mill is available on the south side of Tilden St. off Shoemaker St. NW.

The Anacostia River Trail (see page 235) offers outstanding views of both urban and natural landscapes.

Jimmy O'Connor

Index

Support Rails-to-Trails Conservancy

Rails-to-Trails Conservancy (RTC) is a nonprofit organization working to build a nation connected by trails. We reimagine public spaces to create safe ways for everyone to walk, bike, and be active outdoors. Since 1986, RTC has worked from coast to coast, helping to transform unused rail corridors and other rights-of-way into vibrant public places, ensuring a better future for America made possible by trails and the connections they inspire.

We know trails improve lives, engage communities, create opportunities, and inspire movement. And we know these opportunities are possible only with the help of our passionate members and supporters across the country. Learn how you can support RTC, and discover the benefits of membership at **railstotrails.org/support.**

Rails-to-Trails Conservancy is a 501(c)(3) nonprofit organization, and contributions are tax-deductible.

Love Reading About Trails?

In each issue of *Rails to Trails* magazine, you'll find:

- Features on transformational trails around the country
- Travel recommendations for hot trail destinations
- Insider info on developing trail projects
- Gorgeous photos, trail maps and more!

Subscribe at railstotrails.org/magazine.

rails·to·trails
conservancy

SHARE THE TRAIL

Be nice.
Trails are for everyone.

Calling all trail users! Rails-to-Trails Conservancy
challenges YOU to be the best you can be on America's pathways!
Remember—safe + fun = a great time for everyone!

#sharethetrail

Visit **railstotrails.org/sharethetrail** for more.